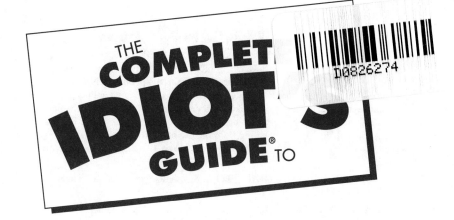

THE
COMPLETE
IDIOT'S
GUIDE® TO

Consulting

by Robert Bacal

ALPHA

A Pearson Education Company

This is a CWL Publishing Enterprises book developed for Alpha Books by CWL Publishing Enterprises, John A. Woods, President, 3010 Irvington Way, Madison, WI 53713-3414, www.cwlpub.com.

International Standard Book Number: 0-02-864271-6
Library of Congress Catalog Card Number: 2001099414

04   03   02   8   7   6   5   4   3   2   1

Interpretation of the printing code: The rightmost number of the first series of numbers is the year of the book's printing; the rightmost number of the second series of numbers is the number of the book's printing. For example, a printing code of 02-1 shows that the first printing occurred in 2002.

Printed in the United States of America

Publisher: *Marie Butler-Knight*
Product Manager: *Phil Kitchel*
Managing Editor: *Jennifer Chisholm*
Senior Acquisitions Editor: *Renee Wilmeth*
Development Editor: *Nancy Warner*
Production Editor: *Billy Fields*
Copy Editor: *Diana Francoeur*
Illustrator: *Chris Eliopoulos*
Cover/Book Designer: *Trina Wurst*
Indexer: *Ginny Bess*
Layout/Proofreading: *Ayanna Lacey*

Contents at a Glance

Contents

Appendixes

Foreword

We live in a Golden Age for consulting. Almost every company and government agency today uses consultants to advise, perform work, or create new ways of doing things. Consultants are in great demand across all industries and professions. They range from the "one man shop" to services companies of over 100,000 employees. Consulting has become the career of choice for millions of people. Consultants are essential to the functioning of modern economies.

That is why a book such as *The Complete Idiot's Guide to Consulting* is so useful. Consulting is a profession with its best practices, its time-proven ethics, and critical purposes. Some of the smartest, hardest-working people I have ever met in nearly thirty years in business were consultants. I have seen them make profound contributions to the welfare of companies, almost single-handedly. How? By employing a solid body of proven techniques, consultants can solve problems, create new approaches, teach, and move people and organizations to new levels of performance.

Robert Bacal has written a practical guide to how successful consultants operate, whether they work in small consultancies or in large services organizations. He has clearly laid out the tasks and attitudes needed. It is fresh, fast-paced, and clear, useful for both the novice "green bean" MBA or the "gray head" veteran managing principal. What I particularly find useful in his book is the breadth of coverage; it's all here, from starting a consultancy business to figuring out how to grow it. He knows his business.

There have been many books published over the years on the art and practice of consultancy, and many are quite good. However, most are long, technical, and too detailed for most of us to read. This one distills the essence of what you need to know, and, for the experienced consultant, is a reminder of how best to consult. Robert Bacal wrote this book in such a way that anybody contemplating consulting will find it of value, whether you are doing process reengineering, running seminars, giving advice, or facilitating transformation projects. The point is, there exist a set of universal practices all effective consultants carry out, no matter their field of expertise.

I have long argued that those who hire consultants need to know what consultants do. Understanding their role helps clients appreciate what they can realistically expect consultants to do and the reasons for their actions. It is all about effectiveness. It is also useful as a body of best practices that anybody who works can apply to their daily activities because this book speaks to such issues as how to organize and manage work, budget costs, meet deadlines, and so forth, all things everyone deals with on a regular basis. This book is, therefore, as useful to a client as to a consultant.

For both consultants and clients, the book is a nice blend of "what to do" with tips on "how to do." That is an important balance because the one thing consultants constantly face is the combination of questions about what needs doing and the approaches required to come in on time, within budget, and effectively. Those issues never go away, which is why experienced consultants constantly look for best practices, tips, and "war stories" of what has worked or failed. So when a book comes along that recognizes that delicate balance, we should pay attention to it. This one delivers. Read and profit by it!

James W. Cortada

IBM Global Services executive, and author or co-author of dozens of books on business management, including *21st Century Business: Managing and Working in the New Digital Economy* and *Into the Networked Age: How IBM and Other Firms Are Getting There Now*.

Introduction

More and more people are choosing to move from being regularly employed to running their own consulting businesses. There's probably dozens of reasons why, not the least of which is that the market for consulting services has expanded over the last decade and continues to expand. There's no doubt that in some ways this is the best time to be a consultant.

Other reasons to join the consulting ranks include a desire to control one's destiny, the anticipated freedom, wanting to make a difference, and to make more money. Since you are holding this book in your hands right now, you obviously have an interest in starting or increasing your success as a consultant. And I'd like to help.

Whether you are beginning or in the midst of building an ongoing consulting practice, and regardless of whether you want to offer consulting services to government, corporations, or just plain old regular people, there's lots of things you need to know to succeed. As with many small businesses, there's a fairly high failure rate for consulting businesses. I don't want you to be one of them.

What kinds of things do you need to know? What skill do you require? Well, the more you know and the more you can do in areas like communication, business strategy, marketing, your specialization, group skills, and client management, the better off you will be. I can also tell you that your attitudes and values will impact your ability to build a long-term consulting career.

In writing this book, I wanted to produce material that would help both those who want to be consultants and existing consultants looking to improve their businesses. For those of you in the first group, I also wanted to help you develop realistic expectations and a sound understanding of the consulting lifestyle, since there's a tendency to see consulting as some kind of "personal Nirvana."

No matter where you are now, I'm sure you'll learn something by the time you've finished this book. I'll tell you what it's like to be a consultant, what to expect in terms of setting up your business, and you'll also learn about the business aspects of the profession. But probably just as important, I'll teach you about the process of consulting, working with clients and doing your best to ensure that every project succeeds. And, I tell you about professional ethics and values and why they are important.

How to Use This Book

I have divided this book into five sections. I'd suggest you read all of the chapters in sequence, regardless of whether you are a beginner or a more experienced old hand, because you'll find all kinds of tips you may not have known about.

Here's how the book is set up:

Part 1, "Foundations—Getting to Know the Consulting Business," is where we start. The first several chapters explain what consulting involves, who purchases consulting services, and some basic business issues. Other chapters explain what "success" means in consulting and give you specific examples of how others have succeeded (and failed).

Part 2, "The Consulting Process," describes the progression of events in consulting from the time you first have contact with a potential client to the "end game" when you offer your recommendation and/or further services. I've begun this section with a very important discussion of ethics in the business because that is the foundation of any long-term successful consulting relationship.

Part 3, "The Start-Up Business Side," not surprisingly, is about getting into the profession (transitions), and describes a process for defining your niche and your services. The purpose of this section is to help you build a firm foundation from square one, since weak foundations are the largest contributors to consulting business failures.

Part 4, "The Ongoing Business Challenge," deals with issues consultants face throughout their consulting lives—marketing, growing and expanding, getting contracts, and issues about fees.

Part 5, "The Client Relationship," deals directly with how to develop good working relationships with your clients. From what to expect from your client (and what you'll really get), to facing resistance and impossible clients. The issues dealt with here are those you *will* come up against numerous times in your consulting career. The last chapter provides additional resources we think are useful in helping consultants update your skills.

Extras

In addition to the regular text, this book includes four extra features designed to help you learn more about how to succeed as a consultant.

Working Words

These boxes include brief definitions of terms you need to know as a consultant. Often this isn't just a word or phrase, but a concept that provides a perspective on the consulting profession and successful consulting behaviors.

Between Colleagues

These boxes include practical advice and suggestions that you might find helpful in undertaking your consulting practice. They are succinct and directed at the point being discussed in the text.

Consultant Crashing

These boxes serve up cautions to help you avoid actions and mistakes that can lead to problems big and small. Pay attention. They are the voices of experience.

Consulting Confidential

Think of these boxes as insider tips and special asides, consultant to consultant. They provide little insights that I have garnered in my years of practice and are designed to stimulate your thinking as well.

Acknowledgments

Special thanks to my wife, Nancy, and to my cats, young Griffey, big ol' Tobin, and the queen of the domain, Moondance. All have been supportive but in different ways. My wife never sat on my keyboard wanting to be petted, although one can always hope.

Also a thank you to mentors and colleagues from the past who have helped me develop my own skills in consulting. You can't grow in the consulting business without interaction with others in the field, and those more experienced.

I also want to thank John Woods of CWL Publishing Enterprises for asking me to write this book. It's the third book we've worked on, and I think we've just about got things right. And thanks to Renee Wilmeth at Alpha Books, who thought this would be a good title to add to *The Complete Idiot's Guide* series.

Trademarks

All terms mentioned in this book that are known to be or are suspected of being trademarks or service marks have been appropriately capitalized. Alpha Books and Pearson Education, Inc., cannot attest to the accuracy of this information. Use of a term in this book should not be regarded as affecting the validity of any trademark or service mark.

Part 1

Foundations—Getting to Know the Consulting Business

What does it mean to call yourself a consultant? What do consultants do and how do they provide value for their clients? In case you're wondering, those are a couple of the questions I take up in Part 1 of this book.

If you want to be a consultant, you need to look at what you have to offer in the way of skills, knowledge, and expertise. Chapter 3, "Prerequisites for Success," will help you make that assessment. The fact is that not every person who decides to be a consultant succeeds, and many find themselves hurrying back to the fold of corporate employment. Chapter 4, "Of Successes and Failures," provides some profiles in success as well as failure. You can learn from those who have succeeded, but you can learn even more from those who haven't.

"The more certain a consultant is, the more likely the consultant is going to be wrong, and therefore a danger to himself or herself and the client." That's just one of my "laws" laid out in Chapter 5, "Bacal's Laws of Consulting." It's a bit tongue-in-cheek, but trust me, this is serious stuff I've learned through the years. Understanding these laws can make your life as a consultant less stressful and more successful.

The What, Who, and Why of a Mysterious Profession

In This Chapter

- ◆ The meaning of an ambiguous word ... consulting
- ◆ How consultants spend their time
- ◆ The reasons why consultants get hired
- ◆ The good and bad news about the consulting market

If I ask you what a police officer does, you'd be able to give me a coherent, informed answer. It's the same with other occupations, whether accountant, doctor, or janitor. Explaining what each of these occupations entails would be pretty easy. Not so with consulting. When someone says, "I'm a consultant," strange things happen. Tell an inquiring and sociable partygoer that you are a consultant and you're likely to see a look of puzzlement, usually followed by the question, "Yes, but what do you really do?"

The reality is that the word *consultant* can mean almost anything. If you want to be a consultant (or if you are one already), you must be clear about the various meanings of the word, and what it means to be part of the consulting profession. That's what this chapter is about.

What Is Consulting—What's in a Name?

What's in the name "consulting"? Not much, really. One consultant offers advice to high-powered executives of major companies, charges large fees, and does very little but advise. That person is known as a management consultant. Another offers help in redecorating houses and receives a much smaller fee. That person might be called an interior design consultant. An Internet web design consultant might advise clients about how to create a top-quality website, and actually build that site for the client.

The range of fields in which you can specialize is huge. The services you offer are limited only by your imagination and what clients will pay for.

Even though an exact definition of consulting is difficult to give, here is one that has worked well for me. *Consulting* is a process undertaken by a disinterested party with significant expertise and experience, and involves offering advice and problem solving to the client or customer using a well-defined consulting process.

Between Colleagues

Whether you want to consult, or whether you are already working as a consultant, it's absolutely critical that you understand what your job entails—the roles you are expected to take on, your responsibilities, and your function.

Let's take a closer look at this definition, keeping in mind that a general definition of this type will be a bit vague. I'll remedy that in a moment.

First, what's a "disinterested party"? It's simple. A consultant (or disinterested party) is someone who has no vested interest in exactly how the client's problem is solved. Typically, the consultant is from outside the organization or client's world and provides an objective approach to the client's problem.

This objectivity is very important and touches on the value of a consultant to the client. As a consultant, you will be expected to provide one or more of the following:

♦ A fresh look at the situation

♦ An unbiased view of the situation

♦ An innovative way to approach the problem

Second, what do "significant expertise and experience" involve? Anyone can call himself or herself a consultant, but that doesn't make the person one. A consultant brings to the client a significant body of skills, or *expertise*, in the field in which he or she works. And, generally, the consultant also has a deep and broad range of experience related to the needs of the client.

For example, an Internet website consultant would need expertise in a number of areas. These might include knowledge about sound graphic design, ability to use web development tools, and a broad understanding of how websites can contribute to business success for the client. And that's just scratching the surface.

In addition, a client would expect an Internet website consultant to have designed and implemented successful websites. That's the experience part.

In short, as a consultant you need to have enough expertise and experience to identify the client's problem and solve it, while at the same time inspiring confidence on the part of your client.

What Do Consultants Really Do?

Someone once characterized consultants as follows: "A consultant is like a seagull. He flies in, buzzes around crapping all over the place, then flies out leaving a royal mess in his wake."

Strictly speaking, that humorous definition would be fairly accurate, except I'd hope that, upon flying out, the consultant would leave less mess than when he arrived.

Traditionally, consultants have been advice givers and not doers. But that view is a little too restrictive for us. Let's look at the different roles that consultants can choose.

> ### Consulting Confidential
>
> Consultants may work as small business owners in that they work on their own or with associates. They may also work as regular employees for small or large consulting firms. I'll focus on consultants as small business owners.

Consultants Who Advise

The advisory role is probably the classic one for consultants. Generally, a consultant is retained to achieve some goal the client wants to reach; that goal may be specific and defined up front, or it may be much more vague, requiring investigation and refinement.

For consultants who work solely in advisory mode, their involvement ends when they present their recommendation. That's it. They're done.

Here's an example. A government is considering whether it should build a new bridge to improve traffic patterns in the city. Not being traffic engineers, the politicians are obviously not able to assess the total impact of such a bridge. Neither do they and their employees have sufficient experience in building bridges to know whether or not building the bridge is a wise decision.

The solution, of course, is to hire a consultant to conduct a feasibility study. In this case the government contracts with an engineering consulting firm that is independent and has experience and expertise with bridges. The firm's mandate and goals are clear: to determine whether the bridge is cost-effective and worthwhile to build.

As far as the consulting firm is concerned, once the report and recommendations are presented to the client, the job is done. The firm doesn't actually build the bridge. If it's done its job well, it will have provided the government with the information and analysis necessary to make an informed decision.

In the bridge-building case the job is advisory, but let's look at another example—one closer to home. Let's say you are thinking about starting a consulting business. You think there is a market for the particular service you could provide, but you've never planned or actually run a business before. So, you look for someone with expertise and experience in small business planning who can offer an unbiased and independent perspective.

Between Colleagues

There is no need to limit yourself to advising only, or doing only. Your role will depend on your skills and abilities. Whether you advise, do, or both, you must acquire whatever skills are needed to complete the task with a high level of expertise.

Consulting Confidential

Most governments offer assistance in developing business plans for small businesses because new business helps support the community's growth. If you are thinking of starting a consulting business, find out what kinds of free services are available to you from government organizations.

You might hire an independent consultant to work with you to prepare a business and marketing plan. You may have specific questions you need answered, for example:

♦ Is there a market for my services?

♦ What services make sense to offer?

♦ How can I best market my consulting business?

In short, you want a professional business plan to guide you in building your new business.

The consultant you hire will answer your questions and help you develop a business plan to start and build your business. This person isn't going to run the business. He or she functions as an advisor to you. In some cases you might look to the consultant for ongoing advice, but generally, once the business plan is completed, the consultant will not be involved in the day-to-day decisions you must make as a businessperson.

Consultants Who Advise and Do

While the "pure" consulting role may be one of providing advice, the reality is that restricting yourself to advice giving may not be a good thing to do. Much depends on the field you work in. Sometimes it makes sense to both plan and advise, and then actually carry out the plan. Providing the work yourself may be more efficient for the client.

Let's look at some examples. Suppose you want a website related to your business. You have no web development experience or skills, and except for some casual web surfing you don't know much about how it all works. Nor do you really want to invest the time in learning to develop the site yourself. So you find an individual who will advise you on the how's, why's, and wherefore's of building and running a website. Part of what you want from your consultant is a sample of what your finished website will look like.

Once that phase of the consulting process is complete, you have a much better idea of what your website can accomplish, where it can be hosted, and a lot of other critical information. But (and it's a big but), you still lack the skills to actually build and run the thing. As the client you have two options. Retain the original consultant to build and maintain the site for you, or hire someone new to build it consistent with the recommendations you received from the original consultant.

Which makes more sense? In this case (and in many others), it makes more sense to stay with the original consultant and have that person actually do it. After all, he or she developed the look, the feel, and the philosophy behind your site.

The point here is that "advising and doing" are often in the client's best interest. The one drawback is that there is some loss of objectivity on the consultant's part, since his or her initial recommendations can be tainted by the possibility of future work with the client.

Let's consider this job from the consultant's viewpoint. What are the advantages of "advice + doing"? First, there's a bigger money pot. The consultant gets paid for the advising and for the doing. Second, it's far more satisfying to be in at the start of a project, when you can plan it and then see it through to the results stage.

There is something very important to consider here. You may have sufficient skills to advise on something but not sufficient skills to implement that advice. For example, if you are a graphic designer, you may be able to map out a "look" for a website but have no skills in coding to make that website come into existence. Likewise, you may be sensational at marketing strategy but lack the skills to implement that strategy on the Internet. There are ways around this deficiency—for example, subcontracting—but nevertheless it's an issue you need to be aware of.

> **CAUTION**
>
> **Consultant Crashing**
>
> One of the worst things a consultant can do is claim to have sufficient skills to accomplish something when he or she does not. Learning on the job does a disservice to yourself and to the client.

Consultants Who Do

I've included consultants who "do" more to clarify an aspect of consulting rather than to suggest that you be "only a doer." The best way to explain this is to use an example from my own field, which is providing training solutions.

Part of my business involves delivering training to staff to help them deal more effectively with difficult and angry customers. When I started my business, I needed to make a critical decision. Would I package a training program and deliver the same thing in the same way to all my clients (which would be "doing")? Or would I treat training as a consulting intervention, in which I would help identify what clients really needed, help them define the best way to address those needs, and custom-design something specifically for them (consulting + doing)?

I chose to do the latter, although many trainers do the former. Why? I felt it would be unethical to do a one-size-fits-all training approach, since I knew that such an approach would be effective for some clients but would not fit all clients. Such a canned solution would not have maximum effectiveness. I anticipated that it would damage the reputation of my company.

> ### Consulting Confidential
>
> Here's something you probably haven't thought about. Consulting involves identifying client needs and figuring out how to meet those needs. Almost any job can include a consulting component, even if the job is focused on "doing." Consulting principles have even been applied to sales jobs. The term "consultative selling" means incorporating consulting principles into selling almost anything.

The point here is that no matter what specific services or products you offer, using consulting principles and processes will increase the value of what you provide to clients. If you recognize this fact, then you can treat everything you do as a consulting process. By clarifying customer needs and then, and only then, delivering solutions, you create higher levels of customer satisfaction.

Bottom line. Without including the consulting process in the project, there are very few situations in which you can just "do" while still pleasing your customer.

Money Tree?

Now that you know what consulting is, let's get to what you're probably really interested in—the money. What's the most common myth about consultants? Despite popular belief, most consultants aren't rich, and neither do most consultants charge the fees bandied about by those outside the industry. Yes, there are consultants who can charge $3,000 a day. But for every one of those, 20 or 30 other consultants are receiving fees in the $300-a-day range.

Think about it in terms of movie actors. For every Tom Cruise or Harrison Ford, who can command multimillion dollar fees for movies, hundreds of other actors are working for peanuts, hoping for a break—or, worse, waiting tables or standing in the unemployment line.

Have I burst the bubble for you? Good. Because there is no point in thinking about being a consultant unless you have a realistic and clear set of expectations about what you can expect to earn. I hope you eventually command large fees, and I'm sure you hope so too. Just be prepared to struggle, at least for the first few years. Be prepared for the possibility that you can't "make it" financially as a consultant. Hope to make a comfortable living if you can cut it. Anything beyond that, consider it gravy.

> **Consultant Crashing**
>
> Realistic financial expectations are important for any new or growing business. Just because some consultants earn huge sums of money, don't count on being one of them. If you count on being a "consulting star" and this doesn't come to pass, you may end up bankrupt. Keep your financial expectations reasonable and on the low side.

Some Good News

If I've dashed your hopes of millionairehood, hold on a minute. There is some good news. Ready? The consulting sector is booming! Some have estimated that the consulting sector is growing globally at a rate of 16 percent a year. That figure may be a bit overly optimistic since it applies primarily to the consulting market with respect to services rendered to other businesses. Consulting to individuals (for example, decorating, fitness) will grow only as individuals have money to spend.

Consulting to business will continue to grow, provided that consultants offer services that are cost-effective and meet the needs of clients better than other alternatives.

There are a number of reasons for the boom, many of which have to do with the shifting economics of doing business. Hiring consultants to do the work has a built-in degree of efficiency and cost savings. No benefits are paid. A consultant can be hired without committing to long-term expenditures, whereas hiring a full-time employee involves an outlay for benefits. And companies often need help that is simply not available within the company, or perhaps is not worth keeping within the company on a permanent basis.

The Bad News

By now you may be thinking that reading this discussion of the financial side of consulting is like riding a roller coaster. Bad news, good news, and more bad news. Life's like that. Okay, here's the bad news. While the consulting market is growing (more customers), tons more people are working in the consulting field. It's a heavily competitive business, not only in terms of fees charged, but also in terms of visibility, reputation, and skill.

It's likely that whatever field you choose as your specialization, there will already be a number of established consultants trying to do almost the identical work. A few of those will be direct competitors if they are geographically close to you, and there will be other competitors who aren't even in your geographic area.

The bottom line on earnings? You just might make it. Not only might you make it, but you might make it big. Or you might end up writing a book. But be prepared. This isn't a get-rich-quick profession, and for many, it may not even be a get-rich-slow profession.

Between Colleagues

Competition. Should you worry about significant competition in your chosen field? Probably not. Here's how I figure it. I want to be the best in my field, and I want to prove to potential clients that I am the best. The fact that hundreds of companies are doing the same thing as I am means nothing to me. None of them have "me" or my expertise.

Why Do People Hire Consultants?

Knowing the reasons why people hire consultants is important. As a consultant, or for that matter as any small business owner, you need to understand your potential clients or customers. After all, if you don't have a clue as to why anyone would pay you for your expertise, then how can you define what you do? How can you market your abilities? You can't. So here are the major reasons why people hire consultants.

Objectivity

Some situations, particularly when they occur in large organizations or organizations somewhat political in nature, are best addressed by someone from outside the organization—someone who has no apparent bias and can be trusted to provide independent advice.

Let's consider an example. Acme Incorporated is facing an economic crunch. Its revenues are down and expenses up, and it needs to do something to remedy the situation or it will go under. The management of Acme has some ideas about what they should be doing to turn the company around, but they disagree about how to do it. They decide to hire an independent and expert consultant to come in, diagnose the present state of the company, and suggest actions the company can take.

Between Colleagues

It is critical that consultants take any steps they can to ensure their independence and an unbiased approach. The reason is simple: trust. Clients must be able to trust the advice of the consultant.

Let's assume that the consultant suggests a number of actions. One of those suggestions involves laying off 15 percent of the staff, a controversial and painful process in any company. Now here's the advantage of using a consultant. Because the recommendation comes from an independent and unbiased individual, it somewhat insulates management from accusations of bias. Also, the use of an independent consultant may make it easier to get all of senior management to support what will be a painful decision.

Here's a simpler example. Husband and wife want to redecorate their home. They disagree on a number of issues. Rather than struggle with those issues, they hire an interior decorating consultant to make some suggestions and draw up sketches. That way, they'll have an objective opinion to draw upon.

Fresh Viewpoint

It's very easy for people to get stuck thinking about things in the same old ways. This happens to everyone. Consultants are thus often hired to offer a fresh viewpoint. Coming from outside the situation, it's likely that the consultant's perceptions will provide a new way of looking at the problem. This input helps companies innovate and come up with new ideas to solve old problems.

Lack of In-house Expertise

One very obvious reason why people hire consultants is that the person hiring lacks the knowledge, skills, and experience needed to solve a set of problems and is not interested or able to learn those skills. The obvious solution is to seek out someone who already has those abilities.

Cost-Effectiveness

Despite some of the jokes about consultants and alleged huge fees collected by consultants, clients hire a consultant with the idea that the consultant will "add more value" than the cost incurred. In other words, it may be cheaper to hire someone outside than to address problems in other ways.

Between Colleagues

Understanding why clients might hire you (and what they hope to gain) is absolutely critical if you are to market yourself effectively. Prove that you can deliver what the client needs, and you'll get the contract.

Completely Lost

Sometimes you will encounter clients who are completely lost. They know they need "something better" than what they have, but they don't know what that "something" is and they don't really know what "better" should mean. So, being completely lost, they look for a consultant to lead them out of the wilderness. By the way, these are the toughest consulting situations, but also the most rewarding if you succeed.

Expert Credibility

Consultants are occasionally hired because advice coming from an outside expert tends to be treated with more respect than the same advice provided from within a company. If you think about it, this preference is rather silly, but it's a reality you can benefit from if you develop a track record as an expert or if your company has a high-profile reputation in the community in which you work.

It is possible that you might be hired as an expert who will confirm your client's course of action. Your confirmation validates the existing ideas of the person hiring you. This is fine except when those ideas are really bad ones. Beware of feeling pressured to provide that expert validation when your judgment says you should go in another direction.

How Do Consultants Spend Their Time?

Exactly how do consultants spend their time? An independent consultant (someone who owns the business in a one-person shop) is going to spend a major portion of his or her time hunting for business and dealing with prospective clients. In other words, this person is going to be marketing himself or herself.

Marketing means developing promotional material, calling prospective clients, taking part in associations where prospective clients may be found, networking, and so on.

You should expect that during the first few years of running a consulting practice, you will spend a good amount of your time in *overhead activities.* These are activities that take up time, don't actually get you paid, but must be done.

The idea is that this overhead time will diminish and your *billable time* will increase. Billable time refers to the time for which you get paid (even if you aren't charging by the hour). It's what puts bread on the table. No billable time? No money. No money? No business, and it's back to finding a "real" job.

Let's talk about that billable time. What kinds of things might you expect to get paid for, keeping in mind that the field in which you consult will determine where your time goes?

Your billable time includes activities you undertake to meet the goals set out in the consulting agreement. It might involve client meetings, data collection, and meeting with other members of the client's organization. It will also involve reporting your advice and opinions in written and/or oral form. Above all, though

Working Words

Overhead time refers to the time you spend that is not directly compensated for by the client. It includes marketing, client meetings, and paperwork (like making sure your taxes are in order). **Billable time** refers to the time for which you will be directly compensated and is the financial bedrock of your practice.

(and surprisingly), you are really paid to think and to draw on your expertise. Always keep this in mind.

As a final comment on the subject of time, if you dream of a job in which you get to do really neat stuff and don't have to do all the junk jobs you hate (like paperwork, selling, and so on), beginning a consulting business is not the way to go. It's not very romantic, and you are going to work harder for yourself than you would ever work as a salaried person for an employer.

The Least You Need to Know

- Have realistic expectations regarding finance and revenue.
- Begin thinking about the consulting roles you want to undertake and for which you are qualified.
- Now that you know the main reasons why people hire consultants, start thinking about how you can mobilize your expertise to meet the needs of potential clients.
- Consulting is not a romantic profession. Evaluate whether you are prepared to spend a lot of time doing very boring and uninteresting things.

Chapter 2

More About the Market, More About the Business

In This Chapter

- ◆ Where to look for consulting clients
- ◆ How the major market sectors differ
- ◆ What the pros and cons are with respect to working for government, large business, small business, and individuals
- ◆ What specialty areas exist for consulting services—ideas for you to consider

Despite being told that you're unlikely to make a fortune as a consultant, some of you are still reading this book. That shows stick-to-itiveness and a number of other prime qualities that will stand you in good stead when you practice as a consultant. For those of you who have given up, good luck. You wouldn't have made it anyway.

Since you are hanging in here, I'll assume you're interested in learning about who might pay you to consult (your possible markets) and the various fields in which you can consult. Knowing the possible markets and deciding on your consulting areas are very important considerations, since the first steps in entering the consulting profession involve deciding where your expertise lies, what kinds of things people will actually pay you to do, and who might pay you to do things.

Let's begin with an overview of the major consulting markets, examining the pros and cons of each of them. Then I'll discuss each market in more detail, including the kinds of services you might offer there. It's not possible to exhaust all the possibilities, but the idea is to stimulate your thinking about your skills and abilities, and how you might be able to sell them.

Between Colleagues

The consulting markets you choose to target for your practice will depend on your particular expertise, the marketplaces in your locale, and your familiarity with each sector.

Four Major Consulting Markets

The consulting market can be divided into four primary areas, or sectors. Each sector operates somewhat differently from the others. For example, getting hired by a government is quite different from getting hired by an individual. Working with small business requires a different perspective than working with a government agency does. There are also advantages and disadvantages associated with the various sectors, and I'll talk about those later in the chapter in connection with each sector.

Government

If you are familiar with the government context, you already know that delivery of consulting services to government should be a prime focus of your business. Here are the reasons why:

- ◆ No matter where you live, you will have governments and potential government clients.

- ◆ Governments often "outsource," or hire consultants on both short- and long-term assignments.

- ◆ Government contracts can be very lucrative (but not always).

- ◆ Finding decision makers is easier than in other sectors since listings of government staff and management are available to the public. This fact makes marketing easier.

- ◆ If you establish a reputation as an expert in government issues and environment, word of mouth becomes very helpful.

A couple of cautions. There is a perception that governments squander money and that government is a gravy train for consultants. That may be true in some cases, but it is mostly incorrect. Don't target government markets simply because you believe they're an easy ride. They aren't.

Consider also that you should have experience working in government if you want to succeed in the government market. Governmental decision makers believe (and rightly so) that the government context is different from other contexts, and they will usually ask you about your experience in working with and helping governments. If you don't have any, then your credibility drops. That means not getting hired.

When considering the government market, take a look at all levels and facets of the sector. It's bigger than you might think. Look at all organizations funded in whole or in part by government funds. These include …

- City and town governments.
- State and provincial governments.
- Federal governments.
- *Arm's-length government* organizations.
- Educational organizations.

Rather than thinking about governments in a traditional narrow way, think about this potential market in a broad way: Any organization that is funded in whole or in part with taxpayers' dollars falls under the government umbrella.

Working Words

An **arm's-length government** organization is one that is primarily or partly funded by tax dollars but is outside the government system. Arm's length organizations often have a board of directors and their own management structure.

Large Businesses

Large businesses and corporations can be lucrative sources for consulting contracts. In this category are multinational companies and other companies that most of us would consider huge in revenue and employee numbers.

Do these organizations hire consultants from outside? Yes, indeed. And contracts with large corporations can be quite large.

As with government, the more experience you have with respect to large corporations and how they work, the better placed you will be to grab contracts. And if you understand the specific industry of the potential customer, that's an immediate plus.

You should know that in both government and large business sectors, competition for the larger contracts is often fierce.

Between Colleagues

When you are starting your business, consider contracts (large business and government) that are smaller in monetary value. The larger contracts are difficult to get until you have an established track record. Don't be afraid to start small.

Small Businesses

Small businesses constitute a large sector of the consulting market. By small business, I mean businesses ranging from one or two people (just like you) up to hundreds of employees.

Did you know that small businesses are considered the backbone of our economy? This market includes literally millions of potential clients. What's interesting is that many small businesses that could benefit from consulting services don't realize their own needs and are less likely to know where to get help.

While specializing in consulting work for small business has some advantages—primarily stemming from less competition for contracts—the marketing costs to reach small-business decision makers can be higher. Contracts will generally be smaller, depending on the size and resources of the small business customer.

If you already have a reputation within the small business community in your area, then this may well be a good place to start your consulting business.

Individuals

The last sector of the consulting market is perhaps the most challenging: that of individuals. Just plain folks like yourself. Typically, you'd provide some form of personal service to people in need of that service. For example, a personal fitness trainer consults with individuals to tailor a fitness program for the customer, and may also supervise workouts. An investment consultant works with individuals to develop a financial or retirement plan and to provide advice.

Consulting to individuals is like retailing in that you work with a number of individuals, whereas in consulting to large corporations you work with a smaller number of customers. However, consulting to individuals means you need to have a larger number of customers, because your fees and contracts are going to be much smaller.

Therefore, unless you are well established in marketing to individuals, much of your time will be spent in continual marketing, and word of mouth can be helpful in this sector.

Differences Among the Four Sectors

To help you understand your potential clients, the following table sums up some important differences among the four consulting sectors. The upcoming discussions will further expand these differences, detailing issues like marketing and the pros and cons of each sector.

Differences Among Consulting Sectors

	Government	Corporate	Small Business	Individuals
Red tape level	Usually high	Also can be high	Low	None
Contract size	From low to high	From low to high	From moderate to low	Low
Difficult to get paid?	No	No	Higher chance of problems	Higher chance of problems
Moves quickly	Decisions and projects move slowly	Tend to be slow, but often faster than government	The smaller the business, the faster it tends to move	Fast—get the agreement done and get to work
Ease of contacting decision makers	Very easy	Difficult	Difficult	Depends on marketing
Requires formal proposals?	Often yes and may be extensive	Often yes and may be extensive	Unlikely, and may be shorter	Not usually
Formal qualifications a factor? (e.g., academic degrees)	Possibly	Possibly	Less important	Not usually important

Government Contracts

What's it like to provide services to governments and other publicly funded organizations? Well, it can be lucrative and it can be exceedingly frustrating. Here's why.

Consulting to government is unique in almost every respect. Don't assume you have an understanding of government processes simply by virtue of being a citizen. To succeed in government consulting, you have to understand government from the inside. When dealing with government staff, listen and learn; make sure you understand any specific constraints and requirements associated with working with your government clients.

Since governments have a responsibility to ensure that the public's money is spent effectively (hard to believe, but it's true), the process of getting a government organization to make decisions or sign a contract can be lengthy and annoying. For example, any specific potential project may require getting the approval of a large number of decision makers—a process that slows things down. It also means that your "done deal" consulting arrangement can be shot down by any one of the decision makers involved.

There's another thing you should know. Governments need to be seen as awarding contracts in a fair way. Hence they use a process called *tendering*. This means you may be asked to write a tender, or detailed proposal, and compete with other consulting vendors. Proposals and tenders are often tedious to develop, and carry no guarantee of getting the job.

Working Words

Large government contracts are awarded through the **tender** process. This involves submitting information (as requested by the client), such as price and basic project details.

Luckily, small projects often do not involve tendering. Most government organizations have a money figure that serves as a cutoff for the tendering process. If the money figure is under the cutoff point, you don't need to do complex tendering. Over that amount, and you will be required to do so. The exact cutoff point will vary from organization to organization, but the important thing to remember is that it is a whole lot easier to get small government contracts than large ones.

Getting Government Contracts

There are two basic ways to obtain government contracts. The first is through a *request for proposal*, often abbreviated as *RFP*.

Most governments will publish requests for proposals for specific projects. Generally, the RFP will contain basic information and explain the format in which to submit your proposal; this format must be followed exactly. You then submit your proposal and wait until a decision has been made, or until you are asked to present your proposal to decision makers in person. The proposal tends to be long and drawn out. Sometimes no one is hired if budgets change or political factors intervene. For more details about requests for proposals, see Chapter 19, "Getting the Contract." The second way to obtain government contracts is less formal, involving much more face-to-face contact. I'll call these *relationship-based contracts*. Contracts received this way tend to be smaller in value.

Typically, in relationship-based contracting, you'd market to individual decision makers in government organizations, and you would develop more personal relationships with those people. For example, if you were in the human resources consulting business, you'd want to build relationships with the human-resource department managers or executives.

In relationship-based contracting, you receive the contract because you …

- ◆ Are in the right place at the right time.
- ◆ Have created confidence in your abilities over time.
- ◆ Are the first to come to mind when a need arises.

Here is the fundamental difference between formal approaches, such as RFPs, and relationship-based contracting. With formal processes your first contact with the customer is through a paper process, and the decision to hire you is slow and delayed. With relationship-based contracts, often the decision to hire you has already been made (at least tentatively) from the time a potential client contacts you about a possible project.

Government Marketing Issues

One of the most challenging tasks for any consultant involves finding and communicating with the people who have the power to hire. How do you find the right people to talk to in any organization?

Finding the decision makers becomes much less of an issue with government, and the reason is simple. Government organizations generally list their employees, managers, and decision makers in directories (both on paper and on the Internet). Directories are available to the public; not only are names listed, but job titles also. To someone familiar with government and how decisions are made, it's a simple matter to identify the key decision makers and contact them to begin creating a positive profile.

Helpful Qualifications to Have for Government Contracts

Are there any special qualifications needed to consult with government organizations? It's hard to generalize, but the following qualifications are good to have:

- ◆ An understanding of how government works
- ◆ A previous track record working with government
- ◆ A university degree or professional certification
- ◆ A reputation as an expert on government *and* an expert in the area of practice you specialize in

Pros and Cons of Government Contracts

Here are a few of the positives about working with the government:

- ◆ You'll get paid. You don't have to worry about deadbeat governments.
- ◆ There's a possibility of large contracts that can sustain you for a long time.
- ◆ Access to government officials (potential clients) is relatively easy.
- ◆ Once you develop a profile as an expert who serves government, word of mouth makes marketing easier.

And of course, here are a few of the negatives you'll encounter in the government environment:

- ◆ Approvals are typically slow.
- ◆ Payments are slow (you'll get it, but it takes a while).
- ◆ Doing business with government clients often requires large volumes of paperwork.

Large Businesses (Corporation) Contracts

Of the four major consulting sectors, businesses that fall into the "large business" sector are probably the most difficult to characterize or describe. They can be all over the board in terms of who and how they hire. Often they resemble government organizations in that they may be inflexible and slow to react, but there are many exceptions to this.

Consulting Confidential

The major difference between working with governments compared with large businesses is that governments rarely, if ever, violate their own rules regarding hiring consultants. Large businesses, on the other hand, make their own rules, and they can alter them or make exceptions. It's easier to negotiate with large businesses for this reason. Don't assume that client rules are etched in stone.

While large businesses may need to comply with some regulations regarding who and how they hire consultants, they can generally make up their own rules. Hence, you will find companies that will hire on the basis of the say-so of a single decision maker, as well as companies that must have a large number of people involved in hiring. Some large businesses may require formal proposals and client meetings before contracting, whereas others may not. Some may need or want fancy contracts, and others may work on a handshake basis, very informally.

A definite advantage of consulting for corporations is that they have the resources to contract with you at a rate higher than you might receive working for small businesses or individuals. If you work for a large corporation, and provided everything goes as planned, you will likely get paid without having to chase your money.

Getting Corporate Contracts

Since corporations make their own rules about how they hire consultants, you will find both formal and informal processes for hiring. Some corporations are easy to deal with. Others will be more like government bureaucracies.

In general, personal relationships become more important as organizations give more flexibility and authority to their individual decision makers (managers and executives). Even in the corporate world, a good percentage of consulting contracts are awarded because the consultant keeps his or her name and expertise in the minds (and hearts) of prospective clients.

It's not unheard of for a consulting project to emerge out of casual conversation between a potential client and a consultant, and for that project to end up in a request for proposal written specifically for the consultant involved in that discussion. When this happens, you want to be "that consultant," since you'll have the inside track.

Corporate Marketing Issues

Dealing with large corporations involves a major marketing challenge. Unlike government organizations, who publish directories that make it relatively easy to identify key decision makers, corporations don't do that. You probably won't have access to the corporate executive and management directories, since they aren't available to outsiders.

In marketing to government, it's rather easy to send out 1,000 promotional letters and brochures targeted to government decision makers. It isn't so easy to do so for corporate organizations. Often, the only way you can figure out who you need to contact at a potential corporation is to call and ask. Even that's no guarantee, since you have to ask the right questions of the right people—not an easy feat.

There's a balancing force, however. Corporate decision makers tend to join professional organizations more often than their government counterparts do. For example, you aren't likely to find government personnel actively involved in the local chamber of commerce, but you will almost certainly find corporate representation there. Or, for example, if you provide financial services, you are more likely to find corporate decision makers at financial association gatherings than you are to find government financial personnel. Thus, you'll find that networking through associations (wherever corporate business people gather to learn or socialize) becomes very important for this sector.

Advertising in trade publications may also work well for corporations, since decision makers may be more likely to read trade material and pay attention to ads in those publications.

 Consultant Crashing

Don't assume that because you have made one contact with a potential customer, you have marketed to them. You haven't. Marketing requires consistent contact over time to develop a positive reputation and profile with prospective clients.

Helpful Qualifications to Have for Corporate Contracts

Are there special qualifications necessary for corporate contracting? It's hard to generalize on this one. Corporations are usually more likely to hire you if you have a background in and demonstrated experience working in their business area. Are they a lot more likely to hire based on that background? Probably not. Certainly it's less important in this sector than in the government sector. For example, let's say you are a human resources consultant who works with companies to help them hire the best new employees. Provided you are expert in that particular area, you can offer the same service to an insurance company or a manufacturing company. The actual business doesn't matter much.

Are academic degrees or professional certifications good to have? Yes, but they are likely going to weigh less in the decision to hire you than they would in the government sphere. If you have them, you put yourself one step ahead of those who don't.

Bottom line: You need to know your stuff and prove to your potential client that you can do the job the client needs.

Pros and Cons of Corporate Contracts

A few of the positives related to working with larger companies and corporations are …

- You'll likely get paid without having to dun deadbeat clients.
- The possibility of large contracts is enticing. You need score only a few major contracts to live.
- While you can't count on corporations being more flexible than governments in their consultant hiring processes, they often are.

And what about the negatives? There aren't a lot of negatives here, although the situation is affected by whether the particular client is flexible or is bound by rule after rule:

- There is a potential for some corporations to be slow moving, particularly if they are bureaucratic and highly controlled by executives at the top.
- Competition is heavy.

Small Business Contracts

There are literally millions of small businesses, ranging from small mom-and-pop outfits to companies that employee 100 or 200 people. And of course the range of business types is huge. No matter if you are in a city the size of New York or a very small town, small businesses will be there, which means a significant local market for your services.

The huge size of the small business market seems to make it a prime focus for consultants—a market of considerable value. It may also be the case that this market is one of the more underdeveloped sectors and is overlooked by consultants.

Definitely consider this market, but pay special attention to the marketing needs and the challenges of small business contracts.

Getting Small Business Contracts

Getting a small business contract is, in fact, the chief challenge of this sector. Small-business consulting contracts tend to be small because of the relatively limited resources that small businesses have. Of course, this factor depends on the size of the client company. The mom-and-pop store may be in dire need of marketing or personnel help from consultants but probably won't have the money to pay a consultant any significant fee.

At the larger end of the small business spectrum, resources may be less of a concern. A company with 100 employees is going to be able to contract for services over a longer time and a more lucrative fee level.

The other factor to consider is that small businesses are less likely to hire a consultant proactively. They are less likely to understand what consultants can offer them and are less likely to know where to go for consulting help if they recognize the need. They are also accustomed to doing everything themselves. As a consultant to small business, you will probably not be invited to consult with them. Marketing, then, becomes paramount.

So what does this mean in terms of getting small business contracts? You'll find that contracts with small businesses come largely from personal contacts and networking. And that fact has profound implications for how you market.

> **Consulting Confidential**
>
> How can you contact small business owners? Apart from carrying out the usual advertising and marketing approaches, become a member of your chamber of commerce. Find out whether any organizations in your area offer free help to businesses, and offer to volunteer. Volunteering, even though it's free, often helps you break into a new area.

Small Business Marketing Issues

It's hard to generalize about marketing to small business, because much depends on the size of the business and the nature of its business. However, your marketing thrust must emphasize two things. The first involves educating small business owners about how you can help them succeed in their businesses. The second involves establishing personal relationships that inspire confidence and trust on the part of your potential customers, who are not accustomed to asking outsiders for help.

My bet is you'll find that marketing tactics useful for government and corporations (for example, Internet initiatives, fancy brochures) are going to be less important and that personal contact (for example, telephone calls, involvement in chambers of commerce and other networking venues) will be more important.

Helpful Qualifications to Have for Small Business Contracts

With respect to really small businesses, academic qualifications are unlikely to be important. What will be important is an understanding of the concerns of small businesses and of the kinds of people who own and operate them. Of course, experience in the particular business (for example, retailing, manufacturing, restauranting) is also important.

Pros and Cons of Small Business Contracts

The pros of working with small businesses can be summarized as follows:

- Numerous small businesses are to be found in your local market, regardless of where you live.
- There is usually less red tape to deal with.
- This market is an underexploited one for consultants.
- The competition from other consultants is less.

Most consultants tend to underexplore the small business market because of certain difficulties associated with this sector. Here are the cons of working with small businesses:

- Contracts are smaller due to fewer resources.
- Small businesses tend to lack an understanding of the value of external consultants.
- This sector is difficult to market to. You have to market one small business at a time, often on a one-to-one basis.
- You may encounter difficulty in collecting fees.

Personal Service (Individual) Contracts

The fourth market sector is individuals. Obviously, individuals don't purchase the same kinds of consulting services that companies purchase. This market does, however, purchase services related to finance and investment, employment, health, and the home.

If your areas of expertise match these services, consider this market.

Contracting with Individuals

Contracting with individuals is relatively straightforward, and in many cases business can be done on the basis of verbal agreement or a simple contract. You don't need the approval of a dozen people to put together a contract, and you will be dealing directly with the recipient of the services. In some ways it's simpler to do business in this sector than in any of the other ones.

On the other hand, your contracts will be very small, and your market will be limited to individuals wealthy enough to purchase your services. Although at first glance the individual market seems huge, it is smaller than you think.

Finally, individuals are used to doing things themselves. For example, if you offer interior design services, you will be competing with other interior design experts and also with those homeowners who are handy at doing such things on their own.

Personal Service Marketing Issues

Since fees from individuals are going to be smaller than those from the business and government sectors, you need a lot of customers, and that means extensive volume-based marketing. You need to make yourself visible to as many potential clients as possible while paying special attention to individual customer satisfaction. Word of mouth is very important in this sector.

Your advertising options are more numerous in this market, since your potential clients are likely to pay attention to ads placed in mass media (radio, television, newspapers, and magazines) but less likely to be reachable through the Internet, professional publications, and organizations.

Between Colleagues

Some services marketed to individuals can serve as springboards to providing services to companies. For example, if you do individual financial counseling, your clients may be able to give you an entrée into their respective companies, where you could deliver group training on the same subject.

Between Colleagues

Marketing to individuals is a mass-marketing process. Since most of us aren't expert in this process, you might want to consider working with a marketing or advertising specialist to devise a marketing plan.

Helpful Qualifications to Have for Personal Service Contracts

Perhaps the most important qualification associated with working with individuals and providing personal services to them is a true enjoyment of working with people one-on-one. After all, that's what you are going to be doing. Not everyone likes this kind of interaction, which can be more personal than the interactions you may have with corporate staff.

When you enjoy working with individuals, you are more likely to be seen by your clients as interested in them as human beings, and that's critical to the personal services relationship.

Generally, you have to be a good conversationalist, and know how to draw people out of their shells so you can get the information you need to help them. Conversational skills like asking questions in a gentle way, and encouraging people to talk are useful.

Apart from that you also need whatever certifications or licenses that are required by law to work in your chosen field, and sufficient credentials and experience to convince your clients that you are worthy of their business.

Pros and Cons of Personal Service Contracts

Working directly with individuals can be very satisfying, particularly if you work with the same customers over time. In some cases you may form friendships with your customers. The following are some other pros and cons to consider:

- This market is satisfying to work with.
- The potential clients are numerous (but the market for your services may be smaller than you think).
- Contracting hassles are few, and there is little red tape.
- There is a much higher probability of difficulty in collecting your fee.
- Contracts are typically small, thus requiring you to have a large client base.
- Sustained and sophisticated marketing is necessary to reach a large number of potential clients.

Possible Areas of Specialization

Now that you have a clear idea of the various markets available to you, it's time to find out what areas of specialization exist in the consulting world. Because there are hundreds if not thousands available, it's impossible to list them all, so this section must confine itself to just a few major areas of specialization. My hope is that this discussion will stimulate your thinking about where your skills and expertise might lead you in the consulting world.

Management and Business

Management consulting and consulting in business areas are prime areas of practice for consultants. The markets are significant, and businesses have money to pay consultants. Consider the following as potential consulting areas, but keep in mind that you must match your expertise and background with the consulting areas:

◆ Providing training and development

◆ Designing marketing and business plans

◆ Helping organizations turn around financially

◆ Providing help with, or offering human resource services in, the areas of recruiting and hiring, application of regulations, and payroll

◆ Facilitating internal development such as strategic planning sessions or team building

◆ Diagnosing organizational problems

◆ Creating policies and procedures

◆ Implementing and planning ad programs in various media

Technology/Computers

Technology and computer-related consulting is a growing area, and one that is likely to continue to be exceedingly lucrative. This is due partly to a move to "outsource" various technology projects, enlisting the help of programmers and designers on an as-needed basis. In fact, almost everything companies do related to technology and computers can be hired out to consultants.

Here are some examples of jobs that can be hired out to consultants:

◆ Computer programming of every sort

◆ Internet website design and implementation

◆ System design advice and planning

◆ Hardware installation and maintenance

◆ Computer and network security

◆ Internet marketing and search engine optimization

> **Consulting Confidential**
>
> Don't box yourself in too rigidly regarding your specializations. You know more than you think. For example, you might see yourself as a human resources expert, but you may also have skills unconnected with this job that are marketable—writing, training, and interviewing skills. Don't forget to consider those skills.

Financial Services

Financial services and advice are areas in which consultants are in demand. Many of these services are offered specifically to individuals (for example, financial and retirement planning, investment advice), but companies use consultants in financial specializations as well.

Some examples of financial services are as follows:

- Investment and retirement planning
- Advising on taxation issues, which can include filing tax returns on the client's behalf
- Personal finance and debt counseling, including things like developing household budgets and debt consolidation
- Providing computer support and installation for financial record keeping

Personal and Home-Related Services

The areas of personal and home-related specializations usually involve offering services directly to individuals rather than to businesses. Examples include:

- House inspections
- Relocation assistance and advice
- Food services (catering, menu planning)
- Job-search advice and assistance
- Editorial assistance
- Fitness and health advice and services
- Interior design and landscaping

Other Professions

Finally, most professional activities can be undertaken on a consulting or freelance basis, for example:

- Consulting engineers (to conduct feasibility studies)
- Architectural services
- Clerical and administrative tasks (for example, stenography, language translation, dictation)

The Least You Need to Know

- ◆ Don't rule out any particular sector or market. Consider the pros and cons of each.

- ◆ Your ability to market to particular sectors should be a major determinant of where you focus your practice. Evaluate where your contacts and network will be most useful.

- ◆ Practicing in an area where you are already known and have a positive reputation is a good idea.

- ◆ When deciding which areas you wish to specialize in, take into account the market conditions, both in your geographical area and beyond; your expertise; and your ability to market in that area. All are important.

3

Prerequisites for Success

In This Chapter

- ◆ Finding out the essentials for success in starting and running a successful consulting business
- ◆ Understanding the breadth and depth of knowledge
- ◆ Looking at your attitudes and values
- ◆ Surveying the personal skills specific to the consulting industry

As you consider a career as an independent consultant, you need to know what elements are essential for success. And, boy, there are a lot of things you need to know, a lot of skills you must have, and a certain outlook you need to cultivate.

Ideally, you will have many of these elements before you hang out your consultant shingle, but it's not necessary to have absolutely everything. You are going to learn as you go. However, the more resources and skills you bring to the table from the start, the more likely you will reduce your number of growing pains, mistakes, and hard economic times.

If you are a practicing consultant, this chapter is also important to you. It's an opportunity to begin a self-assessment to identify any gaps in knowledge, skills, and attitudes that you may have. And we all have them.

In this chapter I'll cover the basic elements you need for success.

Specialty-Related Skills and Knowledge

Specialty-related skills and knowledge refer to those basic and advanced skills and knowledge that are required in your chosen field, and that are needed by you in order to provide expert advice to clients and to be seen as credible by prospective clients.

I can't tell you exactly which skills and knowledge this entails, because obviously your needs depend on the field in which you want to practice. However, I can tell you that you'd better know your field well and what it requires before you market yourself as a consultant.

Regardless of whether or not you know your field, try to identify four or five consultants who work in your field. Find several consultants who work in your geographic area, but also track down one or two who work outside your area. This provides some balance.

Explain that you are considering starting a consulting business in this particular field and that you would like 15 to 20 minutes of their time to ask them some questions. When they agree, make sure you ask the following two questions:

- What skills and knowledge have you found most valuable in running a successful consulting business in your field?

- Before I start a new consultancy, are there any absolutely essential things that I need to know and understand in order to have a good chance of success?

If you are wondering whether potential competitors will be willing to help you, don't worry about it. Even though you may find a few consultants who guard their secrets, those really aren't the ones you want to talk to and learn from. The majority of consultants (provided they have the time) will be glad, even honored, to give advice, and that advice can be golden.

Listen carefully. Ask in humbleness.

This picking of consultants' brains allows you to get some other perspectives on your business, something we all need.

> ### Consulting Confidential
>
> While consultants are generally honest people and will give you the "straight goods" on most questions, there's one area in which you will likely get inaccurate information. Probably every consultant on the planet is going to exaggerate his or her own success. For good reason. If a consultant is known to be struggling, clients hear about it and shy away. So take statements about the great success of small consulting businesses with a grain of salt. The consultants aren't being dishonest so much as protecting their businesses.

When discussing specialty-related skills and knowledge, you must consider two significant questions: How broad should your knowledge be and how deep should it be? The answers will be the topics of the next two sections.

Breadth of Knowledge and Skills

What is breadth of knowledge? *Breadth of knowledge* refers to the number of different areas in which you have expertise. Let's say you're a financial consultant. You need a wide range of skills and knowledge so you can provide your clients with high-quality advice and service. For example, you might have significant expertise in the following areas:

◆ Tax laws

◆ Stock market investment strategies

◆ Retirement plans and funds

◆ Mutual funds

Every time you learn something new, you increase your breadth of knowledge. The broader the range of things you know, the better off you are. Why is that?

Because consultants sell their knowledge, the more you have the more you can offer to your clients. Keep in mind that clients looking for consulting advice want someone who has more knowledge in *more* areas than they themselves have.

There's another reason why breadth is important. Our world is complex, and giving good advice requires that you look at a number of interrelated factors. Let's look at the tale of two financial consultants.

Our first financial consultant, Fred, knows a great deal about tax laws, mutual funds, and stock market investment strategies. However, he isn't familiar with retirement plans and regulations. Jane, our second financial consultant, has a wider range of expertise. She's got all the areas of expertise that Fred has, and more. Now which consultant do you think is going to be more successful over time? All things being equal, Jane's got the upper hand, because she's able to offer more complete advice—advice that takes into account more options and possibilities.

The bottom line on breadth of knowledge and skills is that you need to know way more than you might think. And you must strive to increase your breadth of knowledge throughout your career as a professional consultant.

Depth of Knowledge and Skills

If breadth of knowledge is about how many relevant skills and how much information you have at your disposal, *depth of knowledge* is about how well you know each area. You can know a lot of things superficially, but that kind of shallow knowledge isn't what clients are paying you for. You have to have depth to your knowledge.

To use another financial consultant example, imagine a financial consultant who knows just some of the tax laws relevant to financial planning. Would you take advice from that person? Maybe initially, but as soon as you got dinged for a big tax bill, you would be telling that consultant Sayonara. You'd also tell your friends not to hire the person.

Make sense? You don't want to be a consultant who can offer only inferior service because the breadth and the depth of your knowledge falls short of excellent.

As a final point on both depth and breadth of knowledge, consider that you can't ever know exactly how deep and how broad your knowledge and skills must be. However, the market and your clients will often give you important clues:

- Keep in mind that you have gaps in breadth and depth of knowledge and be aware of situations in which they interfere with providing great consulting services. Identify them and address them.

- Be a continuous learner. It's essential that you commit to learning constantly. Think of what you learn as your knowledge inventory. The more you have to offer and sell, the more likely you will be to succeed.

Process Skills—Tools of the Trade

Let's say you have 20 years' experience in your consulting area, but no actual experience as a consultant. Is that enough? Absolutely not. Consultants require a number of other skills and expertise in the consulting process. I call those process skills.

Process skills are those skills that help you identify client needs and wants, build relationships of trust with your clients, and ensure that you offer each client exactly what the client needs.

Working Words

Process skills refer to the tools all consultants need and use to ensure that their advice and recommendations are as informed as possible. These tools include interpersonal communication, group facilitation, data gathering, and diagnostic skills.

The process of determining what your client needs (and delivering it) is what sets apart the consultant from a salaried employee in the same field. An employee is often told what to do by a manager or boss. It's expected that the employee will do what he or she is told to do.

Not so with a consultant. While your client may have an idea of what she wants you to do, it's your professional responsibility to assess whether what the client wants is what the client needs. And the two are often not the same.

Your process skills allow you to make that assessment. Let's look at the essential process skills.

Interviewing Skills

To succeed as a consultant, you need to build trusting relationships with your clients. You also need to get the information necessary to make judgments and offer advice that fits the individual customer. You can't make use of your specialized knowledge if you don't understand the client's situation.

To complicate matters, clients are not always able to provide this information without guidance. It's your role to provide that guidance through the interview process, by asking questions, helping the client clarify his or her needs, and conducting discussions that will elicit the information you need without being confrontational or alienating your client.

Group Skills

Unless your client involves only one person, you are going to be working with a group of people. Groups can be as small as two (for example, a husband and wife) or as large as several hundred people (for example, employees at a large corporation).

Groups skills refer to the tools and techniques a consultant uses to obtain information from groups, but they also include

- Creating an atmosphere so group members feel comfortable speaking and participating.
- Dealing with group disagreements.
- Using techniques to keep group discussions on track and positive.
- Employing public speaking skills.

Not only do you need these skills during the consulting project, but they are also absolutely essential in the front-end phase: getting the contract. That's because the process of getting a contract often involves interacting with a group of decision makers to convince them they should hire you.

Consultant Crashing

A consultant ill-prepared to deal with group dynamics and the anger, resistance, and confrontation that can occur in group meetings is likely to crash and burn, first temporarily, then permanently. Difficult situations will occur, and your skill in dealing with them constructively will determine failure or success.

Data Collection and Observation Skills

Suppose a client contacts you with this complaint: My staff turnover is high. Every year we lose about 50 percent of staff, and it's killing us to hire and train new people every year.

A poor soon-to-crash-and-burn consultant may take a quick look around and tell the client to increase salaries. But a good consultant avoids the quick and easy answer and instead investigates. The first question that must be answered is, "What is causing the turnover?" Without knowing this, it's impossible to suggest informed solutions. The consultant needs to collect data and make observations regarding the work environment.

The skills needed to get the pertinent information or data on which to base recommendations are known as *data collection and observation skills*.

Consultants have a wide range of tools they can draw upon to collect data. The more tools you can use and the more expert you are (there's that breadth and depth thing again), the more likely you will hit the mark with your advice. Here are a few of those tools:

- One-on-one interviewing
- Small group discussions (facilitation)
- Small- and large-scale surveys
- Direct observation of how people work, behave, and interact

Interpretative, Diagnostic, and Logic Skills

No question that getting information is absolutely critical to providing a great consulting service. However, information on its own is not enough. You must interpret the information to provide an accurate diagnosis. That requires diagnostic and logic skills.

What do these skills comprise? Giving a complete list is difficult, but here are the major abilities they include:

- Delaying judgment until all available data have been considered
- Weeding out the relevant from the irrelevant
- Using different sets of data to confirm or disconfirm a tentative diagnosis
- Applying statistical techniques to large quantities of data
- Putting your personal biases on hold
- Knowing when to follow your gut feeling

CAUTION **Consultant Crashing**

A common consultant error involves developing a "pet way" of seeing things, and then seeing every consulting project in terms of that one way. For example, a team development consultant might tend to see all problems as related to faulty teams. A human resources consultant might look at exactly the same information and see the problem as one of hiring the wrong people. Be aware of your pet ways. Recognize that you need to be flexible.

Negotiation Skills

Consultants are always negotiating. You negotiate a contract, a time span, and fees. If you are involved in the implementation of a solution, you negotiate how the implementation should be carried out—who is responsible for what, when, and how it should occur, for example.

Project Management and Time Management

Finally, consultants need the ability to manage their time and to complete projects on schedule and on budget. Although most of us think we are fairly organized and systematic in our personal lives, consulting tends to highlight any project- and time-management flaws.

These flaws become apparent because a successful consultant juggles several projects and tasks at once, and it seems that everything needs to be done yesterday. The consultant's task is to make sure that if something really needed to be done yesterday, it was done yesterday.

Project and time management thus require the ability to prioritize tasks, develop plans of action that make sense, and maximize personal productivity. Wasted time and missed deadlines mean lost money (and lost future contracts).

Experience and Contacts

The more experience you have in your chosen field and the more contacts you have, the more likely you are to start your consulting practice and quickly generate revenue. In addition, extensive experience and contacts help you do the job well.

Experience and Getting the Job

Think about a time when you worked for someone else. Can you recall when you were asked to do something new, something you didn't know too much about? If you're like most people, you learned on-the-job and hopefully completed the task successfully. When you work for someone else, you have some leeway to learn as you go and still get paid.

When someone hires a consultant, he or she wants a consultant who will walk in the door with the experience and skills required to do the job. That's why experience is so important. The client will want to know whether you've done "this" before. Where have you done it? In the client's sector? With what level of success?

The client will avoid hiring someone who needs to learn on the job or whom the client sees as inexperienced. That's one reason why a consultant who has worked in his or her chosen field for an extensive period of time is likely to be more successful, as compared with, say, a recent university graduate having limited experience.

If there's something to be learned here, it's that you should choose areas of practice in which you actually have significant experience. By that, I mean real experience, not just "book learning."

Experience and Doing the Job

The more experience you have in your field, the more likely you are to complete your consulting assignment so that the customer is delighted with the results. Experience helps you in diagnosing and in suggesting solutions that have track records. Experience also enhances your credibility in the eyes of the people you must have as partners in the project.

If a single piece of advice fits here, it's that you must be very careful not to accept assignments way beyond your experience levels. However, do accept assignments that stretch you and give you new experience to use in future projects. In other words, take moderate risks, always trying to ensure you will succeed and please your client.

> **Consulting Confidential**
>
> The greater your experience, the greater your ability to identify patterns and situations you have seen before. For example, experience in working with groups helps you identify the early warning signs that sometimes appear in group dynamics—signs that indicate problems under the surface.

Contacts Keep You Alive

Contacts are your lifeline in the consulting business. Let's say you are a fitness fanatic. You even have a degree in physical education, and you've been working as a phys. ed. teacher. You're tired of the school system and want to do what you love—help adults become healthier and physically fit. So you quit your teaching job and become a "fitness consultant," offering to develop and supervise personal fitness plans for individual clients.

You're going to be in big trouble. You may be fit and skilled and have all the knowledge you need, but if you don't have the contacts in the field (both practitioners and potential customers), how do you let people know you can help them?

Well, you market. You place ads. And you struggle.

Now suppose you plan ahead and develop important contacts before you leap into the business. You might instruct at a fitness gym as a contract employee, join local fitness professional associations, and so on. The situation has now changed immensely. Because you've taken the time to develop some contacts, you at least have some easily accessible sources for potential clients when you do hang out your shingle.

It doesn't matter which field you work in. Your initial contacts in the field are going to allow you to generate income much more quickly than if you had no contacts. They will tide you over until your other marketing techniques kick in and start generating business.

Contacts aren't important only at start-up. They are also important when you've been in business for a while. They help generate income during tough times when business is slack. Keep in mind that many consulting assignments come as a result of word of mouth rather than aggressive sales and marketing. Your contacts are your livelihood. Cultivate them before you start your business, and continue to expand your contacts whenever possible.

> **Consulting Confidential**
>
> In the first few years of my consulting practice, almost all my income came as a result of the contacts I had. People who knew me from previous jobs knew I was good at what I did. It took several years for the effects of more aggressive marketing techniques to bear fruit. If I hadn't had those contacts when I started, I'd have given up or gone broke.

Personal Qualities

Okay, you've got breadth and depth in the knowledge and skills in your chosen practice area. You have a good grasp of the process skills specific to consulting (but you continue to learn). You have experience and contacts. Is that it? No. Successful consultants tend to have certain personal qualities that stand them in good stead in a tough, competitive industry. What are those personal characteristics?

Willingness to Take Risks

Just making the decision to commit to a consulting business, with its potentially unstable income and hours, requires risk taking. But beyond that, you need to be comfortable with

Consultant Crashing

Don't underestimate the importance of the fit between your attitudes and values and the realities of the consulting business. Do a realistic assessment of yourself and what you want from your life, and compare it to the life you anticipate as a consultant.

taking risks, making mistakes, and having to pay the price when things go wrong. The success or failure of your business is almost entirely up to you. You are responsible for it. If you are uncomfortable living with risk and errors, running your own consulting business is not going to work for you. There is no net to fall into.

Apart from your attitude about risk, you need to have the resources to recover when things go wrong. If you are flat broke and have to provide food for your children, you can't afford the risk if your consulting endeavor fails. That kind of pressure causes bad decisions, and bad decisions cause failed businesses.

Ability to Tolerate Insecurity

Can you live with the idea of having your professional and financial life "ride the roller coaster"? If you can't, you'd better choose another profession. You will have lean times and good times. You'll have elated times and depressed times. Above all, you will rarely know whether the next six months will be lean or good. Until you are well established, there is no security except that which you generate.

Desire to Learn Continuously

One key to successful consulting is to slowly and cautiously add more services and expertise to your "inventory." That requires continuous learning of new things.

Learning in an ongoing way is also critical because most consulting projects are going to put you face-to-face with situations or contexts in which you must learn (and learn fast) in order to succeed.

Your curiosity and desire to learn will be essential for long-term success.

Strong Interpersonal Skills

No matter what your field of expertise, your most important set of skills and knowledge has to do with people. The essence of consulting is about communicating, generating trust, and getting information from people who don't even know they have it. You must have the necessary interpersonal skills to know when to press, to be aggressive, to just listen, and much more. And above all, you need to get along well with people. That includes being comfortable with conflict and being able to deal with it when it occurs.

People Orientation

I've met a number of people working in the technical areas (notably computers and Internet specialties) who have huge amounts of technical skill. Some of them are people-oriented. Others would just as soon be left alone to fiddle on their computers and would prefer not to talk to anyone at all.

A solitary personality in an employee who is relied upon for his or her technical wizardry will be tolerated, but this kind of personality will not work if you want to run your own consulting business. No matter how technical your field, if you don't like working with people, and lack the required people skills, you'll have an uphill battle in the consulting business.

Strong Support System in Place

Running your own consulting business can be an isolating endeavor. You'll do a lot of your work (for example, thinking and analysis) on your own. To counteract the possibility of becoming socially and professionally isolated, you need a good support system. A support system involves people whom you can meet, talk to, consult for advice, or even just complain to about life.

And speaking of support systems, let's not understate the importance of a spouse who is supportive of your endeavors and who can live with the insecurity and ambiguity of your new career.

Between Colleagues

Whether you realize it or not, your spouse is an important part of your consulting business. Spouses offer valuable support. They are also asked to tolerate the uncertainties of your business, including the need to travel. Include your spouse in decision making.

Commitment to Personal and Professional Integrity

For some reason our society seems to undervalue qualities such as integrity, ethical behavior, and a commitment to honesty. Remember this: Your consulting lifeblood is your reputation. Your reputation is built on your integrity, honesty, and ethics. If you aren't prepared to set the highest standards for yourself, your customers and prospective customers will find out. Cut corners to make a few bucks, and eventually you won't have any clients.

In consulting, integrity is much more than a nicety. Honesty isn't optional. Your integrity and honesty have profound implications on your bottom line.

Accepting a consulting contract for which you are ill-prepared is an action lacking in integrity. Making promises you can't possibly keep to a client is a dishonest action. Don't kid yourself. Do these things at your own risk. Your reputation is your lifeblood. Protect it even if you must turn down a project.

Working "with" People

Some people work best when they work *for* someone else. They are most comfortable being told what to do. Some people work best when they feel *above* others in authority or skill. Others (and I hope you're one) like to work *with* people, as relatively equal partners. Working "with" means respecting and valuing the abilities and perceptions of your partners (that is, your customers). It means not appearing to place yourself above them, and not waiting for them to tell you what to do. Consulting requires that you deal with your clients as partners in a process.

Business Acumen

Finally we come to the last set of prerequisites. You need to know how to run a business and you should have the required skills to do so, or else make sure you have access to people who have the skills you lack.

You can't hire someone to exercise good business judgment in your stead. Neither can you rely on someone else to make decisions based on sound ethics and principles. You can hire other people to handle some of the business procedures in which you lack the expertise.

Between Colleagues

You might consider hiring a marketing expert (or consultant) to help you develop a marketing plan for your business. This type of investment can really pay off and is particularly useful at start-up since it will help you learn about marketing and get your business off the ground. Make sure the person you hire is familiar with your target market and area of specialization.

The following descriptions provide a quick list of the skills you will need to succeed in business.

Marketing Skills

During the first year, you will be spending a good deal of your time figuring out how to market to your potential clients. That means you have to know something about sales and the marketing process, and about the various options you have at your disposal (for example, brochures, cold contacts, networking, associations, advertising, Internet presence).

Don't worry if you don't yet have this knowledge, but do commit to acquiring it as soon as possible. You will learn much as you go along.

Networking Skills

Networking is often part of the marketing process, but it's also an important aid in keeping your sanity and growing your support network. There is an art to it. You have to balance your "sales needs" with the need to establish free and equal relationships with other people. For example, if you use networking as a way to push your services down other people's throats, you soon won't have anyone to talk to. Nobody likes a pushy, self-centered networker.

Think about whom you should be networked with and then decide how to go about it. To increase sales, you need to network with people who are in positions to hire you or advise people who can hire you. Don't make the mistake of confusing networking with other consultants with networking with potential clients. Both are important but address different goals.

Financial Management Skills

Have trouble balancing your checkbook? Ever been late filing or paying taxes? Hate paperwork? Not good. Even though managing your company's finances is a tedious and sometimes burdensome task for which you don't get paid, it must be done. Luckily, some or much of this task can be off-loaded to others (accountants and tax preparers). Decide now whether you want to do it yourself (be realistic here) or have someone else help you out.

Computer Skills

Computer skills are even more important than you'd think. Being able to use computers efficiently to create documents, prepare marketing copy, and communicate with clients (via computer, fax, or Internet) is essential.

Perhaps it's occurred to you that you may not be able to afford someone to handle and create correspondence, operate your customer database, or computerize your billing and accounts receivable. If you don't have the skills to undertake these tasks yourself, consider enrolling in local community college classes to acquire them. If you are well capitalized, you might be able to employ someone else to do those things—but likely not, at least in the early days of your business.

Consulting Confidential

Which computer skills are absolutely essential? The ability to use a word processor package, the know-how to send and receive e-mail, the ability to browse the Internet to accomplish simple tasks, and the ability to use a basic financial management or accounting package are musts. Also useful is the ability to use web development tools and a desktop publishing program.

The more you can do on your computer, the faster you can work. And the less you need to rely on paid help.

Oh yes. You *can* type, right?

Written Communication Skills

Written communication skills are a definite must for consulting with organizations of any size, although they are less important if you are consulting to individuals. You need to be able to write prose that is easy to understand, clear, and precise. You also need to be able to create documents quickly. If it takes you a week to draft a five-page report, you are in trouble.

Your written communication skills are important in getting contracts (both in the marketing stages and in the contracting stage) and completing such documents as consulting project reports to your clients. At minimum, your clients are going to expect something on paper that summarizes your advice. Some projects may require the submission of major reports and also interim reports done during the life of the project.

Presentation Skills

Presentation skills relate to your ability to speak in public to (usually) a group of people. I know some people who would rather have teeth pulled than speak to a group of people. So are these skills essential? Yes, unless you work only with individuals.

When is it likely you'll have to do group presentations? Often, this is something you'll have to do right up-front. Corporate clients in particular may ask you to speak to a group of people about what you can offer. Next, it won't be uncommon for you to have to speak to a group of people during a contract, either to report on progress, to present interim advice, or simply to get information from them. Finally, you will want the opportunity (yes, opportunity) to speak to clients in order to present your advice in ways that will encourage them to use and implement it.

Proposal Writing Skills

Finally, if you plan on working for clients who may require you to respond to requests for proposals or who want fairly detailed plans about how you can help them, you need to develop skills in writing proposals. For some consultants, especially those who consult to government and corporations, these skills are essential. The ability to give proposal reviewers exactly what they want and little more is invaluable. A combination of writing skills like concise phrasing and document organization along with a knack for understanding what proposal reviewers are looking for will help you compete for contracts.

For others, such as those who consult mainly to individuals, they may be irrelevant.

The Least You Need to Know

- ◆ Assess your knowledge and skills in your specialty areas in terms of breadth and depth.
- ◆ Pay special attention to identifying where you may need to develop your consulting process skills.
- ◆ Before making an irrevocable decision to start a consulting business, be clear about the challenges involved and examine your own values and attitudes. Is this something you will *really* enjoy?
- ◆ Begin thinking about the business skills you may lack and consider filling in the gaps or deciding where you can find the expertise you lack.

Chapter 4

Of Successes and Failures

In This Chapter

- ◆ What it means to succeed or fail
- ◆ Why it's important to know what success means for you
- ◆ Where John the consultant went wrong
- ◆ Where Robert the consultant went right

In this chapter I'm going to discuss success and failure in the consulting business. What kinds of things contribute to success as a consultant? What are the common causes of consultant failure? You probably realize the importance of these questions. Knowing how people succeed and fail will help you avoid common pitfalls and plan for success.

I'll start by getting you thinking about what success and failure mean. It's important that you have your own idea of what success as a consultant means to you. By having a clear vision of where you want to go with your career, you are much more likely to get there. And you may be surprised at how "unsimple" these ideas are.

Then I'll present some case examples for you to read. While you read them, be alert to both the good things and the bad things the consultant does. I'll ask you some questions to test your ability to recognize pitfalls and good consulting practice. Then you can compare your interpretations with mine.

What Does It Mean to Succeed? To Fail?

Everyone talks about successful people without being clear what "successful" means. When you think about success in your own career, it's absolutely critical that you have a clear and realistic set of criteria or a target to aim at—a measure against which you can evaluate your success (or failure, for that matter). Knowing where you are going and where you don't want to go will help you make any necessary midcourse corrections.

I've divided success into three categories: business success, professional success, and personal success. I'll point out that you need to consider all three, and not just the usual money-based indicators of success.

In a Business Sense

For almost everyone, business success is the most obvious kind. It's often what we have in mind when we call someone else "a success."

What is business success? It's easy to define success in monetary terms: We all have to eat. If you make the amount of money you want or need, and if you can do so for a sustainable period, you have achieved a measure of business success. You want to stay in business, right? Feed yourself and your family? Of course. Business success relates to the bottom line of your consulting business.

Failure, of course is also easy to define. If you go broke, that is a business failure. If you can't maintain the standard of living you want, then your consulting practice is helping you meet your life goals. If you focus too much on immediate or short-term financial success and start cutting corners, you jeopardize your chances of long-term success and risk failure.

Between Colleagues

When considering what business success means to you, be realistic and think long-term. Sustainability is the key here. Not just what you earn this year, but whether you are going in the right direction over time.

In a Professional Sense

Defining professional success is a little more complicated. That's because it's possible to succeed in a business sense, at least in the short term, but fail in a professional sense. In a moment you'll see that if you fail in a professional sense, it will eventually impact your bottom line. The two are related.

What does professional success mean? Obviously, what it means to you is different from what it means to me. But here are some criteria or targets that you ought to aim for in your consulting business. If these aren't important to you, you're likely to get into trouble.

First, professional success (in consulting) means making a difference and knowing that you have helped an organization or an individual. Professional success directly affects your satisfaction with your own work, regardless of whether you are making a lot of money or not. If you feel you are wasting your time, then it's difficult to put in the time and effort required to run a consulting practice.

Professional success is more than just satisfaction on your part. If you do not care whether you are doing something useful or helpful (and yes, there are consultants who think that way), here's what happens. You may earn a decent living for a time, but eventually your lack of concern for making a difference will become apparent to your clients, and word is going to get around that you aren't worth whatever money you are being paid. Bottom line? Ignore this aspect and your business success will not be sustainable over time.

Second, professional success means being highly regarded in your community and, more important, highly regarded by your past and present clients. Another word for this is respect. It is a measure of professional success that you should value.

For yourself, the regard and respect you generate in your community helps you get over the business rough spots. It affirms that what you are doing is important, even though you may temporarily struggle in a business sense.

Ultimately, though, if you don't attend to the way you are perceived by your clients, you are going to end up without clients. Word gets around, and that will hit your bottom line—your business success—over time.

You may have other criteria for professional success. Take a moment to think about what specific things indicate professional success to you. Here are some indicators that might be important to you:

- Being asked to speak at conferences
- Being in demand: clients come to you
- Being asked to write articles
- Having a book accepted for publication
- Receiving awards

Remember, if you focus solely on business and financial success, you probably won't be around in 5 or 10 years. You must take into consideration issues of professional success.

> **Consulting Confidential**
>
> Success in the consulting business requires a balanced perspective. By paying attention to business success, professional success, and personal success, you can develop a consulting business that will grow over the years. Attend to all three and you will be less likely to experience burnout.

In a Personal Sense

Now we come to the third area of success: personal success. Here I am talking about lifestyle and quality-of-life issues. Some examples?

- A reasonable number of work hours
- A stress level that is manageable
- A balance of personal life and business life

In other words, your personal success refers to the things you need to enjoy your life. If you are a hard-driving individual, you might say, "Heck, I'm committed to making my consulting practice work, and I'll do anything to make it work." While that sentiment appears admirable, it's probably a huge mistake. Here's why.

If you do not attend to your life as a whole—in other words, your mental, physical, and emotional health—you may be able to succeed professionally and businesswise for a time. Ultimately, though, you'll break down from stress or isolation from an imbalance in your life as a whole.

Consultant Crashing

It's easy to want to succeed so badly that you neglect family, friends, and the things that contribute to your quality of life. Sometimes, wanting to succeed too much is as dangerous as lacking the motivation to succeed. Don't sacrifice your personal and social life at the altar of monetary success. It doesn't work.

Your work and energy levels will drop, and your success will slowly ebb away. Your life may become miserable. Here are some results of a failure to consider and balance personal success or satisfaction with other business considerations:

- Alienation of family and friends
- Sense of isolation and loss of support network
- Overwork and loss of perspective
- Depression and anxiety
- Less-effective work habits
- Dislike of your job

I'm sure you can see that none of these is conducive to success in any area.

Bottom Line on Success

Let's pull all this together. Success is a question of balance. Although you can succeed in one area while ignoring the others, you won't succeed over the long haul unless you pay attention to all three success areas. Don't allow yourself to sacrifice one area because it appears you are succeeding in another. Don't look only at financial success—the most seductive of the three. Here are some practical suggestions:

- If you are beginning in your practice, sit down and map out what success (and failure) means to you in each of these three areas. Be specific.

- If you are already practicing, do the same and evaluate where you are in those three areas. Do you need to change things? Do it.

- Always think long-term. Aim to succeed in all three areas (by your own criteria) and you will be much more likely to develop a sustainable long-term business.

Oops! What Went Wrong? John's Story

One of the best ways to understand what goes into both success and failure is to look at real-life cases in which consultants have failed miserably, or succeeded wonderfully. I've put together some examples for you based on real-life composites. While the components of the cases are real, the cases do not represent any specific person.

Let's look at John.

John's Story

Middle-aged and hitting a bit of a midlife crisis, John worked as a human resource professional for a large company. Due to a number of factors, including economic climate and some of his own limitations, John found himself laid off at a time when he and his wife had just had a "late" addition to their family. In weighing his future, John decided to hedge his bets by continuing to apply for other jobs while, at the same time, beginning the process of building a consulting practice.

Unsure of who would pay him to consult (and for what services), he anticipated the best approach would be to offer a number of wide-ranging human resource consulting services, hoping that the shotgun approach would allow him to hit more potential customers' needs. John also decided that he needed business cards and brochures to establish a professional presence, and he spent as much money as he could on exceedingly high quality material, which, although expensive to produce, presented the image he wished.

> **Consulting Confidential**
>
> It makes sense to take care of what you sell whether it's automobiles, pianos, or other material goods. Since consulting involves being paid for who you are and what you can do, it's important to take care of yourself. A healthy lifestyle and good support network are invaluable for long-term success.

His marketing strategy included visiting a number of his former colleagues and employers, including those that either did not have the power to hire him or did not think highly of him in the first place.

John was able to land a few very small short-term consulting projects, as much the result of his contacts in the industry as anything else. But they were insufficient to carry him over the slow period experienced by most new consultants.

After about nine months, John, who had continued to search for a regular job, was offered something in his field. He had little choice but to accept for financial reasons, and he closed his consulting practice. Unfortunately, the new job didn't work out well, and he was eventually "released" due to what could be best described as "being difficult to work with." Stuck without income, he again tried to breathe life into his consulting practice.

Where Did John End Up?

Sadly, the financial stresses and strains took a toll on both his mental health and the health of his family life. Unable to exist solely on consulting income, he popped between finding a regular job and running a consulting firm. By any criterion, John failed in terms of business, professional, and personal success.

Be the Consulting Detective

From the brief information given in this case, you should have picked up enough clues to figure out what John did that contributed to a very serious failure. Take a few minutes to identify some of the factors that contributed to the outcome. Write down your ideas; when you are finished, read on.

What Went Wrong?

A lot. First, consider John's decision to start a consulting practice. There are two mistakes inherent in his decision. It was made as a result of a layoff, a *reaction* to his life situation rather than a *proactive* decision that allowed proper planning and laying the foundation for a successful practice. Notice also that John, for understandable reasons, hedged his bets. He didn't commit to a consulting practice, and due to financial considerations he had to focus more on where his next meal was coming from than on establishing a professional profile that would stand him in good stead.

Perhaps the major mistake John made was in timing and planning. His family situation and his financial situation made it very unlikely that he could succeed.

What else? John's attempt to offer a wide range of services, the shotgun approach, was problematic.

Between Colleagues

The decision to start a consulting business should be made with a long-term intent and commitment and way in advance of hanging out your shingle. The decision *must* take into account financial issues. As with any business, being underfunded sets you up for failure.

Understandably, he felt the more he offered, the more likely he'd receive contract offers. But that was incorrect. In effect, he was focusing on business and financial success rather than creating his niche of specialization or his professional reputation. The result? Potential customers admired his promotional material but asked questions like: "Can he really do all this?" or "How can one person be good at all of this?" Potential clients could sense his desperation from his personal attitude and his approach to marketing.

Finally, there's something subtle that you might have missed. John assumed that his decades of experience in his field would give him credibility in the marketplace. His attitude was also that he expected a high level of remuneration for his services. In fact, his expectations were way above the normal rates paid to beginning consultants.

He overvalued himself in his own eyes and misread his status in the community in which he wanted to practice. In consulting, more than in other jobs, you must have an accurate idea of your own skill levels and how your contacts already perceive you. In John's case, word of his track record circulated freely (as is the case in many fields) and became an unanticipated barrier to success for him. We all have baggage, but to be ignorant or unrealistic about how we are seen is a fatal problem in the consulting industry.

So, how did you do? Here are the main points to derive from John's case:

♦ Decide to enter consulting from a position of strength rather than necessity. Plan for your consulting career at least one or two years in advance.

♦ Lose the attitude that you are valuable. You may very well be, but in the eyes of your clients you must prove yourself.

♦ Consider finances and your family situation before you commit to a consulting career.

♦ When you commit, *commit*. It's possible to enter slowly, but at some point you will have to make a commitment.

♦ Don't pretend that you can do everything well. Learn about your prospective market. Find out first what people are hiring consultants for; then tailor your services. Shotgun approaches make you look bad.

Consultant Crashing

Without an accurate, honest, and realistic assessment of your strengths and weaknesses, you may offer consulting services in areas that fall in your "weakness area." That's going to damage your reputation with customers.

Yes! The Stars Are Aligned

John's mistakes are quite common, but I don't want to depress you too much. The truth is that while successes may be outnumbered by failures, consultants are succeeding. The trick is to know some of the ways you can create this success for yourself. Let's look at Robert's story.

Robert's Story

Robert joined the sphere of government as a trainer and instructional designer. Never considering himself a civil servant, he planned to stay no more than two years. The position was rewarding enough financially and in terms of the job activities. He ended up staying for six years.

About four years into his employment, Robert became concerned that his work lacked the kind of meaning he was looking for in a profession. He saw corners cut and customers not receiving the benefits they deserved. At this point Robert began considering the possibility of running his own consulting business. And he began preparing.

Financially, he started saving money so he could survive at least one year with no income whatsoever. He also began to acquire the equipment he would need to run his own consulting business, and did so in a leisurely way, first acquiring a laser printer, then a fax machine, an updated computer, and so on. The fancy word for this activity would be *infrastructure development*.

Perhaps more important, he began learning the new skills he would need to succeed. Writing skills, desktop publishing, and Internet skills, for example. He undertook projects while he was still employed (writing and editing a newsletter) to learn and polish various skills. And, of course, he took every opportunity to observe other consultants in action.

> **Working Words**
>
> **Infrastructure develop-ment** means acquiring the equip-ment you need to succeed.

> **Between Colleagues**
>
> When you start a consult-ing business, you will make decisions that need to be changed later on. Be alert to signals that your initial decisions are not getting you where you want to go. Then change them or shift directions.

In his sixth year of government employment, Robert became convinced that he had become ineffective in his current position, and taking into account a deteriorating relationship with his boss, he resigned.

At that time Robert was passionate about a management process called Total Quality Management, and for the first six months he tried to crack that market within the environment he knew best—government. It didn't work. He found that he was competing against established consultants who, in truth, were better at it and deserving of the contracts they received.

Since Robert had a fairly high profile within government, he would occasionally receive calls to do other things, particularly related to what he did when employed by government. He accepted those at relatively low fees. In his first year of practice, he netted a grand total of only $7,500.

However, not overly discouraged, Robert positioned his company in a particular niche, and business increased somewhat. Meanwhile, he started publishing a free newsletter to establish a profile in his local community. The next step was to move outside of his geographical area by creating a killer Internet website and participating in professional forums. He maintained his niche while gradually expanding the extent of his services.

Finally, rather than becoming discouraged at the relative lack of income, he used his down time to write articles and books, both to generate more income and to increase his visibility.

Where Did Robert End Up?

Well, ultimately, writing this book! This one is my story. I've made a lot of mistakes over the 10 years of my consulting career, but, as I like to say, "I'm still standing!" I now make a decent living and can charge 10 times more for my services than I could when I started. But perhaps more important, I've been able to establish a professional reputation that leads to financial gains and a level of personal satisfaction I can live with.

Okay, Your Turn

Now it's your turn to think. Take a look at what Robert did and identify some of the critical factors you feel contributed to Robert's success. Make some quick notes before you continue reading.

What Went Right?

First and foremost, Robert struggled both financially and personally for several years. Let's not forget this. But two things stand out here. A commitment to long-term success, measured not only in money but also in professional status and recognition, and an outlook that was not short-term. There are a few other things to note.

Robert took his time. He started his preparation for entry into the consulting business a full two years before the decision point came. Many (probably not all) of the resources or infrastructure he needed for success were in place at launch: sufficient finances, a reasonably established professional profile, and at least some of the skills and hardware needed to succeed.

Something else to note is Robert's flexibility. Initially he chose a practice area that could not

> ### Consulting Confidential
>
> Do consultants who own their own teeny business have any competitive advantages over larger high-status consulting firms? You bet. Aim at high flexibility in what you do, offering quick decision making to clients and working cost-effectively.

succeed for him. Rather than overvaluing himself in this area, he realized it was a no-go and listened to the market, working off of his existing abilities. When the market told him they would not pay him to do Total Quality Management, he moved his niche.

Related to this is the idea that the consultant's stock in trade is his knowledge, skill, and experience and that learning new things, even if their immediate usefulness is limited, results in doors opening in the future. When doors open and you have the skills, you can create additional services people will pay for. In Robert's case he moved from offering training services to also becoming a book author and Internet publisher. Thus, by acquiring new skills and being open to possibilities, he was able to take advantage of opportunities in writing and in public speaking to broaden his delivery of services.

One final point on flexibility: Robert's business strategy was to create a clientele beyond his geographic area. Initially he targeted the market he knew, but he moved to larger ones over time. Rather than concentrating on a local market niche (which was somewhat limited), he moved toward a broader market.

Success Points

Let's summarize the main points of Robert's case:

- Prepare in advance. Get all your ducks in a row *before* you embark on your consulting career.
- You may not understand your market completely, so you need to be prepared to be flexible and listen to what the market tells you as you go.
- Constantly learn new things and skills. You'll be amazed how often opportunities can pop up. You want to be ready to take advantage of them.
- Be slow to commit to your consulting business. But once you do commit, do it for the long term. Put aside immediate concerns about money for as long as possible.

The Least You Need to Know

- Develop a clear target by defining what success means for you.
- Consider the three success areas—business, professional, and personal—and work to get them in balance.
- Capitalize on your ability to "turn on a dime," and be fast and flexible. Be ready to change directions if you take a wrong turn.
- Keep learning. You'll be amazed at how often something you learn on the way becomes incredibly valuable to your business.

Chapter 5

Bacal's Laws of Consulting

In This Chapter

- ◆ Having a sense of humor
- ◆ Viewing certainty as a constant threat
- ◆ Making yourself unnecessary
- ◆ Creating your own body of wisdom

Consulting is a serious business. You have the ability to help or harm your clients. As a consultant you will be confronting career and financial issues. You will also have responsibilities, and carrying them out will be challenging.

In the midst of all this seriousness, you need to inject some levity into the proceedings. In fact, one of the best things you can bring to your consulting career is a sense of humor. The ability to laugh at some of the situations you get yourself into is going to make the difference between total frustration and burnout, and consulting success. Your clients and, yes, you too are going to do silly things once in a while. Seeing the humor in these situations really helps.

The reason humor is so important is that it helps you forgive, forget, and move on to constructive things. It counters the tendency to become angry when things go wrong. Being angry about something a client does, or even some mistake you make, reduces your ability to exercise good judgment.

This chapter is consistent with the idea that we have to have a sense of humor. It will look at some fundamental facts of life—of consulting life—but will treat them in a lighthearted manner. Although the presentation takes a light approach, the points made are nevertheless very important.

> **Consulting Confidential**
>
> Ever hear the expression: "Mama said there would be days like this"? Well, now your author, Bacal, also says you'll have "days like this," and one of your ways of coping is to have a sense of humor about your own mistakes and those of the client.

You're probably familiar with Murphy's Law, which goes like this: Anything that can go wrong will go wrong. Bacal's laws are similar. They are comments on the consulting business, but they extend much further. Consulting is about people and organizations. The consulting voyage will bring you in contact with all the quirks involved in human enterprise. And of course, consulting is about ourselves and who we are as people, warts and all. So Bacal's Laws comment on these issues. Each law does have serious implications, which I'll point out.

Bacal's Laws on the Consulting Process

The next few sections address some real issues about the consulting process. I call them "Consulting Process Laws," and there are five of them.

Consulting Process Law #1

The more certain a consultant is, the more likely the consultant is going to be wrong, and therefore a danger to himself or herself and the client.

When I talk to people wanting to hire a consultant, here's what I tell them: If you see a consultant who is sure of his or her conclusions, run as fast as you can in the opposite direction. Really fast. Quick as a bunny. Don't come out until the consultant goes away.

When I talk to consultants, I tell them this: If you are dead certain about how to solve a problem, it's almost guaranteed that you are wrong. Plan on getting your professional head bashed in.

> **Consultant Crashing**
>
> Are you sure you are sure? If you are sure you are sure, it's a sure thing that you shouldn't be sure.

Why? Because consultants who are "sure" usually are consultants who have only one way of looking at a consulting problem—"a one-trick pony." Since they have only one solution, they apply it to every problem they see. It's easy to be completely certain about the one solution, because the one-trick pony doesn't have any others.

Consulting by its very nature is about dealing with ambiguity and fuzzy situations. Thus, a "certain" consultant isn't grasping the central elements of consulting.

If your client starts hopping around, be assured that they've talked to me and that you've been too certain and too sure.

Consulting Process Law #2

From 10 feet away, everyone looks normal.

I've borrowed this line from a longtime friend, Alan Ennist, who missed his calling as a philosopher. What does this law mean?

Simple. From a distance, you can't see the various quirks and foibles of people. Ten feet away is a fair distance, and from there you can't see people very well.

Now, of course I'm not talking about real distance. Rather, I'm referring to what we learn about people as we get to know them—as we decrease our "distance" from them. It's like going on a date (that's a full 10 feet). You see only what the person lets you see. Only later do you discover what's strange about the person. Hopefully that discovery occurs before the marriage, but (sighing) that's often not the case.

If we apply this analogy to consulting, you start a consulting intervention from 10 feet away, not knowing much about your client, the organization, or what's wrong with them. As you work in partnership with your client and close the distance, you begin to discover that your client has quirks.

The consulting implication is this. In initial meetings with clients, you'll be at 10 feet. That personable CEO may appear great, until you find out that ... well, he's a nasty S.O.B. Don't be fooled by first impressions. Everyone, including your client, is less perfect than he or she seems. And, in any significant consulting project, you *will* find out about the imperfections. Be prepared.

A scary thought. If your first impression of a client is negative, imagine how much worse it's going to get after you've worked with that client for a while.

Between Colleagues

Embrace the idea that consulting involves getting progressively closer. It's like peeling away the layers of an onion. Be prepared to alter your assessment of your client and the situation. And know that sometimes the process will bring a tear to your eye.

Consulting Process Law #3

A consultant's main goal is to make sure the client never needs him or her again.

Scary thought. If you do your job well, you put yourself out of a job—at least with that one client. And that's how it should be.

What a deal. You spend all this time and effort on marketing, only to do your job so well your client doesn't need you anymore.

Actually, that statement is not true. You want to solve the client's problem so well and be so absolutely wonderful that the client never has to deal with the same problem again. Of course, the real idea is that you are so wonderful that the client brings you back to help with a different problem.

Consulting Process Law #4

The ability to make very complex situations seem simple is a well-cultivated skill of the idiot.

Oversimplification is not a good thing! I'm speaking here of consultants who are so simpleminded they oversimplify complex situations. Jack, our prototype simpleton, knows how to use a particular consulting technique and simplifies every situation so that the tool fits. Only it doesn't.

> **Consulting Confidential**
>
> Clients also tend to oversimplify complex issues and problems, at least initially. Your job is to peel away the simplicity so you can expose the real issues and causes of the problems.

The reality is that when you are talking about real live people in real live organizations, including families, you are talking about a great deal of complexity.

So if you think you've found a simple solution to something, beware. You might just be right. Or you may be thinking like an idiot.

Consulting Process Law #5

It may be darkest before the dawn, but a consultant who waits for the sun to rise is going to need to buy a lot of light bulbs.

> **Consulting Confidential**
>
> Positive thinking is a good thing provided it pushes you to do something to bring about positive results. There's a difference between saying "I can make this work if I do the right thing" and saying "I'm sure this will turn around." Positive thinking should never be an excuse for inaction.

That's a mouthful. You know the expression "It's always darkest before the dawn"? I suppose it means that we can be assured that whatever the situation, the sun will rise tomorrow and things will get better.

Heck, there are days when I tell myself that things are bound to get better, or the sun will soon rise, or I'll be hitting the light at the end of the tunnel any minute now (or some other cliché). Thinking like that helps me get out of bed in the morning.

Consultants, however, can't wait for the sun to rise. We can't afford to wait for things to get better. Our job is to make sure the sun rises, to be proactive and exert significant control over our projects.

I once met a consultant who took the attitude that things would turn around if he waited things out. He set the course and followed it regardless, being pushed and pulled by events because he wouldn't take control of his consulting projects. For this he got paid? Well, no; or rather, he got paid only for a little while—until prospective clients heard of his consulting disasters.

In consulting, things don't "get better" on their own.

Bacal's Client Laws

In my consulting career, I have found that client issues can be grouped into four laws.

Client Law #1

The more important the project is to the client, the more likely some doofus will try to screw it up.

In organizations, consulting projects that have little effect on employees appear more benign to them. When the project is important, with wide-reaching effects, that's when people start to do dumb things to mess it up.

A project worth doing (that is, one that will have an impact) is a project that will bring out all the hidden agendas, aggressions, and past histories of people in an organization.

On the other hand, a project that creates no ripples or is a total waste of time (that is, having no impact at all except to line your pockets) is easy to do—boring, pointless, even fraudulent, but easy to do.

Perhaps when you hit resistance, you know you're doing something important.

Client Law #2

What the client thinks is the problem is never the whole problem, except when it is.

Here's a conundrum. On one hand, the client has the most knowledge and understanding of his or her situation, and the consultant needs to respect that knowledge and make use of it.

On the other hand, while the client may be the most knowledgeable person (at least at the beginning of the project), the client is likely to be wrong about his or her problems and, more specifically, about what causes those problems.

Faced with this paradox, the consultant's job is to get to the point where he or she has a better understanding of the client's situation than even the client, and then share that understanding with the client. Then, at some point, both consultant and client end up with the same understanding. If you can get to that point of shared understanding, really good things happen.

Between Colleagues

What's your *real* job as a consultant? Hear the client. Disbelieve the client. Find out where the client's understanding is incomplete. Teach the client.

Remember, one of the reasons clients hire consultants is because they need help in developing a course of action, and they need a different perspective—the perspective of someone with no agenda or biases in the situation.

Client Law #3

It's better to have a totally confused client than a sure one.

Working with totally confused clients can be challenging. They don't have a clear idea of what's wrong, let alone why things are going wrong. They don't know where to start. Interacting with confused clients is like sifting through a pile of sand to find one particular grain of sand. In this case, you are looking for the client's real problem.

But that situation isn't so bad, because there's something worse: the client who approaches you with a preconceived idea of the problem *and* has a plan of action to solve the problem. This type of client presents a much more difficult situation. Watch out for these folks, because they may actually be more confused and may be totally oblivious to their confusion.

Such clients are difficult to lead in any direction other than the one they started from. On the other hand, a totally and openly confused client, willing to be led, is much easier to work with. And the chances of success are greater because they listen.

Client Law #4

Clients confuse wants and needs.

Sometimes I *want* a piece of cake, but I tell myself, I *need* a piece of cake. Or I might *want* a new gadget for my computer, having convinced myself I can't possibly live without it. I suppose I'd make an ideal consulting client, because I do what most clients do: They confuse what they need with what they want. And of course, being human, you do the same thing.

Here's an example. A client may want you to do some team-building seminars, and the client believes that this is what he or she needs. But is it? Perhaps the real need—the action that will solve the client's problem—lies elsewhere.

You go into consulting projects with the expectation that your client is going to confuse wants and needs, and has hired you to help him or her tell the difference between the two. No client is going to admit this, but you need to keep it in mind nevertheless.

It's your job to distinguish between the two. Sometimes, telling a client that his or her needs are something different from what he or she wants is a challenge. It's like telling your child she doesn't need a cookie but needs broccoli instead. Needless to say, your child is not going to be happy with this consulting advice.

Between Colleagues

One of your major tasks, early in the consulting project, is to help the client identify which of his or her "wants" are really needs, and which of the wants are not necessary at all.

Bacal's Laws About Consultants

Clients aren't the only ones who have quirks and foibles. In fact, consultants can be their own worst enemies. Let's take a look at my three laws about consultants.

Consultants Law #1

The attractiveness of doing dumb things is inversely proportional to the consultant's bank balance.

For those of you who have a fear of mathematical terms, I'll rephrase this without the fancy-pants wording. It means this: The less money you have, the more likely you are going to make decisions you regret.

Falling into this situation is understandable, but it's still stupid, because you are sacrificing the future for the present. Here are examples of things cash-poor consultants have regretted doing:

 ♦ Taking a project they weren't qualified for
 ♦ Making unwarranted claims about their services
 ♦ Cutting corners on things that cost money and need to be done right
 ♦ Cutting back on marketing

Consultant Crashing

If you don't plan your entrance into the consulting profession, you are much more likely to make poor decisions and end up with a small bank account.

If you are serious about a consulting career, you are better off looking for temporary measures that won't have a big impact on your business. For example, it's better to curtail your lifestyle for a little while than to sabotage your infant business.

Consultants Law #2

The more areas you specialize in, the more people will see you as expert in none.

The old saying "Jack of all trades, master of none" is true, although it's possible that over time you may well become a master of many things. Of course, you need to know your own limitations, but Consultants Law #2 is more about how you present yourself to potential clients and to your colleagues and peers.

If you make claims about your ability to do everything, you will appear deluded, arrogant, or desperate, particularly early on in your consulting career. Write to me if I'm wrong, but the following aren't strong selling points to make to a prospective customer. "Hi, I'm Robert, and I'm deluded, arrogant, and desperate for your business, so let me tell you what I can do for you."

It sure doesn't sound right to me.

Consultants Law #3

The start-up consultant spends most of his or her time not earning money.

If your son or daughter came up to you and said: "Guess what? I've decided on what I want to do with my life. I'm going to do something and plan on *not* earning money." You'd, well, wonder about your child's sanity, wouldn't you?

It's an odd idea … this planning not to make money, but it's something you have to do as a start-up consultant. Sometimes you have to plan not to make money even after you are established.

I'm not saying you need to accept not making money, but you have to be prepared not to make money. Unless you are one of an extremely small group of consultants who prove to be exceptions, you are going to spend much of your first year worrying about money. Get used to the idea. If you can't get used to the idea, then perhaps you should have a regular job with a bit more security.

Plan for this eventuality from the very beginning. If it turns out you make scads of money from day one, more power to you. If you don't, you have the wherewithal to get through the tough times.

Stress-Busting—A Cool Learning Technique

There's some method to this chapter. Some might say there's a method to the madness. Throughout this chapter, at the same time that I was explaining some of the realities of the consulting arena by applying various "laws," I was also demonstrating a creative and humorous way to look at frustrating and sometimes anger-provoking situations. All of my laws arose out of my own efforts to decrease my stress and condense my experience into helpful rules.

As I've said, humor is a tool. By using this tool, I've lightened up the chapter but also helped you learn in the process. Now you can develop your very own "Bacal's Rules of Consulting."

Here's the technique. It's simple and fun.

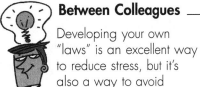

Between Colleagues

Developing your own "laws" is an excellent way to reduce stress, but it's also a way to avoid repeating your mistakes. Commit to coming up with your own laws (or something similar) on a regular basis.

Creating Your Own Rules of Consulting

Why should you create your own consulting rules? There are several reasons. First, coming up with your own rules helps you put disturbing events into perspective if you can summarize the situation in one or two funny or amusing sentences. Second, it's a way to keep track of what you learn about your clients, the consulting process, and yourself as a consultant.

Here's how to do it. Put aside a few minutes a day, a week, even a month. Turn off all the noise around you and think. Think about the last week or month and identify one stupid thing that you've done, that your client has done, or that has occurred as part of the consulting process.

Once you've thought about that stupid event or decision, try to summarize in one or two short sentences what you've learned and write it down somewhere. Indicate the date of writing. It's like having a "Laws of the Universe" diary.

Over time, you will have created a rich storehouse of wisdom that you have created for yourself.

Consulting Confidential

Recording what you learn as you go means you are consciously and intentionally creating your own wisdom. We tend to remember what we create, as opposed to what others create. That's why this technique is so useful.

What Do You Use Your Laws For?

Now that you've begun writing your own "Laws," try to allot 15 minutes a month or week to leafing through them. Think of the writing process as note-taking, and your review of the laws as a way to refresh yourself about your observations and what you've learned on the way.

The point of this exercise is to ensure that you make the same mistake once and once only, and that you forgive your errors, provided they occur only once. There's another purpose. By recording the weird behavior of clients, you will be better able to recognize that behavior the next time it occurs.

You never know. Maybe one day your "Laws" will be so good you will be able to publish them and make a million dollars. Please keep in mind that I expect 10 percent of your gross sales.

The Least You Need to Know

- ◆ Humor provides a means of reducing stress, forgiving yourself and your client, and even learning.
- ◆ The consulting process involves people. All of us are flawed in some way or another. Get used to it.
- ◆ You can't control your client's quirks, but you can learn, over time, how to deal with them more effectively.
- ◆ Create your own laws and you'll create your own personal body of wisdom.

Part 2

The Consulting Process

What's a consulting engagement like? Understanding that is what Part 2 is all about. But before discussing the consulting process from beginning to end, I want to start you off with a chapter on ethics, because ethics, along with solid expertise, are the foundation of any successful consulting practice. You want to do the right things and you want to get things right. Learn more about what that means in Chapter 6, "Ethics: Doing the Right Things, Getting the Right Things Done."

The consulting engagement starts with an initial meeting in which you explore the problems you might be hired to solve. After that, you move on to contracting, then to the work of figuring out what's actually going on, and finally to what improvements you can suggest that will make sense. Besides the legal contract, I call your attention to the psychological contract you're making with your client and help you make sure you're both on the same page with that as well.

The last chapter in Part 2 gives you advice on laying out your solutions to the client and how the company might go about implementing them. The client doesn't always want to hear what you have to say, so I explain how to undertake this step so your advice will actually be listened to.

Chapter 6

Ethics: Doing the Right Things, Getting the Right Things Done

In This Chapter

◆ Why it's important to do the right thing

◆ Why you need etched-in-stone ethics and principles

◆ What your rights are

◆ How to prevent problems with clients

Why on earth would anyone introduce a section on the consulting process by presenting a full chapter on ethics, principles, and rights?

Good question. People are funny sometimes; they don't always begin at the right place. They want to learn the nuts and bolts of a subject—how to write a contract, how to submit a proposal, how to interview, and all that sort of thing. Of course there's nothing wrong with this approach, because these things are important.

But, in the consulting business, knowing the nuts and bolts is useless unless you have a strong foundation on which to place them. They may be the tools of your new trade, but what will guide you in your decision making and thinking is a firm grasp of the mandatory ethical considerations of consulting and an understanding of your own ethical position regarding your work.

In this chapter I'll talk about several topics, beginning with the importance of ethics and principles. I'll talk about your ethical obligations to your clients and why they are critical to your financial success. I'll also explain that, in addition to your obligations, you have rights, as does your client. I'll discuss some common ethical dilemmas you will face and how to deal with them. By the end of this chapter, you will have explored some aspects of your ethical self.

The Importance of Ethics and Principles

If having a high set of ethical standards were some abstract topic, with few practical considerations, it would make more sense to bury it in the back of this book. It's not abstract though. In fact, it's likely that your ethics and principles will be a major determinant in whether you succeed or fail over the long haul. They affect some fundamental issues:

- Your satisfaction with your consulting career
- Whether you develop a positive reputation (that means contracts and money) in your field
- The decisions you make before, during, and after a consulting project

---

Consulting Confidential

In a sense, ethical behavior is important to any business, and to life in general. Someone totally lacking in ethics will end up dealing with crisis after crisis, regardless of profession. Some professions require higher standards of conduct, particularly those that rely on reputation for success or are subject to government regulation. Consulting falls into the first category.

Consulting As an Ethical Practice

Some ways of making a living have less to do with ethical behavior than others. For example, playing baseball doesn't really require baseball players to adhere to high standards of ethical conduct. In fact, these days, we're surprised when sports figures do so.

Selling soap doesn't require high ethical standards. Working in a manufacturing facility doesn't require them. That's not to say they are irrelevant, but they are less relevant than for other occupations. Jobs where there is concern about safety and well-being or that rely on the establishment of good working relationships tend to have higher ethical standards. In these contexts, those standards are enforced more rigorously.

For example, lawyers, doctors, psychologists, and psychiatrists must adhere to the ethical standards set forth by their governing bodies or else risk losing their license to practice.

While consultants do not have a legally mandated set of ethical considerations, such considerations nonetheless exist and are important.

Ethical Behavior As Marketing

What do you think consultants sell? Is there a difference between selling soap and selling consulting? Of course there is. If you sell soap, there are some primary consumer concerns. Is the soap good? Is the price right? If you address these concerns, then chances are good you will sell the soap, all other things being equal.

As a consultant, you sell your expertise, experience, judgment, skills, and usefulness. In a sense, the package you sell is … well, you, as a professional person. If that package is corrupt, sloppy, overly selfish, or otherwise tainted by suspicious or questionable decisions, what do you have left to sell? Not much.

Don't delude yourself on this point. Don't ever assume that you can cut corners with clients and get away with it. Clients talk to other clients. Bid for a contract and it's almost guaranteed that the client is going to do a little background research by talking to other clients you have worked with. Remember this rule: A dissatisfied client may not tell you that he or she is unhappy, but the client will, almost certainly, tell other prospective clients.

Thus, your reputation as being ethical (or not) can be either a marketing tool to be used for your benefit or a negative that will cost you clients. If you develop a good reputation as being ethical and concerned about what you give your clients, your clients will "sell you." Grow a negative reputation and no amount of marketing will counteract the effects of negative word of mouth.

Between Colleagues

Consider your work as a consultant as being similar to acting in a Broadway play. Everything you do is being observed by your audience. If you cut corners or act in unethical ways, not only will your audience know, but you will also receive horrible reviews in the word-of-mouth world. And your show just might close.

Ethics As a Guide to Making Decisions

As a consultant you are expected to make informed, expert decisions on behalf of your clients. The decisions you will make are profoundly influenced by your guiding principles and ethical standards. Let's consider a common example.

A client approaches you with a specific request to do a particular task. Let's say it's working with a group of people to improve their abilities to work together as a team. The client is adamant. "This is what I want," he says.

As you prepare to undertake the task, you discover that the team-building process will not solve the client's problems. In fact, as you gather more information, you discover the real problem doesn't lie with the team but with the manager/client who hired you. What do you do?

A consultant with low ethical standards, more concerned with getting the cash and getting out, might deliver exactly what the client asked for, despite the fact that the client will receive no benefit from it. Take the money and run.

CAUTION

Consultant Crashing

Greed is a poor foundation on which to build a consulting practice. Your job is to work with the client for their benefit in return for fair compensation.

A consultant with higher ethical standards would make different decisions. Recognizing that consulting means creating positive results for the client, the consultant would go to the client and explain (gently and diplomatically) that the path he wants to take won't get him to his destination. Perhaps the consultant would make some other suggestions as to better paths to the goal. If the client remained resistant to those suggestions, the consultant might refuse to continue, and repay any money already received for the project. Ouch!

Here's another example of how ethics affect your decision making. A client asks you to do something completely outside your field and offers you a significant amount of money to do it. What's your decision? On what basis do you make your decision? An ethical consultant is going to have in place a framework of principles upon which to make that decision.

Considering the possibility that someone else might be better able to meet the client's needs, the ethical consultant might recommend someone else the client can contact. The consultant could also refuse the assignment or perhaps agree to do it in partnership with someone more expert in the task.

The unethical consultant might say, "Heck, I can learn this on the job, and I need the bucks."

Keeping in mind the importance of your reputation, who do you think will be more successful in the consulting business over time? The ethical consultant or the unethical consultant?

Good answer!

Fixed-in-Stone Consultant Ethics

Some ethics and principles are of the "fixed-in-stone" variety. That is, we'd consider them as essential and necessary.

Before I discuss the ethical commitments you must make, keep in mind that the details of your ethical commitment depend somewhat on the context. Sometimes you will come across situations where one ethical commitment conflicts with another.

Put the Client's Welfare Above Your Own

Put the client's welfare above your own. I've put this ethic first, because most of our fixed-in-stone ethical principles derive from this golden principle.

I'll explain. There will be situations in which it will be to your short-term personal benefit to do something that will not be in the client's best interest. It might involve taking a contract for which you aren't sufficiently qualified or doing something you know is not going to benefit the client, even though it's what the client wants.

By putting the client's welfare above your own, you focus on generating results, which is a good business practice.

Between Colleagues

While the client's welfare is paramount, that doesn't mean that you allow the client to take advantage of you. The consulting relationship is a partnership in which both parties must benefit.

Respect and Adhere to Principles Regarding Client Confidentiality and Privacy

Prospective clients and contracted clients deserve and expect that what they tell you, and what you discover, will remain exclusively between you and the client. That means you don't do any of the following:

- Discuss one client's affairs with another.
- Discuss client's affairs with colleagues or family members.
- Write or disclose information about a client in any way that could result in the identification of that client to others.
- Provide client contact information to prospective clients without first obtaining permission (this applies to references).

Charge Fair, Consistent Fees and Expenses

Although I'll talk more about fees and expenses in Part 4, "The Ongoing Business Challenge," it's appropriate to discuss them here as well. Commit to the general principle that you will charge equitable and fair fees to clients and that you will strive to maintain consistency in what you charge different clients for the same work. Resolve that you will charge expenses on a fair, reasonable, and honest basis.

Consultant Crashing

Consultants have a tendency to discuss other consultants' work with peers or clients. You may have information about other colleagues in your field. If you share this information, you may be seen as a gossip or as trying to damage the reputation of your peers. Use discretion if asked directly about a colleague.

Consultant Crashing

Here's something to ponder. Some consultants, because of their status as "gurus," can charge up to $50,000 for a one-hour speaking engagement or charge $3,000 dollars and up for consulting work. How do you feel about that? Is that ethical? If you are ever in this position, you'll have to decide for yourself. It's not a simple decision.

As you'll see later in the book, setting fees so they are fair is less science than art. There is no one way to do so. With that in mind, consider the following guidelines:

♦ Do not charge fees way above what the work requires (contract padding).

♦ If billing by the hour, charge for work of value to the client. Do not charge for time spent acquiring the skills you need to do the job.

♦ Just because a client is willing to pay you a huge unrealistic sum of money doesn't mean that's what you should charge.

♦ Use flexibility in fees as is required, but keep fees relatively consistent for similar projects.

♦ Ensure there are no "fee surprises." Clients should know what they will be paying in advance. If those figures change, they should be discussed with the client.

What about expenses? Same thing. Charge only for reasonable expenses or direct out-of-pocket expenses. Don't be overly concerned with nickels and dimes. For example, it's tacky to charge a client 25 cents for the pay phone call you made on her behalf. Bottom line: Don't charge any expense that will make the client, or anyone with half a brain, go "huh?"

Avoid Conflict of Interest and Perceived Conflict of Interest

What does *conflict of interest* mean? If you stand to benefit personally from information you might receive in the course of a consulting intervention, you could very well be in a conflict-of-interest situation. For example, suppose you consult for an investment firm and have access to information that can earn you significant profit on the stock market. That is a perceived conflict of interest. If you use that information to realize a profit, that's also illegal.

You consult for a company to help them downsize their staff, and you have family members who work for that company and who will be affected by your recommendation. That's conflict of interest.

Here's a different kind of example. You are retained to consult for two different companies in direct competition with each other. That might be conflict of interest.

Between Colleagues

Be alert to conflict-of-interest situations. If you have any concerns, you can (a) refuse the contract; (b) provide full disclosure to the parties and let them decide to hire or not; or (c) include clauses in the formal contract that specify what you will *not* do to obtain personal gain.

Before I leave this subject, here's an important point. Not only must you not take advantage and receive inappropriate personal benefits, but you must also avoid the *appearance* of conflict of interest. Your actions may be completely honest and aboveboard, but if you have placed yourself in a position of conflict, you will create doubts about your trustworthiness.

Respect Copyrights and Ownership of Materials

I'm constantly amazed at the number of consultants who "borrow" (actually the word is plagiarize) forms, articles, and other material that is copyright protected by other consultants.

Do not use any written material owned by someone else without obtaining permission first, preferably in writing.

Learn and understand copyright laws, both to protect your own material and so you will not inadvertently tread upon the rights of others.

Finally, even material you create for one client may not be usable with another client. It depends on how you contract ownership. If you create material for clients, make sure your written contract specifies who owns that material, and respect that agreement.

Create Client Independence

Some consultants on the shady side attempt to increase their revenue by creating situations in which the client must continue to pay them. They create a dependence for financial gain when that dependence is not in the best interest of the client.

That's not ethical.

Create Realistic Expectations

There's a temptation to "sell" a client by claiming you can accomplish things that are, in reality, impossible. Exaggerating the benefits of your service is a path to disaster. Apart from the fact that it is dishonest, it guarantees you will have an unsatisfied client when the expectations are not fulfilled.

Open and Regular Client Communication and Access

Your client deserves regular, honest, and open communication with you. You will be accessible within a reasonable time to discuss issues with the client. You don't withhold information that is due the client.

Client Ethics

Treating people honestly and ethically is critical to your success as a consultant—you are responsible for this. However, there's a flip side to ethics in consulting. What should you expect from a client (potential or current) in terms of how they deal with you?

Between Colleagues

Consider drafting a short one-page document outlining the ethical expectations you have of your clients. Couple this with a similar document outlining your own ethical obligations to your clients. Append this to the formal contract, use it in preliminary meetings, and ensure your client understands the meaning of both.

Before I discuss these ethical expectations, realize that your clients are not always going to act in ethical ways. It's sad but true. You can't control the actions of clients, but by being aware of possible unethical behavior, you can at least minimize the impact on your financial and professional bottom lines.

Keep in mind that your client's ethical conduct is important for various reasons, but perhaps the most important is that you can't help the client if he or she is acting in unethical ways.

Following are discussions of some basic ethical principles that you may expect clients to adhere to in dealing with you. Be alert to violations of these principles. Treat such violations as red flags or danger warnings, and deal with them as soon as possible.

Contracting Forthrightly and in Good Faith

Clients should not enter into discussions with you about contracts and projects when they have no intention of hiring you. This also applies to requests for proposals.

Yes, it happens. Some clients will go fishing for free advice by asking for proposals and, without hiring a consultant, will use the information they collect to do the work themselves. It's brain picking.

Disclosure of All Factors Impacting the Project

While it might seem stupid for a client to keep vital information from a consultant, it happens. For example, a company might hire you to do team-building work but neglect to mention they plan to lay off 30 percent of their staff. See the issue? How can you work to achieve the client's goals if the client keeps things from you? You can't.

Prompt Payment Without Hassle

Payment for services should be made on time, in accordance with the written or verbal agreement, so that the consultant is not required to spend valuable time obtaining his or her fees.

The problem of slow payments, particularly interim payments during a project, needs to be addressed immediately.

> **Consulting Confidential**
>
> Blindsiding occurs when, intentionally or unintentionally, the client does not disclose critical information to the consultant. The consultant gets blindsided by factors unknown to him or her, often resulting in disaster. It's a dual responsibility. You need to ask the right questions, and the client needs to provide you with the right answers and information.

Work in Partnership

Earlier I suggested that consultants need to take the position of working "in partnership" with clients. But partnership requires two partners working together. If your client seems to be trying to take advantage of you or exploit you, you have a problem. For example, a client retains you to do some specific tasks. As you progress on those particular tasks, the client starts asking for little extras to be included, in effect expanding the project without offering additional payment.

This is a common occurrence and may not be intentional. However, if you observe this occurring, you need to broach the subject with your client.

Client Violation Prevention

In Chapter 24, "Facing and Dealing with Resistance," I'll discuss in more depth how to deal with violations

> **Between Colleagues**
>
> Preventing problems is far more efficient than fixing problems. Your most powerful tool to prevent problems is to make sure that you understand your client's expectations and that your client understands your expectations.

of these basic principles and how to deal with clients from the dark side. But let's face it. Once problems occur, it's far more awkward and time-consuming to address them than it is to avoid them in the first place.

The question is, are there things you can do to prevent problems from occurring? Yes, and that is the subject of the next section.

Make Expectations and Principles Explicit Up-Front

As I mentioned earlier in this chapter, lay out your expectations of the client early in the process. Draft a basic and simple document that explains the responsibilities of both sides. You can make this a standard document reviewed with prospective clients.

It may not occur to you that doing so is an important marketing tool. Most clients will respect and welcome clear expectations, even when they touch upon their own responsibilities. If they balk at discussing their responsibilities in the process, it's time to question whether you want to work with them.

Act Early on Potential Problems

The more consulting experience you have, the more you will acquire a kind of extra sense, an early warning system that sounds in your head at even the slightest hint of potential problems. This early warning system is useless if you don't pay attention to it and take fast action to place concerns on the table.

For example, having contracted to undertake a consulting project at the behest of a corporate executive, you find difficulty in communicating with him or her. Calls are late being returned, and meetings are delayed or cancelled. What do you do to prevent what might be a disaster in the making?

First, when you finally do contact your client, lay out the problem. Explain that you can't help him or her without faster response time and increased access.

Second, identify why the problem is occurring (a starting point is to broach the subject with your client!), and work with the client to develop a workable plan to overcome the potential barrier.

> **CAUTION**
>
> **Consultant Crashing**
>
> Two common mistakes are made by neophyte consultants. First, they place a bit too much confidence in the client's ability to be a good partner in the project without help. Second, they wait too long to address even the hint of a problem.

Check Your Assumptions

Your dealings with clients are influenced by your assumptions. If you believe that most clients try to exploit you, you'll see small problems as indicators your client is not trustworthy. The reality is that most clients will *try* to deal in good faith, and you need to work on that basis. They may, however, not know exactly what your expectations and assumptions are, unless you explain them. When clients act oddly it is sometimes because they don't know what you need or how to work with a consultant.

If, for example, payment is late, do you assume the client is trying to take advantage of you, or do you see the situation as something that needs exploration? Does it mean your client is "evil"? Don't make assumptions about your client's intent or ethics without checking them out. By doing so, you will be less likely to show you mistrust the client, therefore avoiding additional problems and preventing the escalation of problems that are, at least on the surface, trivial.

The Least You Need to Know

- It's in your best interest to act ethically in everything you do. It will affect your bottom line.
- As a consultant, your decisions and judgments will be made within the context of your ethical code.
- While you have your own ethical obligations, your clients also have obligations. It's a partnership.
- Preventing problems is much easier than solving them, especially when they've been left to fester too long. Act fast.

Chapter 7

Beginning the Consulting Intervention

In This Chapter

◆ Consulting as an iterative process—who cares?

◆ Purpose of the initial contact

◆ Importance of the first meeting

◆ Preparing and managing the first meeting

As is true for many things in life, a good beginning to a consulting project is the key to success. It makes your life (and the client's life) much easier. Consulting is like building a house. If you start with a badly made foundation, the rest of the house will never turn out well. Without a strong foundation, the house will shift and walls will crack. It becomes far more expensive to fix the problems that have occurred than it would have been to build the house properly in the first place.

In this chapter I am going to teach you how to put down a good foundation for your consulting project.

Before we do that, though, I'll introduce a concept that sounds intimidating but isn't really that complicated. It concerns the nature of consulting projects.

Consulting Projects Are Iterative

Now, stay calm. If you haven't heard the words *iterative* and *iteration* before, don't panic. They are actually borrowed from a concept in mathematics. It's really an easy concept, and I'll explain it.

An *iterative process* is simply one that repeats. In mathematics an iterative process might require you to take the square root of the number 81 (answer = 9) and then take the square root of that answer (answer = 3). It's the process that repeats. The results or answers usually do change.

Working Words

An **iterative process** is one that repeats; the answers may be different each time, but the process itself is the same.

Consultant Crashing

Don't conclude that iterative processes give you license to guess or use trial and error. The idea is to hit the mark the first time. However, even when you hit the mark, you may have to refine the plan.

The reason why the consulting process is an iterative one is that successful consulting requires that you refine the goals and consulting approach you use. Let's take a simple example.

Say you are a physical fitness consultant. Jenny comes to you to map out an exercise program designed specifically for her. Her goal is to lose 20 pounds. Based on your initial consultation, you design such a plan. (That's probably not a good solution to her problem, but I'll get back to that.) After three weeks, Jenny returns, complaining your plan hasn't worked. What do you do? You *repeat* your diagnostic process. You decide that an exercise program, on its own, won't help Jenny meet her goals, so you add some pieces to the project (for example, an eating plan, weekly meetings with her to motivate).

You may "iterate" several times, each time getting closer and closer to getting the plan just right. Think of the process as a spiral. Each iteration narrows the spiral as you get closer to the right solution.

Here's another example. A corporate client requests that you do some team-building work. In the course of your data collection to determine the exact nature of the team-building process you should use, you discover that your client needs to change his leadership style to one that is more supportive of his teams. So you add this to the project. You have repeated the decision-making process.

Basically the template to follow is this:

- Make initial decisions (plan).
- Act (or collect additional information).
- Observe and repeat the decision-making process.
- Repeat.

The Initial Contact/Approach—A Two-Way Process

Now you're ready to walk through the birth of a consulting project. Obviously there has to be a starting point. That starting point isn't when you sign a contract; rather it occurs at the instant you have initial contact with a prospective client. Why? Because, as I said earlier, you must build a good foundation, and that process begins at the first contact.

Regardless of who initiates the first contact, you and the prospective client are evaluating each other. That's why the initial contact is a two-way process.

Typically a consulting project begins when your prospective client contacts you. It may be on the phone, by e-mail, or through some other communication method.

This initial contact varies a lot, because each client approaches with a different frame of mind. Let's characterize where a prospective client might be coming from:

- Client knows little about you.
- Client has vague idea about the problem he or she faces.
- Client has preconception about problem and solution.
- Client is repeat business and knows you well.
- Client is completely lost.

Purposes of the Initial Contact

Your goal is to manage the initial contact so both you and the prospective client achieve the desired goals. Those goals aren't the same goals. You need to understand what you want to accomplish from this initial contact and what the client might want.

Let's look at the client's agenda. First, the client doesn't want to waste time. He or she needs to determine whether you can help with the

Between Colleagues

Even in the very first phone call or contact, you should be collecting data about the client. The more you know about the client's perceptions before your first meeting, the better.

problem. That's the client's primary agenda. However, the prospective client is also doing some screening. The initial call is to learn a bit about you, your services, and your fees to determine if further follow-up is indicated—in other words, a face-to-face meeting.

Clients, though they may not be aware of it, are also looking at their comfort levels with you personally. That's part of the screening process. If they hit it off with you, they are more likely to pursue hiring you.

Your agenda for the initial contact is a bit more complicated. What do you want?

At one level, you also want to screen the client. It doesn't make sense to arrange further meetings if the client's needs don't seem to match your abilities or specialty. So you want to obtain enough information to determine whether you want to pursue the project. If you can get that information at initial contact, that's great. You have to decide whether you have enough information to evaluate "fit" or whether it's worth additional time to explore.

Consultant Crashing

Because clients don't always know how to define the problem, it can be difficult to determine if there's a fit between their needs and your abilities. Don't make snap decisions based on too little information.

Apart from the screening process, what else do you want from the initial contact? At this point you are still in the marketing phase, so one of your goals is to set up a situation in which the prospective client is favorably disposed to hire you (taking into account the screening process).

Like the client, you also want some sense of whether there is a good match between your style and that of the prospective client's.

Finally, and perhaps most important, you want enough information so you can prepare for the first face-to-face client meeting, which is where the real work begins. Here are some facts that are useful to know:

- The client's perception of the problem or issue
- Reasons why the client wants to do something
- Reasons why the client has approached *you*
- Other things the client has done to address the problem

If you continue the contracting process, you'll obviously have in-depth discussions about these elements. At this point, you want to be able to prepare and plan for a successful first-step meeting.

The Presenting Problem vs. the Real (Root) Problem

Success in the initial contact involves understanding two related and important concepts: the presenting problem and the root problem.

The *presenting problem* is the surface-level issue or problem presented to you by the client. In many situations the presenting problem is not the "real" or root problem. If such is the case, it can be a lethal trap for the consultant. Why?

Because there's usually a difference between the presenting problem and the root problem. The *root problem* is the real reason behind what the client thinks he or she wants to achieve. The scary part is that the client often thinks the presenting problem is "it" and is not aware that "it" is not the real issue. If you take the presenting problem at face value and proceed as if it is the only problem needing solutions, you are likely to completely miss the mark. So keep this in mind: Your job, from square one, is to work with the client to "root out the root problem."

Again, let's use a very simple example … the physical fitness consultant I described earlier. If you recall, Jenny indicated she wanted "to lose 20 pounds." That's the presenting problem. Now here's the question. Based on what we know, if Jenny loses 20 pounds, will she be happy with the result? Is it what she really wants? Maybe. We don't know. Maybe that is her real issue. Or maybe the issue isn't the actual weight, but the fact that she really wants to look trim and improve her muscle tone. The consultant needs to know which it is, as early as possible, because the solutions are different.

If it's simply a numerical issue of weight (it's usually not), an aerobic exercise regimen might be indicated. If it's muscle tone, then a weight-lifting program may be better. The latter might actually limit weight loss since muscle is heavier than fat. The consultant needs to clarify the goals of the client.

Where You Want to Be After the First Contact

Where should you be at the conclusion of the first contact?

First, both you and the client should have enough basic information (that is, you've screened each other) to decide whether the consulting relationship is worth pursuing. Screening is a primary goal for both of you. If you believe the relationship is worth continuing, obtain a commitment from the client to meet (or set a date by which time the prospective client will contact you).

Next, you should have enough information about the client and the presenting problem so you can sound intelligent and prepared at the first substantial meeting. It's important that you do not accept the presenting problem as the root problem—it's too early. It's also important that you have in mind a rough course of action you can explain to the client at the next meeting.

> **Consulting Confidential**
>
> It's important, even at first contact, to create some momentum for the potential project. Try to get a firm commitment for further contact, even if it's just getting the client to call you back by such and such a date to let you know that he or she isn't going to contract you.

The First Substantial Meeting—What's It For?

The next phase of the birth of the project is the first substantial meeting. I call it a "substantial meeting" because it's more than a social call or a get-to-know-you meeting. Generally you'll move from your initial contact point directly to the first substantial meeting. Sometimes there may be a social visit before the real meeting is set.

Before talking about the purpose and conduct of this meeting, I'd like to point out that already you are "iterating." In a sense you are repeating the process of your first contact, but you will be going into much more depth. You (and the client) will still be screening, and getting and giving information.

It's easiest to understand the purpose of the meeting by working backward from where you want to be at the end of the meeting. Here are some of the possibilities:

◆ You achieve agreement in principle to go ahead.

◆ You or the client decides there is no good fit (a no-go).

◆ The client needs more information and requests a further meeting or a proposal on paper.

◆ The client decides to consult other stakeholders before making a decision.

◆ The client offers no commitment, perhaps because he or she is also looking at other vendors.

Thus, as you can see from the preceding list of outcomes, the purpose of the meeting is to enable the parties to come to a decision.

If the purpose is to reach one of these outcomes, or at least the ones that are desirable, then what has to happen to get there? More swapping of information and increased understanding.

At the end of the meeting the client should …

◆ Have some sense of your personal style.

Between Colleagues

If you go into the first substantive meeting with a clear idea of where you want to be at the end of the meeting, you will be much more likely to get where you need to go.

◆ Have a general idea of the course of action you *might* pursue.

◆ Understand your approach to consulting—in other words, your philosophy.

◆ Have a rough idea of cost.

In turn, by the end of the meeting you should …

◆ Have a sense of your client and whether you can get along well with the client.

- ◆ Be able to articulate the presenting problem.
- ◆ Have identified other stakeholders who need to be involved in the process and in future meetings.
- ◆ Obtain a commitment to communicate—a firm date for the next action—even if the client decides not to hire you.
- ◆ Have a firm idea of what's going to happen next.
- ◆ Have at least a preliminary idea as to whether the presenting problem is the whole story, or whether there is a different root problem.

The First Meeting—What's It Look Like?

This initial meeting is *not* a sales meeting. Your goal isn't to sell a service come hell or high water. Your goal is to begin relationship building and to obtain a commitment to continue the infant process you have just begun.

The best way to explain this is to describe the meeting as one that is based on two-way communication and on building increased understanding on both sides.

If you are nodding your head, whoa up a second, because it isn't that easy. It is common for clients, particularly corporate clients, to audition you much as they would if they were hiring an employee—sort of like a job interview. They may ask you to prepare a presentation for them.

This may or may not be a problem, but one thing is certain: It's important to start educating your prospective client right now. Here's what I mean. If you are asked to present to your client, you've been asked to do something that is actually quite silly. It's silly because you can't possibly give the client details at this point. You simply don't have enough information yet. It's like asking an architect to draft a blueprint for a home, without telling him or her anything about what the home-owner wants or needs.

If your presentation is a small part of the initial meeting, with the rest of the meeting focusing on *dialogue*, that's fine. If a presentation is all you are permitted, that may be a red flag that this client

Consultant Crashing

While you usually want the client to hire you, you should limit your selling at the first meeting. If there's a good fit between your abilities and the client's needs, you shouldn't have to sell.

Consulting Confidential

If a client asks me to do a "cold presentation" and restricts the interactions, it tells me that the client probably has little desire to develop a consulting relationship, but may be more interested in buying some prepackaged, one-size-fits-all solution. That's not really a consulting process.

doesn't have a firm grip on the consulting process. This issue will no doubt emerge during any project you agree to for that client.

What do you do when you are asked to do a presentation? You can do it but use it to start educating your client on how a consulting process unfolds. You can't provide details yet, so don't try. Describe the overall process you will use to get to the point where you can provide a diagnosis and set of recommendations. Be absolutely clear that a consulting project cannot be cooked up overnight without having the proper ingredients.

If you are asked to do a presentation, and only a presentation, you should deal with it at the time of the request. Here's how I would handle it. I'd say: "I'm willing to do a brief presentation for you, but there's a particular way I like to do these things. Rather than have me come in and present, I'd like to spend 15 minutes asking some questions of you and the people at the meeting. Then, I'll do a very brief presentation to you."

Notice what I'm doing here. Before I do any presentation, I want to know about my audience. I can't do my job properly without information; if a client is unable to understand that, I don't think I want to work with that client. So I'm gathering information *first*. Then I'll incorporate what I've learned in my presentation. This technique is a bit of a challenge for a speaker because the person has to think on his or her feet to carry it off.

What if the client refuses to allow me to ask questions? If the project is large and potentially lucrative, I might consider doing the presentation. Usually not. This is such a glaring red flag—the desire to not interact with the consultant—that it does not bode well if the contract gets signed.

As to format of the meeting, it doesn't really matter so long as you get to ask questions, they get to ask questions, and the meeting results in a better understanding of each other and provides a foundation for making a go, no-go decision.

As a reminder, end the meeting by asking what's next. In fact, that's often the way I put it. Here's one way of phrasing it: "We've had a chance to get to know each other, and I think I have a starting point and have an understanding of what you are looking for. Where do you want to go next?"

At this point they'll tell you what they want next: more information, a proposal, whatever. Just make sure you all agree on the next step and on a timeline for that next step.

CAUTION Consultant Crashing

If, at the conclusion of your first meeting, a prospective client says, "We'll be in touch," don't go along with it. Such a response is not a reasonable way to do business. If you get that kind of delaying tactic, ask for something firmer—at minimum, a date by which you will hear from the client.

Stakeholders and Who Should Attend the First Meeting

Ideally, your first substantive meeting should include all of the stakeholders and decision makers connected with the anticipated project. The difficulty is that since it's still an early contact, you aren't in a position to determine who those people are. However, the earlier those people are involved, the better.

You have several strategies to address this issue of stakeholders and attendees. First, during the initial contact described earlier, make it a point to ask who will be attending the first meeting and whether all of the people who should be involved will be involved. The client may not yet know who should be there. If that's the case, you can negotiate and advise.

The second strategy is to live with what's possible and what is put on the table. The meeting may not end up including everyone it should. Even though you are doing your best to encourage the client to think about who should be there, this issue is not something under your direct control.

You may have to live with not having all key people at the meeting. Your concern should shift to involving all of the relevant stakeholders as soon as possible. If they aren't in on the first meeting, then they should be involved in the second and subsequent meetings, as is reasonable.

If your client balks at this (it happens sometimes), that's a red flag worth investigating.

Being Prepared

Before closing out this chapter, I want to talk about how to prepare for your first meeting and, for that matter, any meeting.

I'll begin by explaining what you don't want to happen at the meeting. You don't want the meeting to …

- ◆ Meander or lose its focus.

- ◆ Make it appear as if you don't understand the client's business or industry.

- ◆ End without some commitment to further action.

- ◆ Result in your walking out with no more information than when you started.

Between Colleagues

Want to close the deal? The best thing you can do is be prepared and anticipate the questions you may be asked at the initial meeting.

Simply put, you want to appear organized, experienced, and informed; and you want to be able to exert a substantial influence about how the meeting is conducted.

As you can see, going into the meeting you need to know what information you hope to gain. You need to have some understanding of the business and industry related to your client. You need to walk in equipped with questions to ask the client, and you should be clear about how you are going to get the end-of-meeting commitment.

Preparation is the key. First, give enough thought to the meeting so you are clear, in your own mind, what you need at the end. If the meeting moves away from those things, bring it back. If you can't do that at an initial meeting, how are you going to manage the project as it continues?

Try to do some background research on the company and its business. Ask some of your colleagues or people in your network if they are familiar with the industry, or even the specific company. Don't take the information as gospel. It's background material.

Be prepared with a list of questions you want to ask.

Anticipate the questions they may have for you so you won't have to fumble for answers. Anticipate they will ask about your qualifications, experience in the sector, and perhaps even references. Have them available at the meeting and supply them if asked.

Develop your end-of-meeting approach. That's where you get a commitment to the next step, whatever it might be.

The Least You Need to Know

- Even your first contact should provide you with information to prepare you for the next steps.
- In setting up the first meeting, try to guide the client so it's structured and the right people attend.
- Insist on an opportunity to talk *with* people at the initial meeting and not just *at* them.
- Prepare for each meeting as if it's important ... because it is.

Chapter 8

Decision Making and Contracting—Let's Get It On (or Get On With It)

In This Chapter

- ◆ Getting decisions made so you can get going
- ◆ Understanding why the psychological contract is important
- ◆ Covering all the necessary elements of an agreement
- ◆ Knowing your contract options

In the last chapter I covered the initial contact and the initial substantive meetings. These are the first steps involved in starting a consulting relationship or project. As part of these first steps, you may also be asked to attend additional meetings, prepare a formal proposal, or just plain wait.

Whatever the outcome of these initial meetings, at some point decisions need to be made. Either you have a "no-go," in which you and the client go separate ways, or it's a "go" situation. If it's a go, then you begin the more formal contracting phase of the project; and it, like the earlier steps, is part of laying the foundation for a successful project.

In this chapter I'll talk about the decision-making process that kicks in at this point, and the process of putting together an agreement that works.

In the course of the discussion, I'll introduce a new concept—the psychological (or implicit) contract—and explain its meaning and importance.

Do You Accept This Client to Be ... (and Vice Versa)

Once the initial meetings or entrance phase is complete, both parties have some decisions to make. Obviously you understand that the client's decision is whether or not to retain you, so I'll focus on the decisions that you need to make. Consultants often neglect this aspect of the process, because they assume the entire decision-making process lies with the client, and only the client. That's not true.

As I've said before, doing consulting and obtaining consulting contracts are different from selling a "thing." In selling a thing, the consumer is the final arbiter of whether he or she should purchase the product. While a seller may market to the consumer, or even educate the consumer, the seller doesn't usually say: "Well, I don't think that's the right soapcake for you, Mrs. Jones." In a selling or retail relationship, it's often the case that the seller gives the client what he or she wants, and that's pretty much the end of it.

Not so with consulting. With consulting, your goal is not to sell the person something, but to help the person with something. Of course you want to get paid, and you want the contract, but not at the expense of the client's welfare.

> **CAUTION**
>
> **Consultant Crashing**
>
> It's a mistake to take every project that's offered, or to assume that you can proceed with a project without giving it serious thought.

This issue isn't just an ethical one; it's also a practical one. If you provide services the client doesn't need, or services that don't help your client, it affects your reputation, and therefore your future business.

Therefore, after the initial meetings you have some questions to ask yourself (and perhaps the client) and some decisions to make, independent of your client's decisions.

Your First Questions and Decisions

What decisions do you need to make, and what questions do you need to answer in order to come to these informed decisions? Let's look.

First question: Can I help the client, given my abilities and the situation as I know them right now? This is a beginning question. If the answer is no, you aren't done yet, since there are other questions to consider.

If the answer is yes, you are close to coming to your decision to commit to the project if the client decides to go ahead.

Let's consider a situation in which you conclude you can't help the client. In that case, you ask yourself a second question: What needs to change with this current situation so I feel I *can* help the client?

That's a broad question. Your answers may have to do with pursuing more information, augmenting your skills, involving someone with the needed skills, or working out ground rules with the client so you can help.

What you are doing here is looking beyond the surface to see if, given some changes in situation, you can deliver your services effectively.

Now let's say you believe you can help the client. At this point you move to other issues.

Your Next Questions

Okay, you haven't yet decided to accept the contract if offered. You've merely determined that you can help the client. However, that doesn't mean you should help the client.

Turn your attention to your own needs—business and personal. Ask yourself some questions to decide whether you should take on the project. Here are just a few:

- ◆ Is my workload such that I have sufficient time to carry out this project effectively?
- ◆ Is the compensation for the project adequate, taking into account that most projects end up requiring more time and attention than is obvious at the beginning?
- ◆ Are there any red flags or gut feelings that may provide hints as to problems I might anticipate during the project?
- ◆ If there are red flags, do I need to clarify them before accepting?

You get the idea. Based on the answers to these questions, you can now make a decision to accept the project if offered, or to decline it.

It's not likely you will decline dozens of projects, but you must be aware of the option. How do you decline a project?

First, if you've already decided to decline, then decline. Don't decline and then negotiate. If you aren't sure, negotiate and clarify first; then decide what to do.

> ### Consulting Confidential
>
> Once in a while a project comes along that doesn't fit your situation. Consider carefully whether you have the time, energy, and inclination to take on a specific project, and consider its impact on your professional and your personal life.

Second, decline professionally. You have two options. You can decline using generalities without being specific about your reasons. For example, you might say something like the following:

- "After thinking about it, I don't believe I'm the best choice for this project. There are probably people better able to help you."

- "I'm not convinced that if we go ahead with this, it would really help you. You might be able to find someone who is a better fit."

Your second option is to provide chapter and verse about your reasons. Frankly, I don't think that's a wise choice, because it's not really your place. You aren't in the role of helper if you are declining. Therefore, your perceptions and interpretations are not particularly relevant anymore (they would be if you had a project going). Worse, whatever your reasons, is there a point in explaining in great detail? Probably not. In fact, you are likely to anger a prospective client by going into detail.

Between Colleagues

You are better off giving general, even vague, reasons for refusing a project than risking the ire of your "rejected client." Unless there is a compelling reason to go into detail, stay with generalities.

For example, let's assume you determine you simply do not want to work with, and be at the beck and call of, a client you consider an S.O.B. No matter what honest, detailed explanation you provide this client, how can anything good come from it?

It can't. Part ways cleanly and simply.

So where are you now? You've decided, perhaps even before the client makes a decision, whether you want this to be a go or no-go. The rest of this chapter relates to the process of finalizing agreements with the client.

Dealing with the Psychological or Implicit Contract

In the next section I'll talk about the final consulting agreement and the contract. Before getting to that, though, I want to discuss the nature of consulting agreements. A formal agreement is usually in the form of a written document, but sometimes it is an oral agreement. The *formal agreement* sets forth the terms and conditions of the service you will provide.

No doubt you are familiar with that type of agreement. What you probably are not familiar with is the idea of a psychological contract or an implicit contract. I'll use those terms interchangeably.

A *psychological* or *implicit contract* refers to a set of unstated assumptions about the project that may or may not be shared by consultant and client.

Let's look at an example. Jane signs a formal contract with the XYZ Company to examine its operations and make suggestions about how profits might be increased. That formal contract specifies timelines, what the client expects will be delivered and when, and, of course, fees for the project.

However, in addition to that, the XYZ Company has some expectations about what Jane will do and how she will do it. They are implicit, or under the surface. They haven't been discussed, but the XYZ Company assumes there is agreement. Perhaps they might have ideas about how Jane should dress or how she should address senior executives. More seriously, they might expect that Jane will identify any potential "troublemakers" in the company. They may believe, in perfectly good faith, that Jane has agreed to do so, even though it hasn't been discussed.

Working Words

A psychological contract or implicit contract includes the formal arrangements you make with a client, plus a set of assumptions about the project that may or may not be shared by consultant and client.

Can you see the potential problem here?

Pay Attention to the Psychological Contract

In our example with Jane, everything goes along swimmingly until the point when an XYZ executive asks Jane to disclose any employee comments that could be construed as negative. Jane refuses. The executive becomes very angry, indicating it's Jane's job to give him that information.

This serious disagreement could now cripple Jane's project. Its cause? Neither side took into account the unwritten clauses in the psychological contract that may not have been agreed upon in the first place.

The preventive solution is simple. If, at the start of the project, Jane (or the client) had broached the subject of disclosing employee comments to management, this mismatch of expectations would not have occurred. It could have been addressed.

To avoid clashes later on, you must pay attention in the beginning to the psychological content and make explicit any assumptions you have, and inquire as to assumptions the client may have.

Consultant Crashing

The problem isn't something that you agreed to but what each side thinks has been agreed to, though not discussed. Don't assume that because you have a contract all the bases have been covered.

Wonder why psychological contracts happen? It's literally impossible to capture every single expectation, from both sides, related to a consulting project. If you could do so, and make those expectations part of a written contract, the contract itself would be the size of the New York City phone book.

So, we rely on assumed expectations. Your task is to actively look for and anticipate which of these potential assumptions is a threat to the consulting relationship and the success of the project.

Making the Implicit Explicit

If you can't possibly bring all hidden assumptions out in the open, how do you deal with them? Part of handling unstated expectations is knowing your clientele and being able to anticipate where your client may have expectations that don't match what you do. As a mundane example, I prefer to do much of my work dressed very informally. I also know that clients differ in terms of their expectations about "professional attire." I do not assume that wearing jeans to a consulting meeting will be acceptable. Neither do I rely on the client to broach the subject. *My* responsibility.

So, I ask. Or I check it out with the client. It's not uncommon for me to ask what kind of "dress" they would deem as appropriate to the task. I take it into account, and we don't get derailed by unspoken expectations.

Here's a more significant example. A client may indicate that he or she wants a formal end-of-project report, and this is usually stated in a contract. Seems clear? It's not. What does the client want included in that report? Does the client expect a short 3-page report or a 200-page report? Should it include any/all data you have collected?

If you assume that the client's idea of a final report is the same as yours, you have a fair chance of falling short of the client's expectations. For no really good reason.

The solution is to pay attention to assumptions, surface those that seem significant, and clarify them in the open.

In the event that a mismatch of expectations occurs during the project, you deal with it in the same way, and as quickly as possible.

Between Colleagues

When (not if) you run up against unstated assumptions on the part of the client, deal with them quickly by clarifying them. Bring them into the open. When in doubt about expectations, ask. The less you assume, the more likely the project will run smoothly.

The Final Agreement—What Should It Contain?

No matter the means by which you formalize your agreement, the inclusion of certain elements is pretty much mandated for any consulting agreement. While these elements vary, depending on the nature of the project and the client, here are some standard ones to include:

- A brief description of the project and the services you will provide
- A timeline for the project (when it starts and ends)
- What you must "deliver" to the client (outline of any physical things or services, final report, and so forth)
- Fees and timing of payment (specifying any interim payments and when you will get paid)
- For consulting services charged at an hourly rate, specification of "billable" activities and their rate
- A description of how expenses (for example, travel, photocopying) will be reimbursed
- A statement indicating who owns the products of the project (copyright and reproduction rights)
- A cancellation clause that outlines what happens in the event one party or the other cancels the project (either before it starts or during)

These elements are generally mandatory. Although the clauses on copyright and cancellation are often left out of letters of agreement, they should nevertheless be included.

Formal contracts (longer, more legalistic agreements) often will contain a number of other clauses. For example, statements and/or disclaimers regarding client and consultant liability are usually included.

Depending on the situation, you may also want to have something that references the responsibilities of the client, if those are essential to the project. Such issues include communication and having access to the client or access to certain records and information.

Consultant Crashing

Consultants often forget to include reference to ownership of project material and to cancellation requirements. Unless these two areas have been specified at the start, they can become the basis for much conflict in consulting projects.

Contract Options

You are confident that you and the client are on the same wavelength. The client has made the offer of a contract, and you've accepted it. Now what? You've hit the project formalization stage, and you need to sign a contract. What options are there? Who drafts the contract? That's the next topic.

Verbal Agreements—The Old Handshake Deal

I'm not much of a red-tape person. When I can, I prefer to work on the basis of a verbal agreement accompanied by a letter of understanding (see next section). A *verbal agreement* is exactly what it sounds like. You and the client agree to the terms of the project and signify your agreement verbally.

Of course, using only a verbal agreement has risk involved. Unless there is some documentation, you will have no legal recourse if your client cancels, bows out, or refuses to pay you. Then again, any contract is only as good as the willingness to use the courts to enforce it.

> **Consulting Confidential**
>
> In my years as a consultant, I have relied a fair amount on verbal agreements. I can't recall a single instance where problems have occurred. That said, verbal agreements can have substantial risk.

The real drawback of using only a verbal agreement is that things tend to get lost or forgotten. By accompanying the verbal agreement with a letter of understanding that outlines the project basics, it's not likely either side will forget the critical parts of the agreement.

Conclusion? A verbal agreement is not recommended as your sole contracting method. Do not use verbal agreements for large, lucrative projects or for long or complicated ones.

Letter of Agreement

When I have a choice, I use letters of agreement. *Letters of agreement*, or *letters of understanding*, are memos or letters that outline the basic elements of the project, including the dates, times, deadlines, copyright issues, and so on. Many of the agreement documents I am a party to are no more than one or two pages.

> **Consulting Confidential**
>
> Formal contacts can give consultants a false sense of security. While a well-written contract may be important in a court of law, the reality is if you have to go to court, you've already lost. Only the lawyers win.

Typically, one party drafts the letter and forwards it to the other. The party drafting the letter signs it, but generally the recipient does not. There's no reason why both parties can't sign it.

The idea behind the letter of agreement is to save the time and expense of a longer, more extensive contract, which often involves lawyers on both sides. Its primary function is to ensure that the details of the basic agreement are not lost or forgotten. A letter of agreement is often sufficient for a project.

However, if there is a drawback to the use of such letters, it is that they are probably not as legally powerful in protecting you against problem clients. If you have a concern about this issue, it's best to consult a lawyer to get a legal opinion.

Recommendation? A letter of agreement is a fast way to get an agreement done and the project going. It doesn't provide as much legal protection, but it's much better than a straight-out verbal agreement. If both parties sign the document, it becomes, in effect, a contract.

Formal Contract

Formal contracts … I'm sure you know them. These beasts can run to 10 or 15 pages, are written in legalese, and take hours to read and understand (if you can at all). They contain all kinds of disclaimers and clauses, and there is a reason why those are there. To protect whoever drafts the contract.

Formal contracts come about in several ways. The client may have a standard one he or she is required to use. Or the client may have one drawn up especially for the occasion.

On the flip side you can supply the contract, also using a standard one, or a custom-designed one. Generally you should have an attorney review any contracts you want to use.

Is one approach better than another? There are pros and cons. For example, any contract drawn up by the client is bound to be one-sided, at least at first. It will protect the client while giving you virtually no rights or recourse. That is, until you change the clauses so they are more balanced. Whenever the client furnishes the contract, read it carefully and make sure there is nothing in it that has not been discussed or that will involve signing away any of your rights.

On the other hand, if you draw up the contract (or have it drawn up), at some point you have to get it checked by a lawyer. That's an expense and can delay finalizing the project.

Recommendation? If a formal contract is required by the client, then do it. If you have concerns about legal issues, it is the safest way to go. However, if you go this route, make sure you examine the contract carefully since a client-supplied contract will often not provide you with the protection you want.

> **Consulting Confidential**
>
> You may not have a choice as to the exact method used to contract. And neither may your direct client. Most companies of any size have requirements that must be met. Generally, I allow the client to call the shots on how the contract should get done. They have more restrictions than I do.

The Least You Need to Know

◆ Not only does the client have to decide about a go/no-go state, but so do you.

◆ Be alert for, and clarify, any assumptions or elements of the psychological contract that have been left unstated and may impact the project.

◆ While formal contracts may be reassuring, they do not provide as much protection as you might think.

◆ For smaller, less complex projects, a letter of agreement is an excellent course of action.

Chapter 9

The Middle of the Consulting Intervention—Data and Interpretation

In This Chapter

- ◆ Getting information on which to base recommendations
- ◆ Separating objective and factual information from opinions
- ◆ Dealing with human information sources
- ◆ Organizing information to make sense of it

Congratulations! As musicians say, "You got the gig." As a matter of fact, some consultants actually use the word *gig*, albeit in private, rather than with the client!

Now what? You have to get down to business, and your next step is to gather the data, or information, you need to make recommendations or carry out a course of action.

In this chapter I'll discuss the information gathering process and your options, and end the chapter with a section on interpreting your data.

Principles of Data Gathering

If there is a common template for a consulting project, it goes like this:

- Entrance and contracting
- Information gathering (data collection)
- Data interpretation
- Preparation of report or plan of action
- Implementation
- Evaluation

What does data collection contribute? Clearly, in order to exercise informed judgment, you must have the best data or information you can lay your hands on. If your information is bad, you can't make informed recommendations—all you can do is guess. That's not good enough. What principles should guide your data gathering process? Let's consider the first one.

Talk to the Right People

Regardless of the techniques you use to gather information (I'll talk about those in a moment), perhaps the most critical part is that you gather information from the right people. Who are the "right people"?

First, and most obvious, is your direct client. In fact, once you get to the point of carrying out your project, you will have already done a good deal of data gathering through the process of contracting for the project.

Second, and less obvious, targets are other stakeholders. *Stakeholders* are those people who can impact the success of the project and therefore need to be included. They are part of your information gathering efforts because (a) they likely have valuable information and perceptions that you need to have; and (b) they need to buy into the project, and by involving them (asking their opinion and so on) you help that happen.

> **CAUTION**
>
> **Consultant Crashing**
>
> If you have data from only one source (that is, the direct client), you are almost guaranteed to have a skewed perception of the problem and head in the wrong direction. The key to gathering good information is asking the right questions of the right people.

The third source is others in the organization—those with valuable information but who are not in positions of power. Particularly when you are consulting with companies, it's typical for people at different layers in an organization to have completely different perceptions. Sometimes those perceptions contradict each other.

Depending on the nature of the consulting project, you may also want to include the customers of your client. This fits, for example, if you are developing a marketing plan or a customer-service improvement plan.

Objective Data and Subjective Data

The people you gather information from are likely to confuse *objective data* (facts) and *subjective data* (opinions, judgments). You must never lose sight of the difference. In the course of data collection, you will be offered a lot of information. Some of it is going to involve facts (what happened, when, how), but a large part is going to involve opinions (what the facts mean, explanation of causes).

Both types of data are important in different ways, and you consider them differently. Let's take an example. You contract to help the XYZ Company improve its customer service. The client (in this case, the CEO) is of the opinion that there is a problem in that area. He also presents some ideas about where the customer service problems lie. He has no specific data or facts to support his opinion—it's just an opinion. An important opinion, but an opinion nonetheless.

Your task is to collect more factual or objective information to confirm the nature of the problem and then to identify the root cause. To accomplish that, you may choose to talk to other stakeholders (that is, midlevel managers closer to the action), employees, and even customers to determine their perceptions. You might also decide to use some objective measures, such as customer response time, number of complaints, and so on.

The subjective data are used to develop hypotheses about what's happening. The more objective data are used to confirm or disconfirm those hypotheses. In our example, the CEO has some perceptions. You collect data to confirm or disconfirm those perceptions. You never accept subjective interpretations as representing the real situation until you have confirmation from objective data, or unless the subjective information comes from a number of different sources and is consistent.

The Right Questions

Believe it or not, you have to ask the right questions to get the right information. It's one of those "duh" things that seems obvious but is easy to forget. When you deal with people, it's very easy to unintentionally lead them into giving you certain answers. Let's look at two questions and see if you can identify the difference between them.

Consulting Confidential

The line between objective and subjective information is blurry. In a philosophical sense, no information is free from bias or subjectivity, even so-called hard data. That's why multiple sources of data are so important.

Question One: "What's your sense of how well customers are served in your organization?"

Question Two: "Why do you think customers have so many complaints about your customer service?"

Both are valid questions but mean completely different things. The first is a broad, open question that does not imply there is a customer service problem. You aren't really influencing the response as much as you are in the second question. The second question is different. It presumes that customer service is faulty, and you are guiding the answers in a specific situation. It's very easy to color the questions in such a way as to bias the answers.

Working Words

The term **probing** refers to using follow-up questions that are based on what the respondent has told you, for the purpose of refining the person's answer.

The key here in getting information and asking the right questions is timing. If you ask question two first, you are biasing the results. If you ask the first question and follow up with the second question (if it's appropriate), you are less likely to bias the results.

The basic pattern to use when asking questions or trying to identify hard data is to start with a general question and use the person's response to generate a follow-up question (which is a bit more specific). The term for these kinds of follow-up questions is *probing*.

Data Gathering Techniques and Sources

Let's look at the sources of information that are likely to be available to you. Obviously, these will vary depending on the nature of your client. If you are doing interior design work, your sources will be different from those in a corporate situation.

Between Colleagues

When dealing with factual information such as statistics, reports, or financial statements, it's prudent to evaluate the quality of that information by finding out how it was collected. Just because it's on paper doesn't mean it's accurate.

Factual Information and Observation

So far, I've spoken of data gathering as a process you undertake with people, and that's true. What I haven't discussed are the sources of relatively objective and useful information already existing in the hands of the client. For example, if your consulting project looks at why so many employees quit their jobs, you'll likely want to look at the numbers that the human resources department has—the statistics on employee turnover. The department may even have summaries of interviews with those who have resigned.

Suppose you are consulting on a home redesign. There will be existing information that you would prefer to get straight from the source, and not secondhand through the filters of a client's perceptions. For example, you might check zoning regulations, building history, original home blueprints, and so on. Doesn't it make sense to find out exactly how big the house is by looking at the blueprints (or measuring) rather than relying on the client's estimate?

Tapping into such factual information also involves people. For example, if you need information from the human resources department, you'll need to specify what you need. The way you do that is important. Just as with person-to-person interviews, you should start with a general request and refine it if needed. Why? Because people (well-meaning and helpful) will presume to reduce the information they give to you to make your life easier. They often filter it if they have a too precise notion of what you need. As a result, you may miss out on important information.

If you start generally, you may be more in control of the information you receive. The downside is you may get everything but the kitchen sink thrown at you, so you have to weigh the benefits and drawbacks of starting broadly.

Don't overlook another obvious source of data—what you see and hear with your very own eyes. This is called *observational information*, and if you can arrange to see things directly, you are way better off than if you rely on the perceptions of others.

For example, I'm brought in to work with some teams to improve their productivity. I get some information from those involved about how their teams work and don't work. I take their information seriously but treat their conclusions as hypotheses that may be accurate, inaccurate, or partly so.

What's the best way for me to assess this information? Attend team meetings; see how team members interact. It's that simple. Want to learn about customer service in a retail operation? Observe the interactions—even offer to work for a day or two in a menial position. I've actually done that.

The information you get from direct observation is quite different in character from what you collect indirectly. It's like the difference between trying to redecorate a home from pictures and verbal descriptions versus doing it after spending a whole lot of time in the house.

It's obvious with physical objects like houses. It's less obvious with people.

Between Colleagues

There is no substitute for direct observation. Make it a priority to figure out ways you can gather your information directly. Get it on the spot if you can.

Face-to-Face with Client and Stakeholders

Interviews—that's what I'm talking about here. One-on-one, usually private, conversations that involve you asking the right questions of the right people. In this case the interview involves your direct client and stakeholders.

The pattern for an interview goes like this:

- ◆ Allay fears and concerns.
- ◆ Begin with general questions.
- ◆ Solicit both opinions and facts as available.
- ◆ Get more specific.
- ◆ End the meeting by promising to get back to the person and let him or her know how the information was used.

Here's an example of how to allay the fears of a stakeholder:

> "Mary, I know you've received some information about what I'm here for, but I'd like to explain what we are trying to accomplish and why I've asked to speak to you." [Explain in a nonthreatening and involving way.] Do you have any questions or concerns about what we are doing?"

You might also bring up the subject of confidentiality, often a concern in these kinds of interviews.

After you've allayed the interviewee's fears and concerns, you start with broad questions. When you get a response, you probe, trying to get the person to relate his or her observations to specific events or objective information. For example, if you ask someone to comment on the quality of customer service, and she replies, "Well, it kinda sucks; you know, we're really short-staffed," your next question is, "Can you recall any specific instances where you observed poor customer service?"

Between Colleagues

The best way to deal with fears and concerns is to broach them yourself and to provide enough accurate information so the individual has a clear grasp of the purpose.

That's pushing the person to link what she thinks (her opinions) and what she actually sees.

Then get more specific with probing questions until (a) you believe the person is getting antsy or (b) you've got the information you came for. It's important that you end the interview with a closing commitment, such as:

> "Thank you for your ideas, Jackie. What we are going to do next is [explain]. I'd like to get back to you and let you know where things are going and get more of your opinions, so I'll get in touch by [date]."

Face-to-Face with Others (Employees and Customers)

Interviews with employees and customers are generally conducted in similar ways. The pattern is the same. However, you may encounter somewhat different forms of resistance from these groups—less willingness to disclose their opinions and observations. It is understandable that employees would be concerned that their comments might get back to people who could do them harm, co-workers or the boss for example. You might also uncover a considerable amount of venom aimed at someone whom the employee blames for the problem. Just so you know.

The information these people have is valuable because it is gleaned from where the action is—the shop floor, the interaction with customers, and so on. The weakness of this information is that both employees and customers will probably lack the "bigger picture," since they are not privy to the decision-making process or its rationale. That's usually in the hands of managers.

When talking with employees, in particular, it's important to allay any fears and concerns by pointing out how their input can help improve their own situation. I often put it this way (almost regardless of project):

> "Tom, I've been hired to see how we can make this place a better place to work in, and I need your help and opinions. The idea is that I will draft some recommendations, based on what I hear from you and your colleagues, and then push real hard to get them implemented."

Then continue the process already outlined.

> **Consulting Confidential**
>
> Sometimes interviewees express anger aimed at the messenger or interviewer—in this case, you. Never overreact or react emotionally. Don't confirm or deny their conclusions. That's not your role at this point.

Groups and the Group Process

So far I've talked almost exclusively about one-on-one interviews. However, it's not necessary to do your data collection one person at a time, and in some situations it might be advisable to bring people together in a group setting to pick their brains. The advantage is that working with a group can be a huge timesaver for you.

Group sessions have a lot of disadvantages, although a skilled group facilitator can counter most of them. Here's a list of drawbacks:

- Lack of anonymity on the part of the participant can reduce the information you get, sometimes to almost zero.

◆ The group process is less controllable than individual interviews. Things can go wrong, and sometimes things can go wrong in serious ways.

◆ It's not always easy to bring everyone together at the same time and place.

◆ The group process can go off-track, and you are more likely to see open hostility or cynicism expressed publicly.

Facilitating group sessions is a challenge, and I believe most consultants need to build the skills needed. If I can give you just one piece of advise on how to conduct yourself, I would say: "Do everything you can to show that you have few preconceived ideas and that you are open-minded, really want to hear their opinions, and intend on doing everything in your power to use those opinions to improve things."

Try to create some distance between you and management. In many projects, even though you are representing management, your recommendations must work for everyone, including employees. You don't want to be seen as "management's boy or girl." I've done group sessions in which I've specifically requested that the boss not be present or not even introduce me. On the other hand, when I've felt the session would benefit from management's show of commitment to the project, I've asked for a management presence.

> **Consulting Confidential**
>
> The good thing about group processes is that if you are smarter than a pencil, you'll know when you've screwed up. The bad thing is that the process will be painful.

Oh, and never lose your temper or show irritation.

Survey-Based Gathering Tools

This chapter has looked at several data gathering techniques, including collecting information (reports, documents, statistics), interviewing, and using the group process. There's one more method at your disposal: using a survey instrument.

Let's say your task is to improve productivity within a company. The company has 200 employees over several locations in different states. How do you get information from them? One way is to use a survey of some sort, usually one on paper, but it could also be something undertaken electronically or via e-mail.

There are two ways of setting up a survey. One is to use a standard instrument designed by someone else. You (or the client) would purchase the rights to use that. The other way is to devise your own. Which is better?

I think it depends. Purchasing a survey instrument can be expensive, and finding just the right one is difficult. On the other hand, you will at least know the instrument has some sort of track record.

Developing a survey is a difficult task if you don't have any training or experience in doing so. It's not impossible; it's just difficult, and it can be time-consuming. Compiling the information from your own survey can also be hugely time-consuming.

What do I do, you might ask? I have a rather different way of using surveys. First, my starting point is that surveys are great tools but on their own are not very useful. I develop my own short surveys and then use the results of those surveys to stimulate discussion in person-to-person interviews or group settings. In other words, I say, "Okay, this is what you guys said in the survey, now what do you *really* mean?"

Consultant Crashing

Most consultants put way too much credence in the results of survey instruments they purchase. There is no perfect instrument—there are only instruments that are better or worse for your particular purpose.

Since I use the information only as background, I don't have to be as picky about the quality of the survey. I don't expect objective reality to be reflected in the results.

If you are going to use surveys, here are some tips:

◆ You will get a lower return rate than you expect. If possible, set up a follow-up plan to get in touch with those who haven't returned their surveys.

◆ Make the surveys short and simple.

◆ Surveys work best when you have a clear idea of what information you need and know how you will use the information. Surveys that are unfocused don't work well.

◆ Treat all survey information as tentative, and confirm through other methods.

◆ I recommend setting up the survey so that respondents can tick off a box or use some sort of rating scale, and can also append written explanations of their position.

Organizing Your Data

Organizing your data is really the beginning of the data interpretation phase. In talking about interpretation, we are answering this question: What do the data mean with respect to the purpose of the consulting project?

To answer that question, you need some way of organizing and classifying your data, or boiling it down to manageable proportions. Here's one way to do it.

You have a whole bunch of information, and it doesn't much matter how you obtained it. Your first task is to do some tentative filtering. Some information may be irrelevant to the purpose of your project. In the trade we'd say it's *out of scope*—might be important to someone but not to us at that time. You want to eliminate that information at least for now.

Your next task is to look at the information and further sort it into the following three categories:

- ◆ What you are certain is true
- ◆ What might or might not be true
- ◆ Things you've ruled out as not true

In a sense you are doing exactly what a medical doctor does in diagnosing, and diagnosing is probably the best word to use. For example, you go to the doctor because you have a skin rash. The doctor collects a bunch of information from you and mentally orders it.

Between Colleagues

You can organize your information on paper, on computer, or in your head. The important thing is to distinguish between what you know for sure, what's tentative, and what you have ruled out.

The doctor begins with information that is absolutely true. Your age, the fact that you do indeed have a rash, whether you've been in the outdoors, and so on.

Next the doctor is ruling things out. You don't have pets so it can't be an allergic reaction to cats. You haven't changed your cosmetics, so the rash probably isn't due to that.

What's left is what might or might not be true. Hmm? You were recently out of the country? Perhaps you came in contact with some "bug" or parasite? Perhaps. Let's test some more (collect more data).

Eventually, through an iterative process involving repeating the data collection actions, the doctor should arrive at a diagnosis—then a prescription.

The process is really no different with consultants. Why is productivity low? Well, I know it's not this reason or that reason. I am sure the team members lack some important communication skills. I'm not yet sure whether the team leaders are the cause. How can I find out?

That's how data organization works. So, as you classify your information into true, might be true, and not true, you are doing a diagnosis and starting your analysis.

The Final Interpretation

In consulting, you move from having information, to forming a diagnostic opinion, to prescribing a solution. It's difficult to map out how people do this, because we all work differently. Some of us work logically and systematically. Some work on more of a gut feeling.

Your final diagnosis is based on the preponderance of the evidence. That's actually a legal term. You will never reach certainty about your conclusions except in the rearview mirror. You'll never get beyond a reasonable doubt until after the fact.

Before you commit to a final diagnosis, you should consider the following:

◆ Am I comfortable making this diagnosis with the information I have, or do I need more?

◆ Does the information I have to support my diagnosis come from multiple sources and from information collected in multiple ways?

◆ Should I confirm my diagnosis by feeding it back as a preliminary finding and getting feedback from my information sources?

◆ Have I missed anything?

The answers, by the way, should be yes, yes, yes, and no.

Okay, you've interpreted information and have completed the diagnostic phase of the project. In the following chapter you'll move on to the next phase, drafting recommendations, and then on to the reporting phase and finally the implementation and evaluation phases.

Consultant Crashing

Even as you approach a final interpretation, your conclusions should be treated as having the potential to be wrong. Remember, certainty is not a good state for consultants. When you feel really certain, it's time to examine whether it's warranted.

The Least You Need to Know

◆ The more sources you use for data, the more reliable your diagnosis and interpretation will be.

◆ All methods of data collection have pros and cons. Choose what fits best and don't worry about using multiple techniques.

◆ Understand that the information you collect will be part objective or factual, and part subjective or colored by bias.

◆ Know that some of your information will be true or accurate, some may be a bit of both, and some will be totally inaccurate.

The End Game–
Recommending, Reporting,
Implementing

In This Chapter

- ◆ Formulating your recommendations for the client
- ◆ Knowing the difference between an oral project report and a written one
- ◆ Understanding why an executive summary is important
- ◆ Managing project completion—the exit meeting or celebration

The last chapter left off with the consultant having formed a diagnosis of the problem. To use our earlier terminology, the consultant determined the root cause and then guarded against going in the wrong direction by not accepting the presenting problem as the only problem.

Now we move into the end game: the process of formulating recommendations, reporting and presenting them, then implementing and evaluating them.

First, a comment on the end game. Some clients, wanting to reduce consulting costs, will prefer to end your involvement after you have submitted your recommendations and report. That's their prerogative. So if you end up in such a situation, the implementation and evaluation phases will work a little differently for you.

I will say, though, that on a personal level it's much more satisfying to see the project through to completion so that you can see the positive results (or experience and learn from any errors and failures). I'll discuss this further toward the end of the chapter.

Putting Together Your Recommendations

I'd like to say that the recommendation phase is the really tricky part of consulting, but the truth is that all the stages are tricky. The recommendation phase involves putting together a set of recommendations for the client. Let's see how to do it.

You have a diagnosis. You are comfortable that it's accurate. Your first step is to identify as many of the possible remedies as you can. That's actually easier said than done, because you, like all of us, have preferences for solutions with which you are comfortable. The purpose of listing all possible solutions is to counter your own tendency to choose your favorites.

Let's work with an example. Again, you've been retained to make recommendations about how to improve team functioning in Company XYZ. You've diagnosed the situation and concluded that (a) the managers are operating in ways that are not effective in creating smoothly functioning teams and (b) there is a need for team members to develop their skills. What remedies do you consider?

Initially you consider as many remedies as possible, for example:

- ◆ Send managers to leadership and team development training.
- ◆ Work with managers individually to help them refine their attitudes and skills.
- ◆ Fire all the managers and start over.
- ◆ Train team members in groups (there are several variations to this one).
- ◆ Don't do anything at all.
- ◆ Create a team improvement committee to assume the ongoing responsibility of improving team function.

The list could go on much longer. The point is to generate as many remedies as you can, a bit like brainstorming.

Now let's be clear here. The remedies you come up with at this point will range from moronic to excellent, and you aren't going to present all of them to your client. It's possible you may present several, but certainly not all.

You have to decide. Here's the ultimate question: Which remedies will be in the best interests of the client?

What factors do you consider?

- Sustainability of the remedy. (Will it work and continue to work over time?)
- Cost of the remedy. (Consider cash outlay, time, and resources to implement.)
- Any downsides to a particular remedy.
- Palatability of the remedy to the client and stakeholders.
- Is it practical?
- The consequences of doing nothing at all.
- Does the remedy increase the independence of the client rather than create dependence on you?
- Is the remedy ethical or consistent with your principles and those of your client?

These factors are a good starting point, and I'll discuss some of them in more detail.

There's little point in making recommendations that are unacceptable to the client, either for cost reasons, reasons of principle, or because they are just plain unpalatable to the client. While it's remotely possible you can "sell" such recommendations and get buy-in, ask yourself whether there is a better path that will get to the same place.

You can consider doing nothing at all. Such a recommendation is a bit weird. After all, the client does expect that something will eventually get *done*, but that's not always in the best interest of the client. Perhaps you discover that the client's perceptions of the problem are unfounded. Attempting to remedy a nonexistent problem will be a waste of resources and could even create a bigger problem (that happens

Between Colleagues

In choosing among possible solutions, the critical question to ask is, "Which remedies are best in terms of the client's welfare?" By doing so, you are less likely to allow your own biases to push you to solutions that are easier or more convenient for you.

Consultant Crashing

It's pointless to present recommendations that you know the client will find impossible or impractical to implement. Clients tend to interpret such actions as your being "out of touch" with their situations.

sometimes). If doing nothing is your conclusion, then you have the responsibility to lay out that option.

You have to consider the obvious costs of a remedy, but the costs you really need to pay attention to are more subtle and hidden. In consulting, there's a term called *unintended outcomes*. It works this way. For every action there is a reaction, and sometimes the reaction is worse than the original problem.

Working Words

An **unintended outcome** is a by-product or side effect of a course of action, generally not anticipated, but sometimes foreseeable.

An example: there's a small problem with team building. So you send everyone to team-building training, but in the process those that attend feel belittled, angry, and insulted. They believe management thinks they are stupid. That's an unintended outcome. You have to anticipate such outcomes as best you can and factor them into your choice of remedies.

Before I explain the reporting phase, you should know about two more aspects of the rec-ommendation phase. You are not necessarily obligated to provide just one remedy. It's often a good strategy to provide several options, so the client can pick. On the other hand, providing too many options can be confusing and frustrating to your client.

You also don't have to narrow down your recommendations completely on your own. In fact, I suggest you discuss your preliminary findings with the client. At the minimum, your direct client should be supportive of the recommendation and have advance warning of what's going to be contained in the report. In certain situations, you won't be able to give advance warning—for example, if you are doing an audit or performing some similar process that's bound by professional and legal obligations.

So you've chosen your best remedies. Now it's time to communicate them.

The Final Reporting Process

What should go into your final report? The report, whether it is delivered on paper, in a presentation, or via both ways, will contain similar information. However, the amount of information you include differs, depending on the delivery method.

Written Documents

Most projects involve the submission of a written set of recommendations to the client. The length of the report and what is included will partly be influenced by the client's expectations and your initial agreement, by the complexity of the project, and by your determination of what will best help the client understand your recommendations.

First, let's deal with basic issues. I recommend that you have two major components to your report. You will have the main body of the report, which may be extensive and long, and you will also include an executive summary.

The *executive summary* is exactly what it sounds like. It's a summary of the full report, written succinctly and precisely, so people can quickly identify the key recommendations included in the larger report.

The executive summary is obviously there so readers can quickly identify the key points you are making. Some people may not even read the entire report, which means that the executive summary is extra important. Also, if the findings are disseminated to other people, the client may choose to share the executive summary and not the entire report.

What else needs to be included in your report besides (obviously) your recommendations? Well, readers need a context for your recommendations. They need to know why you have chosen particular solutions. They need to know how you went about collecting information to inform your decision. And they need to know why you didn't choose other possible solutions, and the advantages and disadvantages of any solutions you looked at.

So you see, the final report is much more than a set of suggestions. Readers and decision makers need to have enough information to get behind the recommendations. By providing this additional information, you make it more likely they'll implement your recommendations. Giving too little information means you have less ability to "sell" the solutions.

Working Words

An **executive summary** is a short, concise description of the project, the purpose of the project, and your recommendations. It is usually placed at the beginning of your report.

Consultant Crashing

Never provide copies of the report to anyone other than your direct client unless you have been given direct permission to do so. Your ethical and legal obligations require you to guard your direct client's confidentiality.

The major parts of the report can be summarized as follows:

- ◆ Executive summary
- ◆ Brief overview of the project purpose and history (less important in very simple projects)
- ◆ Statement of key questions you set out to answer
- ◆ Summary of the data and information you collected
- ◆ The method used to interpret the data

- ◆ Solutions you considered and reasons why you rejected some

- ◆ Recommendations and pros and cons

- ◆ An appendix containing any data you collected (for example, survey result summaries), if applicable

Of course, you need to judge which parts fit for your particular project.

One last thing about reports: It's up to your client to decide who gets copies of the reports, and in what formats. It's not your place to disseminate the report unless you have been given permission to do so.

The Verbal Presentation

The client may very well ask you to present your findings to him or her or to a group of people. If your client doesn't ask you to do this, I suggest you bring up the subject. Why is it in your best interests to do so? Because paper reports are easily misconstrued. Paper reports lack the power of personal contact and are weak persuasive tools. And persuasion is part of getting your ideas implemented.

Between Colleagues

I have a rule of thumb for verbal presentations of this type. I try to keep the actual presentation under 20 minutes but provide significant time for dialogue and questions.

The verbal, or oral, presentation, contrary to what many consultants think, should be focused less on the nuts and bolts of your findings and much more on the task of getting the people at the presentation to support the recommendations.

The content of an oral presentation is thus different from that of a paper report. In the verbal presentation you will focus more on the specific recommendations and the pros and cons of the solutions. In addition, you want to encourage a dialogue between you and those attending.

Chapter 23, "Getting Your Advice Used," will talk more about how to get your advice and recommendations implemented, but for now keep in mind these points about oral presentations:

- ◆ The written report is for all the details; the oral presentation is for persuasion and discussion.

- ◆ The oral report should be short but heavy on the important points. It need not be "flashy."

- ◆ As with initial consulting meetings, the right people should be party to the presentation—usually all the significant stakeholders.

Implementation–Where the Rubber Meets the Road

The implementation phase presents two situations. In the first one, you are retained to assist in implementing your recommendations. In the second one, your formal involvement ends once you submit your report.

No Formal Implementation Responsibilities?

Let's consider the easier situation of the two: when you are not officially involved in implementation. You should know that if you aren't there to help in the implementation, the chances of the client doing things exactly how you suggested drop significantly. Let's be blunt. They screw up. Not intentionally. Mostly there's a drift away from the original recommendations during implementation.

Even though you aren't involved at this stage, I highly recommend that you stay in contact with your client both through the implementation stage and during any evaluation that follows. It's really almost a "can't lose" effort.

If your client is experiencing difficulty during the implementation phase, and you stay in contact, you may be able to extend or supplement your initial contract. But perhaps more important, you have a bit more influence over the success of the project than you would if you just faded into the sunset. And it's great public relations.

You *Do* Have Implementation Responsibilities

Your contract may stipulate that you are to have formal and active involvement in implementing your own recommendations. In a sense this is what you want, since it allows you to participate in steering the project in the direction you envisioned. On the other hand, you may hit difficulties during implementation that you did not anticipate, particularly if the early parts of the project went well.

Here's what can happen. People are funny sometimes. They tend not to pay attention to things until it's clear that something is going to change and that the change is going to involve or affect them directly. In some cases, resistance will surface during the earlier parts of the project. In

Between Colleagues

Even if you aren't getting paid to provide ongoing implementation support, I think it's in your best interests to stay in touch with the client and offer help as needed.

Consulting Confidential

Just because things go smoothly in earlier parts of the project does not mean things will go smoothly during implementation. People tend to exhibit more resistance once a change is imminent.

other situations, resistance may not be obvious in earlier parts but will emerge, almost full-blown, when it's time to actually make real changes.

In Chapter 24, "Facing and Dealing with Resistance," I'll help you cope with resistance no matter when it occurs, but for now here are two important points about resistance.

First, resistance during implementation requires the same strategies you would use if it occurred at other times. You need to identify it, bring it into the open so it can be dealt with, and have open discussion, either in private or public, with key players.

Second, you have to be alert to the real possibility that problems can occur during implementation. Here are some to watch out for:

- Initial action and enthusiasm followed by "backsliding," or a return to the old ways
- Apparent commitment to implement but refusal to allocate the resources necessary to do it properly
- Flavor-of-the-month mentality, particularly with respect to your direct client

Consultant Crashing

Watch out for direct clients exhibiting a flavor-of-the-month mentality. That occurs when the client tends to have a relatively short attention span, is easily bored, and turns his or her attention to other things, just when the client is needed most—during implementation.

My best advice to you during the implementation stage is, "Keep on top of things even if they look good." There is always a tendency to revert to the old ways. This "going backward" can appear even after you have pronounced the implementation a success.

Evaluation—Did It Work?

Finally, we turn to the issue of project evaluation. It's in your interests to have some way of evaluating the success of the project. If the project has gone well, you'd like to know that, and you want the client to know that. Of course, if the project yields no positive results for the client, that's not a good thing.

Between Colleagues

Remember that evaluation isn't just for the client. A proper evaluation helps you improve as a consultant by identifying things that could be done differently.

Knowing the outcome means you can learn from what went well and what didn't go well. I suggest you negotiate with your client up-front for a project evaluation component and have it in the contract.

By dealing with the evaluation issue up-front, you should have enough input in designing the evaluation that you ensure it's relevant and will be carried out properly, even if you aren't a part of the evaluation process.

In situations where you *are* involved in evaluation, you would probably collect data, interpret the data, and draft another report detailing the evaluation results and also giving any additional recommendations. In other words, you would repeat the initial project process.

Here are a few things you should know about the evaluation process. Even though it seems in the client's best interests, clients often stop short of doing any meaningful evaluation. Cost may be a factor. Time is another factor. Clients tend to assume that doing something is the same as getting results from doing something. I'm of the opinion that part of the consulting job is getting clients to actually measure outcomes.

Further, you should distinguish between different levels of evaluation. The most stringent method involves measuring results. For example, you could evaluate productivity figures before the project and after. If they increased, then the project probably has succeeded.

Or you could use a less-stringent way and measure whether people are *doing* things differently. Are they communicating better? Are the teams more harmonious? That kind of thing.

Finally, you could evaluate the project in terms of people's perceptions. You could use a survey to find out if they are happier in their teams, if they feel the company has become a better place to work.

Whenever possible it's best to measure bottom-line results. If that's not possible, then measure whether behaviors have changed; if you can't do that, measuring perceptions of change is the only thing left.

Managing Your Exit

Well, you've done it. Whether your involvement stops at the presentation of your recommendations or whether you've been on hand for the implementation and evaluation, you're just about done. Not quite done but almost.

There's the exit door, but hold up. Before you go marching out (with your head held high or hanging limply), maybe you should think about managing your exit.

What does that mean?

Think of it like a date. You've been out on the town. Hopefully you had a good time. Maybe not. You don't just walk to the front door and go in (or walk away, depending on whose door it is), ignoring the other person.

Some process of closure is necessary. In other words, there are some courtesies and some things you do intentionally to end the date on the right

Consulting Confidential
No matter if the project went well or not, you should manage the "final exit" so both parties know where they stand and so there is some comfortable end to the project relationship.

note so that either you will have another date with the person or so that you will *not* have another one with this person. Both parties should have a sense of where the other party is at the end of the date.

Managing your exit is a bit more complex than just leaving. There are some questions that should be answered before the contract is deemed to be finished. My recommendation is that this be done in a separate and final meeting between you and your direct client.

What should be included? Here's a list:

- Are we done—absolutely done with this project? Is it truly complete?
- Is the client comfortable with his or her ability to continue and sustain any of the benefits that occurred from the project?
- Should there be any ongoing follow-up to make sure things are still on track?
- In reviewing the history of the project, are there things you feel could have been done differently, and does the client have any perceptions about what could have been done differently.
- Did you find out things during the project that, while not directly relevant to the project, are things the client should know about?
- You may also want to discuss any further projects, and whether your client is willing to act as a reference or contact if other potential clients wish to contact him or her.

The exit process can also involve some sort of celebration or recognition of the contributions of people involved. The celebration, since it's a public event, should be separate from the more formal exit meeting.

Do the exit meeting, have a celebration, and reward yourself somehow for a job well done, or if the project didn't live up to expectations, for the things you learned and the idea that you won't make the same mistakes twice.

The Least You Need to Know

- Recommendations need to be practical and palatable to the client, in addition to being the solution to the client's problems.
- The written report is for detail. The verbal, or oral, presentation focuses more on the key points and on convincing attendees to implement.
- The executive summary may be the only part of your report people see or read.
- Include a final exit process—a meeting and/or celebration to create a sense of closure.

Part 3

The Start-Up Business Side

The idea of consulting is to make a living, and that's what I address in Part 3. As a consultant, there are multiple ways you can make money and leverage your intellectual capital. Chapter 11, "Don't Miss the Multiple-Income Stream Strategy and Other Survival Principles," gives you some ideas about how to do this.

Transitioning from the corporate world to consulting requires some adjustments, and I've devoted a chapter to that process, followed by a chapter on the concept of professionalism and what that means for you as a consultant. Then, what will your specialty be? A good question, and you'll also find a chapter on selecting a niche that's neither too broad nor too narrow—one that will allow you to take advantage of what you know and be paid reasonably well for it.

Legal concerns, financial issues, insurance, copyrights, and more—these are other issues a start-up business owner needs to know about, and so these topics are covered in Chapter 15. I call the chapter "Staying Legal, Solvent, and Sane."

Chapter 11

Don't Miss the Multiple-Income Stream Strategy and Other Survival Principles

In This Chapter

- Diversifying to create more revenue and enhance your reputation
- Understanding the multiple-income stream strategy
- Learning new things—looking to the future
- Examining your options for generating additional revenue

This might be the most important chapter in this book. It also might be the chapter most likely to spark disagreement on the part of existing consultants, particularly those who are established and earning large fees. That's because some of the things in this chapter apply to consultants who have not yet achieved that high-paying position in their fields. If you belong to this group, the principles in this chapter can help you boost your income.

I'll spend most of the chapter explaining two simple strategies: generating multiple streams of income and cascading your skills. Then I'll move on to talk about some basic principles of success that I believe every consultant should know.

Multiple Income Streams

You've defined your consulting niche, gathered your resources together, and hung out your consulting shingle. You are well positioned and have an average number of contacts. What do you expect to happen in the first six months? Well, your business might take off and you might undertake exactly the kinds of consulting contracts you were hoping for.

Or maybe not. You may be struggling and have more nonbillable hours than billable ones. To apply a manufacturing analogy, your production facilities are underused. You need to ask yourself two important questions: How will you use your time during that period and during other slow periods in the future? How will you keep your financial commitments, given that you are in a feast or famine career?

Planning for and creating multiple income streams addresses both of these questions. What does it mean?

Between Colleagues

During slow times, and particularly as you are starting your consulting business, part of your thinking and planning should be directed at creating multiple sources of income. You can use "downtime" (unpaid time) to create other revenue streams.

Multiple income streams refer to different ways and sources of making money. Not only do multiple income streams help you financially, but they can also raise your profile for your main business, consulting.

The Multiple Income Stream Strategy (M.I.S.S.) goes like this. At start-up and during the early years of your business, look for alternative forms and ways of doing business or making money. During the first year of business, allocate at least 30 percent of your unpaid time to developing other income streams.

Some M.I.S.S. Examples

The best way to explain what M.I.S.S. means is to relate a story. As I said earlier in the book, my first year as a consultant yielded very little income. Since I was adept at writing articles and newsletter publishing (and had time), I decided to begin publishing a free monthly newsletter targeted at my potential consulting customers. Having very little money, I produced the newsletter cheaply and invited customers to subscribe, with delivery done via fax.

Let's stop here. Why would I publish a free newsletter? One reason was to use it as an advertising vehicle to let people know about my services. Another was to establish a reputation as being knowledgeable and current. I published the newsletter for several years. It did increase my business. After a while, though, it became a hassle to continue faxing newsletters each month, since the process took up to 20 hours to complete the faxing. So I decided that each and every thing I did should break even or become a source of revenue.

I decided to offer a new option. Subscribers could switch over from a free fax version to a paid "receive in regular mail" version. And about a third of the free subscribers converted.

I had just created an additional revenue stream. I'd like to say I planned it out from the start, but I didn't. But you can.

After a few more years, I tired of the process and eventually stopped publishing. But during the life of the publication, it generated extra income while establishing my reputation in the target market.

Consultant Crashing

If you develop additional income streams, make sure they enhance your reputation rather than diminish it. One "consultant" whom I know of diversified into writing love letters, often erotic ones, for people who lacked the skills to write their own. How do you think that impacted people's perceptions of his main business?

The Saga Continues

The story doesn't end there. During the years I published the newsletter, both free and for fee, I wrote several hundred articles, which I continued to own. Could they have value? Yes, indeed, and in several ways. My thinking was (and now I was starting to catch on) that the articles themselves could be used to further establish my reputation. If I could find ways to distribute them, they would expose thousands of other people to my abilities.

By then, the Internet had hit the scene, so I published many of these articles on my website, where people could read them for free. That didn't create any direct income, but it provided reasons for people to visit my website.

Then an interesting thing happened. A few people from major companies asked if they could use articles of mine in their in-house newsletters. Bingo! Another revenue stream: reprints.

One of the people contacting me about reprint rights wanted to use one of my articles each month. He proposed that they be published in an association magazine distributed to tens of thousands. After doing that for a bit (and being paid for it), I started writing articles specifically for the publication. We maintained that arrangement for several years. Bang! Another income stream: writing new material.

Between Colleagues

You can plan to take advantage of multiple income streams from the start. But also be alert to possibilities that emerge as you go. Many of the income streams I developed came as a result of a client request or as a result of being asked to do something.

I could go on for quite a while about how I've created even more income streams, while at the same time enhancing my consulting reputation. I'll give you one more example.

Another Example

During my first year, I had spare time—time that wasn't filled with direct marketing or consulting service delivery. Most consultants in that position beef up their marketing efforts and use that extra time to call potential clients, meet, and so on. And that's a very good thing to do. But it wasn't what I wanted to do, since I'm not comfortable doing those things.

So instead I wrote and published a small book. It didn't look like much, but it was cheap to produce and the profit margin was huge. I marketed it to my target consulting market and made a bit of money, while yet again establishing a reputation. I wrote another, and yet another. Several of those books are still making money and spreading my reputation, almost 10 years after they were written.

Now, the kicker. I was approached to write a "real" book with a major publisher on exactly the same topic I had written about for my own original short book. Then I was offered another book, and another.

> **Consulting Confidential**
>
> Besides enhancing your income and reputation, building multiple income streams has another benefit. At some point in the future you might find you want to do something different. You might find, as I have, that writing a book is more enjoyable and lucrative than flying around the country doing consulting. I still do both, but I don't *have* to consult.

Let's sum up how I used the M.I.S.S. I started out as a "pure" consultant. Then I evolved new income streams from that main business:

- Newsletter publishing
- Article reprint sales
- Writing original material for a magazine
- Electronic syndication of articles
- Book writing and publishing
- Writing books for major publishers (like this one)
- Electronic sales of books
- Public and conference speaking

Some of these endeavors required almost no extra effort or time. Selling article reprints didn't involve anything but sending a permission letter. But what all these have in common is that each provides additional income, and each allows me to promote my other services. They work in a synergistic way.

By the way, I can add one more item to my multiple-income stream list. I sell advertising on my website. This item is a bit different from the others because it does *not* enhance my consulting reputation. It just generates some money.

Skills Cascading—The Key to M.I.S.S.

Now here's a concept I think is critical to long-term success but is also very important if you want to generate multiple income streams. I call it skills cascading.

What does that mean? Simple. *Skills cascading* means that whenever you have an opportunity to acquire a new skill, you do so. It means you use your existing skills to learn new ones.

Again, an example. Prior to beginning my independent consulting practice, I had acquired a few skills in desktop publishing and writing articles. As I said earlier, once I hung out my shingle I started publishing a newsletter. As a result I enhanced my skills further. In particular, I learned to write quickly, and that skill enabled me to meet writing commitments for my books with major publishers. In other words, it made me more valuable.

Another example. Although I was an established trainer and group facilitator, I had done very little public speaking to large groups of people. When I was invited to speak on the basis of my books, I did so. Now I have the skill down cold and can make money as a professional speaker.

Each time I undertook a consulting project, I learned about my client's business. I learned and learned, and each thing I learned allowed me to do new things and create new revenue streams.

Look at everything you do as an opportunity to become more valuable by learning new things, even if the things you learn don't seem to have immediate economic value. Perhaps you can't imagine ever wanting to do anything but consult in your area of specialization. Fine. However, try to look beyond simply learning about the ins and outs of your clients' businesses. You must learn new things, and you will benefit financially by learning new things. It just might take a while for you to see the fruits of your learning. That's the essence of skills cascading.

Now You Try Using the M.I.S.S.

You have two ways to apply and benefit from the M.I.S.S. The first is to plan to benefit from M.I.S.S. even before you start your consulting business. The second is to be alert to opportunities as they occur (which is what I did). You're better off choosing the first way, which involves doing some planning, so I'll concentrate on that.

To carry out the first way, you should have some idea of where your consulting expertise lies and an idea of the areas in which you want to practice. On a piece of paper, write down the areas you wish to work in. You don't quite know yet whether people will pay you for those things but include ones you aren't sure of.

Now, on a separate piece of paper, write down your other skills and abilities. Include skills that aren't perfected yet but may be valuable if perfected.

For example, on my first sheet, I would list communication consulting (and a few others). On my second sheet, I'd have skills like the following:

- Writing skills
- Desktop publishing skills
- Public speaking skills
- Web development skills
- Marketing strategy skills

Plus a bunch of others.

Once you've completed these two sheets, place them side by side in front of you. Now it's crunch time. How can you combine your area of consulting expertise with your other skills in order to create other income streams? What different things can you do, and who would pay you for those things?

In my case, this is a partial list of what I would come up with:

- Writing about communication for trade journals and popular magazines
- Publishing additional print materials to sell to the general public, trainers, and corporate clients
- Speaking at association conferences on communication topics
- Consulting to small business owners on how to build effective websites

The list could go on and on. Once you have a list of possibilities, cull out the ones that are likely to damage your consulting reputation, or the ones that you simply have no desire to undertake. For example, I have absolutely no desire to consult on website development. I don't want to build sites for others. Period. Out it goes. What you have left is a list of potential revenue streams that you can pursue as you have the time.

Once you have decided on possible revenue streams, you can also plan to build your skills. Perhaps you need to augment your public speaking abilities to take advantage of a potential revenue stream. You would then plan on taking a course or joining a public speaking group. Go back over your list and determine what additional skills you should acquire, and do so.

The process I've just described is the easiest way to plan to generate multiple income streams. Multiple income sources get you through the rough spots, can stabilize your income, and increase business in your consulting specialty. And remember, always learn new stuff.

Other Business Principles for Survival

There are a few other important principles you should apply to your consulting business, particularly at start-up. Let's take a look at them.

Long-Term Thinking Means You'll Be Around a Long Time

When people start consulting businesses, they typically think in terms of the first year and what's going to happen in that important time. Unfortunately, they neglect to think about what's going to happen the next year and the next.

Why is that a problem? Because short-term thinking means that you may be around for only the short term. Look at it this way. You aren't starting a consulting business to survive a year, are you? You want to succeed over 5 years or 10 or 20. So you need to think about your business over that time span.

When you start thinking long-term, you deal with critical long-term issues, like customer retention (that is, getting repeat business). You are more likely to accept the "short-term pain for long-term gain" philosophy, deciding to sustain a few rough years to achieve the long-term success you want. And finally, you make decisions for the long term rather than the short, and those decisions will help you stay around longer.

Between Colleagues

You have a decision to make about how you spend your downtime. You can use it to market in your specialty, or you can use it to develop multiple revenue sources, or some of both. Neither way is right or wrong. You have to decide what suits your personality and your market.

Slow Sustainable Growth

Let's look at an example from the manufacturing and retail sector. A company develops a new product and bets its future on it by investing heavily in marketing. And guess what? It succeeds. Overwhelmingly. The problem comes when the company can't provide enough of the product to customers. It simply can't keep up. I've seen several excellent products go down the tube because of just this kind of thing.

In that company's position, slow, sustainable growth would have been a better course of action. Growth is good, provided it can be maintained over time without creating a situation in which commitments can't be kept.

What could the company have done? Proceed much more slowly with the marketing campaign until such time as the company could meet the demand.

Even though consultants don't sell "things," the same principles apply. In consulting, growth can have several meanings:

- ◆ Growth in services
- ◆ Growth in staff
- ◆ Growth in customer base

Chapter 21, "To Grow or Not to Grow," talks about growth in staff, so I'll look at the other two here. As you move forward in your consulting career, it's likely you will add some services, particularly if you are following the skills cascade approach. You'd want to add them slowly, so you would have time to master each before introducing the next. So rather than unveiling six new services in a month, it's better to pace yourself and do it over a year, instead.

Between Colleagues

Follow this basic pattern for any change or growth. Change → Establish Stability → Change → Establish Stability.

What about growth in customer base? Let's say you have identified some trade magazines that offer advertising at relatively low rates and that target your market. You can afford ads in all of them, but what happens if they succeed beyond your wildest dreams? You could conceivably be inundated by so many phone calls that all you'd do is deal with the calls. Better to phase in customer growth so you won't be trapped and boxed in by success.

Frugal Financial Management

When times are good, there's always a temptation to loosen the purse strings, either to augment your personal life or to purchase business tools that you don't really need.

Consulting Confidential

I have a simple system to reward myself. When I complete a project, I allow myself a few hundred dollars of "fun money." I give myself permission to spend it in any silly way I choose with no guilt. But the rest of the money stays put as long as I can help it. It keeps me sane.

But what happens in lean times? Do you have enough money to tide you over and to ensure that you don't take contracts because you're desperate?

You don't have to deprive yourself forever just because the consulting business has financial mountains and valleys. You just have to be frugal.

Do you really need to buy that 1.5 gigahertz fancy computer, or does the old slower computer meet your needs just as well? Save the money. When you get to the point where you know, with absolute certainty, that you have surplus, fine. But think in one-year chunks. Ask yourself: "If I buy this, do I still have enough money to live comfortably for a year even if I don't make a single cent more?" I know it's conservative. But it works.

Optimizing Time and Outsourcing

The final guiding principle I'm going to address involves the way you use your time. The principle goes like this:

As much as possible, you want to spend your time doing what you, and you only, can do, and outsource or off-load tasks that others can do.

That, in fact, is the principle of delegation, which is applied in most business establishments. The CEO of a major company doesn't usually do his or her own photocopying. Why not? Is photocopying too lowly a task? No, but someone else can do it just as well and more cheaply, simply because the salary of a CEO is so high. An hour of the CEO's time is worth more (monetarily) than an hour of the copy machine operator's time.

The same principle applies to consulting, except that if you are a one-person shop, there's nobody to delegate to. You can, however, outsource or have other companies do low-level tasks for a fee.

Here's an example. You are planning a direct-mail marketing campaign that involves sending out 1,000 brochures. The task involves getting the addresses, entering them in a database, printing the materials, folding the materials, and preparing the envelopes.

Should you do it? Or is it more sensible to have your neighborhood print shop do most or all of it? How do you decide?

A key point: Your time in and of itself has no value. Shocking, isn't it? Your time has value only if it is used to generate income. Therefore, you should spend your time on billable activities rather than on more trivial activities if you have other income-generating activities. Let's say you have to write a report for a client, but you also have to get your marketing material out. Only you can write the report, but a print shop or mailing company can do the marketing part. Clear decision. You write the report, and they do the mailing.

However, if you have nothing better to do, there's no harm in doing the mailing yourself, except of course that it's a dreary task.

 Consultant Crashing

Outsourcing is important, but calculate how much time you have to spend instructing whomever you have hired. It's also easy to underestimate the time involved in meeting, delivering material, and getting outsourced activities off the ground. Sometimes it's faster to do it yourself.

So, prioritize. Do the important stuff only you can do and outsource the other stuff if you have other, more valuable, activities to complete.

The Least You Need to Know

◆ Plan for, and be alert to, opportunities to develop multiple income streams.

◆ A multiple income stream should complement your consulting services, not detract from them.

◆ Use your existing skills to put yourself in position to learn new skills. Cascade your skill learning.

◆ Follow the slow growth strategy. Grow, then stabilize, and then grow some more.

Chapter 12

Getting into the Profession— Making the Transition

In This Chapter

- ♦ The easiest way to enter the consulting business
- ♦ Getting from where you are now to a consulting career
- ♦ Advantages and disadvantages of different points of entry
- ♦ The part-time approach to becoming a full-time consultant

How do people become consultants? you ask. They go to their local print shops and have business cards made up with their names and the word "consultant" printed below. Voilà! Instant consultant.

Okay, that's not a very helpful answer. The real question is this: What's the best way to make the transition from your current situation to being a full-time consultant? That question I can answer in a useful way.

The answer, though, isn't a one-size-fits-all solution. How you manage your transition depends on where you are coming from and on your current situation. Not only that but the strengths and weaknesses of your transition depend on where you are coming from.

For example, if you are a newly graduated bachelor of business administration, your transition path will be different from that of someone who is already a consultant in a partnership and wants to strike out on his or her own.

In this chapter I'll discuss transition strategies in terms of where you are coming from. I'll look at ways to make the transition from different entry points. The following points of entry are ranged in order from easiest to hardest:

- Consulting job—with partners
- Consulting job—working for others
- Regular job—non-consulting
- Straight from school
- Unemployed (or "at liberty")

Consulting Job—Working with Partners

If you are presently (or were recently) in a consultant position, either working for someone else or working in a partnership with others, you will have the easiest road. That's because you have more to bring to the table—more experience and skills that will put you in good stead when you go out on your own. Just as important is that you are likely to have a client list (or list of potential clients), contacts in your field, and hopefully a positive reputation.

What You Bring to the Table

As a consultant (in partnership with others) you are in the best position possible to make the transition to a completely independent consultancy. What are you likely to bring to your new business?

First, if you've been consulting for a number of years, it's likely you will have developed many or most of the process skills you need. It's always possible that the reason you are breaking with partners is that you are incompetent, but if that's the case you have other problems.

Second, if your independent consultancy will be providing services in the same subject areas as you have practiced in before, then you already have experience in that specialization and the required knowledge of that specialization. Not just "book learning" knowledge but knowledge gleaned from real-world encounters.

Just as important as the experience and knowledge you have is the fact that you will begin your business with a wealth of contacts—potential customers—and a positive reputation.

Finally, as a partner in a consulting firm, you've likely had some experience managing a business, although this isn't always the case.

What You Might Lack

In a partnership situation, especially if there are a number of other members of the company, there is often a degree of specialization. For example, one person might manage the financial affairs and billing, while another might manage some other aspect of the business. So it's possible you may lack certain skills and abilities because of the way that business functions were delegated to your partners or employees.

You may also lack the personal preferences or skills to work completely independently and in a somewhat isolating environment. In a partnership there are other people to bounce ideas off of. You have at least one other person to talk to about projects. As an independent consultant, you don't have stimulus.

Consultant Crashing

When moving from a previous consulting position to your own independent consultancy, you will lose your advantages if you change specialties. For example, if you are a human resources consultant and move to running your own Internet consultancy, you are almost starting from scratch.

Getting from Here to There

First, you need to be free of any contractual and financial constraints that remain from your previous partnership agreement. Or you must be able to work within them. For example, you may have a non-compete clause in your partnership agreement.

A *non-compete clause* is an agreement that, if you leave a company, you will not be permitted to practice in the same area (in competition) for a particular period of time. While many non-compete clauses don't hold up in court, dealing with them can be time-consuming.

You also need to know where you stand regarding the contacting of previous clients and the use of proprietary material from your previous company. These issues may be etched in stone via your partnership agreement, or they may be negotiable. Know where you stand before you start your company, and seek legal advice if necessary.

Working Words

A **non-compete clause** is a contractual agreement that you will not practice in the same area of specialization for some particular period of time after you have left a company.

Do a quick and dirty assessment of your skills and knowledge. Is it possible that some of the things you need for independent success are not yet in place? Perhaps you don't have any experience with computers, since someone else did that in your former company. Maybe you need to address that lack, either by learning more or by finding someone to provide that expertise.

Consider also committing to staying in touch with consulting colleagues, and don't allow your network of contacts, both social and professional, to atrophy.

Finally, I suggest that you look carefully at the reasons why you left the partnership. Was it because you couldn't get along with people at work, or is it because you just want to be independent? It may be that the reasons for leaving indicate some small or large failing on your part. If that's the case, you need to acknowledge it right now, before any failing on your part affects your new business. Take a good honest look.

Working for Others—Consulting Job

There are many similarities between making the transition from a consulting partnership and doing so from a consulting job in which you work for others. On balance, the difficulty level for both is about the same, although there are a few differences in the details.

Let's look at what you bring to the table.

What You Bring to the Table

Because you are already working as a consultant, you possess a number of advantages that will make your transition much easier than if you hadn't been working as a consultant. You have the following going for you:

- Developed consulting process skills
- Real-world experience and knowledge in your consulting specialty
- Contacts and potential client lists

What You May Lack

As an employee, working for someone else, it's possible you haven't had the opportunity to develop financial and management skills that could be useful. In all likelihood, a number of business functions haven't fallen within your responsibilities. For example, if you work for a large company, odds are you have little to do with marketing, something you will need to know about.

It's also possible that you are less experienced in an unstructured work environment, where the only person you have to answer to is yourself.

You may be less prepared to work in an environment that's isolated. Like someone coming from a partnership environment, you may find that your new environment takes getting used to. You can't just wander over to the water cooler for a chat, or pop into your co-worker's office to get some advice or intellectual stimulation.

Consultant Crashing

It's not uncommon for people to be unaware that they actually signed a non-compete clause when they took their job. Before you leave your company, make sure you are clear where you stand in that regard. Six months into a new consulting practice, you don't want to discover that your former company is suing you.

Getting from Here to There

Pay special attention to any skill gaps you may have. Look carefully at business functions such as marketing and billing. If you are moving from being an employee to running your own business, I guarantee that you will have to upgrade at least some skills and knowledge.

Make sure you are clear about any non-compete clause that exists between you and your former employer.

Starting Point? Regular Nonconsulting Job

A number of people enter the independent consulting business from regular jobs that have some relationship to their planned specialization. For example, a human resources professional, working in a personnel department, might decide to move into consulting and set up her own firm. A computer systems analyst might do the same, offering to do the same work he used to do for his employer.

That's probably the most common transition path. It's not a bad starting point, but it's a little more difficult than if you have actual consulting experience. For those of you who are entering the consulting field from a non-consulting job, let's look at what you bring to the table.

What You Bring to the Table

Assuming your consulting firm will specialize in the same professional area that you worked in as an employee, you'll have a strong, if somewhat narrow, set of skills, knowledge, and experience.

It's possible that you also have at least some contacts in your field of specialization, links to potential customers.

Between Colleagues

In making the transition from working a regular job (nonconsulting) to running a consulting practice, pay special attention to marketing and to developing your consultative skills.

What You May Lack

Unless your "regular job" involves using consultative processes, you may lack some of the skills involved in creating consultative relationships with clients. You may also have fewer contacts on which to rely to create business.

As with the previous transitions I've talked about, be alert to the challenge of moving from a structured and social environment to a more isolated and unstructured situation.

Getting from Here to There

Begin honing your consulting process skills by attending seminars, reading, and interacting with other consultants. If possible, seek out a mentor, someone who is experienced in consulting and who will be available to provide advice and tutoring related to the consulting process.

Since you haven't been active in the consulting business, your marketing task is going to be more difficult. A major focus for you should be developing a strong marketing plan and implementing it. You are less likely to have a ready-made client pool, so plan on a year or so before you see an increase in business.

Straight from School

It's possible you want to enter the consulting business directly from school. You may have a Bachelor or Master of Business Administration degree, or perhaps some other degree relevant to your prospective consulting specialty.

It's hard to generalize about this situation, since much depends on the type of degree, where the degree was obtained, and what you learned as part of your degree program. With that said, let's see where your degree takes you.

What You Bring to the Table

Compared with consulting colleagues who are long out of school, you may have more current knowledge in your field. For example, you may be familiar with the most recent research findings and ways of thinking. You may be more in touch with what is coming in your field, rather than the historical body of knowledge.

You may also be less constrained by the "usual way of thinking" common in your consulting field, and thus a bit more original in your thinking than colleagues long out of school.

Depending on the quality of your education, you may also bring a more disciplined approach to problem solving. One of the major advantages of higher education, particularly at the graduate level, is that there is an emphasis on thinking skills.

Now I'll talk about an advantage you have that you may not have thought about. Whether you are an older student earning a degree part-time or a younger person attending full-time, you are likely to have significant important contacts. As an older part-time student, you'll find that many of your fellow students are well connected in your field and may even be potential clients. If you are a full-time student, your fellow students (and professors) can connect you to potential clients.

You'll find that your network of fellow students can be a long-term boon, particularly if you and your colleagues are close-knit.

> **Consulting Confidential**
>
> One of the best-kept secret advantages of going to full-time graduate school is that the relationships you begin there can last a lifetime and can be extremely valuable to your career. Some graduate schools (for example, Harvard Business School) function almost like exclusive clubs, bound by the common student experience.

What You May Lack

Ahh … well. Lack of experience and context are major factors in your situation. You may have significant holes in your knowledge. It depends on your academic program and how much real-world experience you've acquired.

You may be a little weaker in understanding what most of us would call real-world situations. There is always a danger that your academic program may not have exposed you to the context in which you wish to practice.

How well do you understand the consulting process? That's important. Keep in mind, particularly if you are younger, that patience and diplomacy are exceedingly important here.

Finally, you may or may not have good contacts within the specialization in which you wish to practice. It depends how involved you've been during your student tenure.

Consultant Crashing

Full-time students, listen up. If you have limited work experience, start with the assumption you don't know squat. Freshly minted students tend to overestimate their abilities. When you graduate, that's when the real learning starts.

Getting from Here to There

While you are studying, keep in mind that your task is twofold. Of course you want to learn as much as possible. You also want to be as active as possible in building a network with both your fellow students and your professors.

Also while studying, take any opportunities to work with real people in real companies. You need this experience and it's a way of gaining a positive reputation. Don't be as concerned with getting paid as with gaining that experience.

Be sure to maintain relationships with professors, even after you graduate. You can learn a great deal from them outside of class and get sound advice even after you've started your business.

So You're Unemployed

Moving from being unemployed to running a consulting business is a special case. That's because much depends on your previous job and how long you've been unemployed. Your strengths and weaknesses relate more to your entire work experience than to whether you are currently unemployed.

The same applies if you are re-entering the workforce, for example, after having left to raise a family.

I have to say that beginning a consulting business after being unemployed for a significant period of time can be exceedingly difficult. You may have a limited network. More important, you may have limited financial resources and really need to make money fast. That's not a good starting point.

If you can, use your unemployed time to build your skills and knowledge. Take advantage of seminars and courses, particularly those offered at low cost to people who are unemployed.

Consider carefully whether the timing is right for you. If you are in debt and cash strapped, it may not be the best time to begin a consulting practice. Consider the possibility of taking a regular job for a year or so to stabilize your economic situation and to plan the launch of your consulting business.

With that said, being unemployed need not be a huge impediment. If you planned in advance, it's hardly different than if you quit to go straight into consulting. However, if you've unexpectedly lost your job and have no plan in place, then it's going to be a struggle.

What Else Do You Need to Know About Transitions?

Now that you are familiar with the advantages and disadvantages attached to different points of entry, let's look at two other transition strategies: part-time/spare-time consulting to full-time, and the semiretirement approach. Then I'll close with some basic transition principles.

Part-Time to Full-Time

Some consultants move into full-time consulting after an extended period of providing services on a part-time basis. For example, a person holding a job as a systems analyst for a major company might spend his or her spare time doing odd projects for other customers—I guess we'd call it moonlighting.

There's a tremendous advantage to doing this approach, since it allows you to plan and lay the groundwork for a full-time practice. You can take your time while still having a financial safety net. Once your part-time business grows to justify quitting your day job, you make the transition.

All is not perfect, however. Consulting on a part-time basis means you probably do not have much of a life outside of work, since you are either working for your employer or working on a part-time project. That's okay for a short time, but over the long haul it may not be a good plan.

Your employer may not be too happy to hear that you are moonlighting. It's even possible you are bound by a contract forbidding this kind of part-time consulting. You also need to be extremely careful about potential conflict of interest issues. You have the option of doing the moonlighting on the sly, but that is fraught with problems and worries, and really not recommended.

Finally, there's a part-time "trap." I know a number of people doing consulting on a part-time basis who have been planning to make the jump to full-time consulting. They've been in the same place for as long as a decade, biding their time until just the right time. It's easy to wait and wait and never come across the right time. So for some, consulting on a part-time basis is a way of avoiding taking the risks necessary for a successful consulting career. If you don't mind consulting part-time forever, it's not a problem. Just be sure you aren't using the part-time approach as a deception.

Between Colleagues

If you want to transition using a part-time strategy, be aware that you'll probably never find a perfect time to quit your day job. Ever. It's like quitting smoking. It's easy to stall, waiting for just the perfect situation.

The Semiretirement Strategy

You've been working for a major company for 20 years. You're within shouting distance of retirement (if you choose) and of receiving a pension that, while not luxurious, will provide you with the basics of life.

But you aren't "old." Rather, you're experienced and skilled, and you've developed a wisdom about how the world works. Can you make the transition to a consulting business?

You bet. The consulting business is one that you can carry on into your senior years. It's not physically demanding, since it's really a brain-based profession. If you can think, you can work. The other huge plus of a consulting business is that you determine how much work you want to do. You can accept projects or not, keeping the precise balance between enjoying life and working enough to keep yourself intellectually stimulated.

So if you are in this situation, consider a semiretirement strategy. As with most transition paths, it's best to plan in advance, prior to your official retirement from regular employment. Get your network in place. Assess your skills and remedy any knowledge and skill gaps.

In addition, it's a good idea to set an upper limit on the amount of work you want to do as a semiretired person. Why? Because otherwise you can actually slide into being a full-time consultant when that's not what you really want. If your business is booming, it's easy to forget the reasons why you semiretired. Don't lose those reasons, and stay balanced. You've earned the right to your leisure time.

Transition Principles

I'll end this chapter with some principles and tips to help you through the transition process:

- The best transitions are planned over a fairly long time span. That's why unemployed people may be at a disadvantage if they are considering the consulting business as a result of job loss.

- No matter where you come from, it's likely you will need to learn at least some new skills and to gain new experience. There's no state of grace when it comes to the consulting business.

- It's easy to forget the importance of your family in the transition process. Factor in whether or not your family supports your endeavors. A supportive family can make a huge difference.

- When marketing your services, key your selling points to your strengths, but pursue remedying your weaknesses. Be aware of both.

The Least You Need to Know

- ◆ Each entry point has different advantages and disadvantages. The key is recognizing your strengths and addressing your weaknesses.

- ◆ Networks are important. Build them before you start your consulting business; maintain and grow them after you've started.

- ◆ A low-risk way of entering the consulting business is to go the part-time route. The problem is you may never go full-time.

- ◆ For recent graduates, be very careful not to overestimate your value. A lack of experience means you need to exhibit a humble attitude.

Chapter 13

The Importance of Professionalism in Everything You Do

In This Chapter

- ◆ Professional image—the key to long-term success
- ◆ The importance of being genuine
- ◆ Enhancing your professionalism
- ◆ The importance of the trivial and superficial

Ever hear someone comment, "He was so unprofessional, I couldn't believe it" or "She's the most professional person I've ever met"? What do those remarks mean? It's hard to say exactly, but one thing is sure: You do not want to be labeled as unprofessional, so you'd better know what professionalism means in terms of the consulting business.

Professionalism is the topic of this chapter, and I'll begin by trying to pinpoint its meaning in the consulting business. There are many ways to define professionalism. One meaning is that you are conforming to formal codes of conduct as specified by governing bodies or professional associations; in effect, you are complying with a code of ethics. Another way to define it is in terms of what your clients and colleagues "believe" professionalism means.

Neither definition is particularly useful, since there isn't a universally accepted code of behavior for consultants. There is also no guarantee that your client's views on professionalism will be reasonable.

I'm going to define *professionalism* as an image, projected through competence, actions, and words, that makes you a trusted and reputable practitioner in the eyes of your clients and colleagues.

Professionalism—Don't Leave Home Without It

Perceptions about your degree of professionalism profoundly affect your ability to succeed over the long haul. You could be the most talented consultant in your field, but if you are seen as unprofessional, your business is going to decrease over time.

Between Colleagues

One criterion that clients use to judge your professionalism is whether you are "easy to work with." It's important that you create that perception by being flexible when possible, without sacrificing the effectiveness of the project.

For example, if you show up for a client meeting dressed in torn and dirty jeans (attire that your client considers unacceptable), the perception of your unprofessionalism is going to spread from your present client to prospective clients. People talk. Word gets around, particularly if a client is angry or upset about an aspect of your behavior.

Other examples of unprofessional behavior are sloppy presentations and reports, failure to show up for scheduled meetings and unreliability in keeping commitments, and an Internet website that is hard to navigate or not properly thought out.

What Does Professionalism Look Like?

What actions are considered professional? Let's see.

Professional behavior involves adhering to ethical standards, whether they exist across the profession or not. You have principles and values. You stand by them. You act in accordance with them.

Chapter 6, "Ethics: Doing the Right Things, Getting the Right Things Done," discussed ethical behaviors, but let's recap here. Behaving in an ethical way means …

- Full communication and disclosure with clients.
- Reasonable and realistic marketing claims.

- Fair and consistent fee structure.
- Avoidance of conflict of interest and the appearance of conflict of interest.

Professional behavior also involves projecting an appropriate image to clients and colleagues. In some ways, that image includes trivial or superficial things, for example, your appearance, your demeanor, and the type and quality of your marketing material.

Professionalism also relates to your reliability and your consistent ability to do what you say and say what you mean. Completing tasks on time is professional. Keeping commitments is professional.

Consultant Crashing

Whether you agree that image is important or not, keep in mind that you will be judged on your professionalism by your clients, and sometimes those judgments will be made based on superficial issues. It's in your interest to pay attention to such issues.

Matching Professionalism with Your Personality

Peter Block, probably the most highly regarded expert on consulting, suggests that it is very important to be genuine with your clients. His position (and I think it's right on the nose) is that you are, in effect, marketing yourself. Consulting relationships work best when you don't play "roles" or try to be someone you are not.

We each have our own personality and style. You may be diplomatic; someone else may be fiery, or laid-back, or blunt. Your personality is your strength, provided there is a match between what the client wants and prefers and your own style. The flip side, however, is that any personality style becomes a weakness if it is extreme.

There is a critical rule to bear in mind regarding professionalism: If your client's criteria about what constitutes professionalism are such that you are forced to try to become something you are not, then you need to consider carefully whether you want to work for that client.

Sometimes the client's preferences may actually interfere with the project's success. If you have to bend too much to meet those preferences, you are no longer being genuine.

Need an example? Let's say your style is to be straightforward and, in some cases, honest to the point of being blunt. A client you are working for has a strong desire to avoid conflict and to gloss over problems. His notion of professionalism

Consulting Confidential

When a client expects you to have a personality style that you are uncomfortable with, you are more likely to come across as phony or fake. That can affect your credibility and ability to create a consulting relationship based on trust.

involves a rather artificial politeness. Still, he hires you because of your appearance of diplomacy during contract negotiations.

As the project unfolds, you discover this client's quirk. You also discover some information that reflects badly on your client. Do you conform to the client's expectation that you will avoid conflict? Or do you use your strengths, honesty and sometimes bluntness, to address these issues for the benefit of the client?

In this case, although you don't want to bludgeon your client, it's probably best to go with your own natural tendency and risk the client's perceptions of unprofessionalism. That way you remain committed to the client's welfare and the success of the project, while remaining genuine.

Between Colleagues

During early contact with clients, it's best to "show your true colors." Be yourself and don't try to become what you think the client wants. If there isn't a good fit, the time to find out is before you sign a contract.

One more example: Your client equates professionalism with wearing a $3,000 four-piece suit. You don't even own a $200 suit, and you think the whole idea is completely silly. Do you conform to this standard of professionalism?

It's obviously up to you, but I'll share my thinking. I'm not that kind of guy. I'd feel stupid and uncomfortable doing it. It's not me.

There's a bit more to this somewhat superficial example. I know that I tend to work well in informal environments, and I get along well with people who don't make judgments based on the price of clothing. What are the chances that my client and I will be able to work as partners if the whole organization is exceedingly formal? How will my rather informal, occasionally undignified, style fit in?

The odds are that my style won't be a good fit. That means the project may end up as a monumental struggle if our values are different, not only on this issue but on more important issues.

So the bottom line here is that you should make reasonable accommodations to fit the client's idea of professionalism, but don't try to become something you aren't. You shouldn't negate your personal strengths, and you need to be genuine.

Now let's take a more detailed look at professionalism in terms of the following areas:

- ◆ Personal demeanor
- ◆ Image in print
- ◆ Image on the Internet
- ◆ Image on the phone
- ◆ Customer service image

Personal Demeanor and Conduct

Personal demeanor covers a wide area. I should warn you that what is considered professional behavior in this area is fairly ambiguous and subject to personal opinion. That's not to say you shouldn't attend to it, though.

Let's start with appearance. Despite what some people believe is a superficial aspect of professionalism, your appearance—how you dress—and your personal grooming affect how people perceive you. In a perfect world you'd be judged on your abilities, but since consulting is a people area, the perceptions that others have of you are critically important.

For example, part of the consulting process involves obtaining honest and open information from people. If you appear as sloppy or inappropriately dressed, people may be less likely to provide you with the information you need. Thus, your appearance can impede your ability to do your job.

Is there a universal standard regarding professional appearance? No, it varies depending on your clientele. A fitness consultant wearing a three-piece suit while leading a workout group is going to be perceived as having an odd professional appearance. In the end, you have to make your own decisions about professional dress, based on your clientele.

More important than your appearance and grooming is how you communicate with clients, what kind of language you use, and the way you carry yourself. Are you overly blunt? Do you tell jokes that are offensive to some people? Are you overly formal or too informal in the way you speak? Do you waste people's time by talking too much and rambling?

There are probably a hundred things that fit into this category, but luckily you already know most of them. If you don't know what is appropriate demeanor, then you aren't going to last long. Since we all have communication quirks that can cause problems, take an honest look at yourself and your past interpersonal history to identify yours. Then fix them. Ask your spouse and your friends to help you identify both your communication strengths and your weaknesses.

> ### Consulting Confidential
>
> I'm an informal guy. How do I figure out what to wear when interacting with clients? I anticipate what they usually wear to work and dress similarly. I balance my own comfort levels with where their comfort zones may lie. I'm not comfortable wearing a tie, but I can still achieve a professional look without one.

Image in Print

The professionalism of your image in print is defined by the print materials you use. Proposals, letters, brochures, and final reports contribute to clients' perceptions of your professionalism.

Here are some general guidelines for print material:

- ◆ Print material should be free of typographical and spelling errors.

- ◆ Print material should present the image you want and need. If you want to portray an elegant look, putting little cartoons or poor-quality graphics on your print material won't work.

- ◆ Writing should be clear and to the point, including only information essential to clients and prospective clients.

- ◆ Jargon should be used as little as possible, except for situations in which a specialized technical vocabulary is necessary for good communication with the client.

What about the "look"? Should your letterhead and promotional material be expensive and slick? Flashy? Understated? It really depends on the image you want to present. What you should know is that generally the flashier your print material, the less professional it appears.

Consulting Confidential

Print material need not be expensive. It does not have to be printed on glossy paper or have award-winning graphics to convey professionalism. However, it does need to be easy to read, free of errors, and provide information that prospective clients want. Expensive-looking brochures may help but may also turn off smaller clients who believe you will be too expensive.

There's one exception. If you work in a creative area, let's say as a graphic design consultant, your print material should be the best work you can do, since it is, in effect, a sample of your expertise.

Should you have your material professionally designed and printed? Although it's not necessary to engage a designer, it's usually a wise investment, particularly if your graphic design skills aren't the greatest. Having your material printed professionally is a good idea, but these days it has become easier to print your own material on high-quality printers. Let the results and your market dictate your decision.

Your rule of thumb as you choose print materials is to keep in mind that your print materials are often the first thing people see and that they should represent you in a way consistent with your specialization.

Image on the Internet

The Internet has become an important tool for communicating with both prospective and current clients. The two components of your Internet-generated image of professionalism are your website and your e-mail. Let's deal with them separately.

A Professional Website

You may be surprised to learn that people often make decisions about a website in less than 20 seconds. That's scary. If your website is easy to use, or user comfortable, and looks good, it encourages people to explore and enhances your image as a true professional. If your website doesn't have these qualities, one of two things happens. The prospective client leaves immediately, never to return; or the client struggles with the website and then leaves, having decided never to do business with you.

Covering all the ins and outs of website design is not possible here, but I can warn you about the most common, or the dumbest, things people do that destroy the value of their websites:

◆ Overhyping the site, making it sound like a hard-sell sales brochure. Click, the viewer is gone.

◆ Flashy design, too many fonts, too many colors. These make it look like you are trying too hard.

◆ Too many banner ads, pop-ups, or sign-in boxes.

◆ Too hard to navigate.

◆ Lack of confidentiality. The site is collecting e-mail addresses and doing dumb things like selling or giving them to someone else.

◆ Typos and spelling errors.

◆ Links and other functions that don't work. If you are sloppy on the Net, people think you are sloppy in real life.

 Consultant Crashing

Over the last several years, the bar has been raised regarding the quality of Internet websites. You can no longer get by with an average web design, since your competitors are creating better and better sites. Don't design your website yourself unless you understand how to do it right. Get an expert to do it for you or help you with it.

What about the "look" for your website? It should look inviting and uncluttered and be easy to navigate. Over the last two or three years, consultants and other businesses have realized the importance of a clean and professional look. That has raised the standard for websites, making older sites look shabby in comparison.

Do you need someone to help you develop a website? Probably. It's hard to do well. Unfortunately, a lot of web design consultants have as little experience in graphic design as you do. When retaining web design help, always ask the designer for examples of his or her work that is currently online. Check out these sites before making a commitment.

People seem to spend even less time thinking about the image they project via their e-mails than they spend thinking about a professional telephone image. But the content and format of your e-mails do matter.

Between Colleagues

With e-mails, simple is best. No fancy fonts, no images, no fancy codes to dress up the message. Just use plain text. Remember that the person receiving your e-mail might have a very simple e-mail program that doesn't support anything but text.

Here are some guidelines for professional-looking e-mails:

- Write concisely. E-mail is the fast food of communication. Don't ramble.

- Avoid using fancy fonts, codes, or colors in e-mail. Some people send e-mail that looks like the letters were cut out of newspapers, like a ransom note.

- Don't send attachments unless the person you are e-mailing is expecting something in that format. Attachments are files attached to plain text messages, and currently they are the most common way of transmitting computer viruses.

- When drafting a response to an e-mail, quote some of the original message so the person you are responding to knows the context. Remember that some people receive hundreds of e-mails a day.

- Be extra careful about the tone of your e-mails. It's easy for an e-mail to be misinterpreted. Reread you e-mails before sending them to make sure your tone is clear.

Remember that your e-mails are a reflection of you and of the quality of your work. A professional e-mail enhances the reader's favorable perception of you and your work.

Professionalism on the Phone

Since I run my business from a home office, and have several cats, it's not uncommon for one of them to interfere with a phone conversation. Occasionally, I do something I shouldn't do. I tell the person I'm talking with that I have to move one of my cats. While that's endearing to some (and reflects my own personality and style), I suspect that some clients find this a little unprofessional.

Consulting Confidential

While mentioning my cats may seem unprofessional to some people, I've found that being open about my situation can endear me to potential clients. I try to talk like a regular person and treat callers as potential friends. That works well for me. Whether it works for you depends on your clientele.

I'm sure that all of you understand the basics of phone conversations, so I won't cover them here. Instead, I'll focus on two important aspects of phone interactions.

First is turnaround time. Thanks to modern phone technology, clients can leave voice mail messages when you aren't available to answer the phone. They then expect a response from you in the immediate future, or else they need to know why there is a delay. Here are a few tricks. In your voice mail greeting, indicate when you will get back to callers, and keep the commitment. No exceptions. You can also state that you will respond within one working day (or whatever fits). Update your voice mail message daily, or as required by your schedule.

The second aspect of phone interactions is the information you leave when you are the caller. Let's say you call your client Jack, and he's unavailable. Do you just leave your name and number? No, you don't. Indicate the reason for calling, including whether it's urgent you receive a callback as soon as possible and when you'll be available for the callback.

Adding this kind of information shows that you consider your client important and want to make it as convenient as possible for him or her to contact you. You are showing respect and consideration for your client, and that will be appreciated.

Customer Service Is Professionalism

I'll end this chapter with some comments on the relationship between offering good customer service and the image of professionalism you wish to project.

As you've just seen, a lot of things contribute to a professional image. Some are trivial and some are important, and I've given you examples of each in this chapter. However, I'd like to leave you with one main thought regarding professionalism. Your demeanor, print image, Internet image, and phone image all contribute to professionalism, but the best way to be seen as a professional is to offer superlative customer service.

Customer service at the highest level means addressing client needs, being reliable and consistent in everything that you do, and being easy to work with.

If you are slow to respond to client queries, you damage your image. If you make promises you don't keep, you look bad. And above all if you provide poor-quality service, nothing else you do will make up for that. You can lower your prices, wear fancy clothes, and have expensive brochures; but it's the quality of your service that will ultimately put you in the elite of the profession.

You can live with a simple business card. You can live with a less-than-perfect website. Great service and expertise can make up for small errors. Nonetheless, pay attention to the big things and the little things, and clients will see you as an established professional.

The Least You Need to Know

◆ Part of being seen as professional is being flexible enough that clients see you as "easy to work with."

◆ Flexibility is important, but so is being genuine and not trying to be someone you are not.

◆ These days, your Internet presence is important in contributing to perceptions of professionalism.

◆ There is no universally acceptable definition of professionalism. It varies from client to client.

14

Start-Up–Defining a Niche, Defining Services

In This Chapter

- ◆ What is a niche, and what does it have to do with me?
- ◆ How can I figure out my competitive advantage?
- ◆ Why should I define my services step-by-step at the end rather than at the beginning?

When you start a consulting practice, you have a number of critical decisions to make. One of your first decisions is determining the services you'll offer and the particular niche you'll carve out for yourself.

What's a niche? A *niche* is a narrow area of practice or a corner of the consulting world where you have special expertise and where you have significant competitive advantages over your competitors.

Why is a niche important? Because consultants tend to, at least initially, develop a better reputation if they focus on a fairly narrow area of practice and mark it out as their own personal territory. Consultants trying to do too much appear as "jacks of all trade and masters of none."

So first you establish or define your niche, and then you define the services you will offer within that niche or specialization.

In this chapter I'll help you define your niche. I'll also explain how an understanding of your target market and your competitive edge will logically lead you to determining the services you will offer.

Defining Your Niche

There are good niches and poor ones. You can figure out which is which, albeit after the fact, by applying a simple criterion. You ask yourself, "Did I make money offering niche-related services?" By then it's too late if you've gone in the wrong direction. Therefore, you need to define your niche ahead of time and move in the right direction from the moment you hang out your consulting shingle.

A good niche for you may be a bad one for me. That's what makes this so tricky. To define a niche, you first need a starting point, so let's begin with your own expertise. In staking out a niche, you need a high level of knowledge, skill, and experience with the services, market, and general environment related to that niche.

Second, you need a market for services within that niche. It's great to define a niche where you want to practice but exceedingly depressing to find out that the market for those services is small or that nobody in your target market has any money to pay you. The larger the market the better, and the more money in that market the better.

Third, a good niche is one in which you have a significant competitive advantage over your competitors. Let me give you an example. You have 20 years of experience working with government departments as a regular employee. You also have significant experience in violence-at-work issues. Now, there are hundreds of consultants who help companies with workplace violence, but few consultants are specifically knowledgeable about the subject within the context of government. Hence, if you define your niche as helping governments reduce workplace violence, you have an edge. You do not have a competitive advantage for the larger and broader niche of workplace violence, however.

CAUTION **Consultant Crashing**

Here are some examples of niches: helping governments reduce workplace violence, assisting nonprofit organizations in their board-of-director development, providing web design help to nonprofit organizations, helping small businesses hire the right staff.

Fourth, a good niche is one in which there is no overwhelming competition. To continue our example, there are few competitors working with governments to reduce workplace violence, but there are many competitors in the wider area of workplace safety. Typically, the narrower your niche, the less competition; but of course, the smaller the market.

Fifth, a niche that works needs to have an accessible market. You need to be able to reach your targeted customers.

To summarize, a good niche is ...

◆ An area in which you have extensive experience and skills.

◆ Characterized by a substantial market with substantial money.

◆ An area of practice in which you have a significant competitive advantage.

◆ An area in which competition is less, or at least not overwhelming.

◆ Accessible for marketing.

Note that there is a difference between your initial niche and your niche (or niches) as it develops over years of consulting practice. A niche should not be etched in stone, but you do need one or two to serve as focal points for your start-up business. As you gain new skills and abilities and become more familiar with the marketplace, new niches may magically appear.

The niches you define at start-up must be considered as beginnings—decisions subject to change. It isn't uncommon to find that the niche you thought had great potential doesn't work for you. If that happens, move in another direction.

Consultant Crashing

A niche that is too narrow means a smaller market but less competition. On the other hand, a wider niche means much higher levels of competition but a bigger market. Don't make the mistake of being too narrow or too broad.

Think of your start-up niches as working hypotheses that you are testing in the real world. Be quick to change direction if you find you were mistaken about what will work for you.

When you define a niche, do it this way: Indicate a general way you will help your client *plus* an indication of the market. Do not specify your services at this time.

For example, let's consider the following as a niche statement: "help governments reduce workplace violence." It contains an indication of *who* you will help and the goal of that help. It does not specify *how* you will help. Why shouldn't you specify how you will help? Because at this point you do not want to narrow your thinking about services. You'll see why a bit later.

Defining Your Competitive Edge

I believe the most significant part of defining your niche and your services lies in the ability to choose areas in which you have a significant competitive edge.

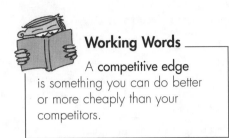

Working Words

A **competitive edge** is something you can do better or more cheaply than your competitors.

A *competitive edge* is something you have to offer or some characteristics of your services and company that competitors do not have. In other words, your competitive edge allows you to provide better value for customers, and it provides the main selling points that answer the customer's question: "Why should I hire you?"

Looking at the Competition

One of the best ways of identifying possible niches and your competitive advantages is to look at the competition. I'm presuming here that you have some idea of the general areas in which you want to practice. Now it's time to check out the competition.

What are your competitors doing? That's a good question, but here's a much more important one: What are they *not* doing? Let's say a major consulting firm in your city works in your specialization area. They are one of your major competitors.

Look for the services the competition offers. Look at what they charge and the markets they concentrate on. Then look for the things they do not offer. Can you offer more value for lower fees? Have your competitors ignored any markets, either because they lack the expertise or because the markets are too small for them to bother with?

You've identified possible areas in which you have a competitive advantage, and you have some good ideas about services you can offer that do not compete directly with established competitors.

Let me give you an example from my own practice. I deliver seminars on defusing hostile customers. Before I began doing this, I looked at what competitors, large and small, do in this area. Here's what I found. Very few competitors know the government environment. (I do.) Very few competitors offer custom-designed seminars done as part of a consultative process. (I could do that.) The major, or actually huge, competitors charged very high fees.

Between Colleagues

In one sense, defining competitive advantage is simple. What can you do that's better, faster, cheaper, more effective, or different from what your competitors can do?

So what are my competitive advantages? By narrowing my niche to government, I've taken advantage of a competitive advantage on my part. By offering custom-designed consulting on the topic, I'm, in effect, eliminating a good part of the competition, because we aren't doing the same thing. And finally, I can charge less money, because I have less overhead.

See how it works? You define your niche by identifying where you have a competitive edge.

Here's another example. Peggy is the owner of a fairly successful chocolate shop on Main Street. However, she's tired of the long hours and, in her confidential moments, reveals she's plum sick of the odor of chocolate. She wants to switch to a consulting career. So, in preparation for selling her business and preparing herself for a consulting career, she studies human resources and receives her certification.

What are Peggy's competitive advantages, and what niches should she look at? Stop here and take five minutes to consider her situation.

Let's look at Peggy's skills. She's run a successful retail business and has hired many staff members over the years. She also has formal training in hiring.

Few firms specialize in helping small retailers hire staff for their businesses. So there's an opening. But here's the real competitive advantage. She *knows* retail business. She can spot a good chocolate vendor from miles away. If she chooses a niche like "help small retailers hire and retain good staff," she'll have an edge over other companies that lack this specific experience. And Peggy knows that small retailers are generally underserved by her competitors.

Consultant Crashing

A common start-up error is picking the wrong niche because of a lack of research, failure to understand the market, unrealistic assessment of skills, or selection of a niche in which the established competition has significant competitive advantages over the start-up consultant.

More Edges—Some Ideas

There are other competitive advantages you can capitalize on. This is where it gets fun and provides an optimistic window on your prospective consulting practice. The most obvious competitive advantage is speed. As a small consultant with a one-person show, you don't have to consult with 16 partners to make a decision. You can decide things quickly, and that makes you somewhat easier to deal with. You may be easier to contact and provide faster response times than your competitors in returning phone calls, e-mails, and other queries. Clients may find it's simpler to deal with you because there is no red tape.

Another potential edge is the one-stop shopping you can provide a client. Clients like to have as many of their needs as possible met by a single consultant. Thus, if you can provide one-stop comprehensive services, that could be an edge. In this same category, clients tend to like

Between Colleagues

"Cheaper" may or may not be a competitive edge. It really depends on the kind of consulting you do and the perceptions of your clients. If you rely on cheaper as your only edge, you'll end up in trouble.

working with the same person in a company. As a one-person shop, you can promise them they will always deal with you.

Here's another kind of competitive edge, just to stimulate your thinking. One of my edges is that I have several books published. If a client likes one of my books and needs help in that area, who is the client going to contact? If a client wants services that mirror the ideas in my book, he or she has to come to me. This is an example not only of identifying a competitive edge but of creating one over time.

Competitive Edge and Marketing

You've seen how competitive edges are important in choosing niches and defining services. How do competitive edges affect your marketing?

The answer is simple. Your competitive edges are front and center in any marketing you do. When you talk to clients, you make sure that you mention what you can do that competitors can't do—or any special features of your company that others lack. Highlight your competitive edges in your marketing material.

Consultant Crashing

Don't oversell your competitive advantages. Make sure prospective clients know about them, but don't flog clients with them.

By now you can see how very important it is to identify your competitive edges up-front when you start your consulting business. Your competitive edge is not something that applies only to deciding what services you will offer.

Finally, What Services to Offer

You've learned about niches and competitive edges. Now you're ready to define the services you will offer.

At the beginning of the chapter when I talked about defining niches, remember that I was very specific in pointing out you do *not* specify your services at this point. Here's why. There is a tendency for consultants to develop a sort of tunnel vision in terms of the services they provide. Most often tunnel vision restricts consultants in their thinking, usually limiting them to providing direct consulting services. That can result in missing out on significant revenue streams.

The best way to explain this is to look at two different consultants working in the same niche. Both have considerable expertise in their fields, which happens to be human resources and hiring and retaining staff. Both have experience with small business. Both have defined their market as small business.

Bill started out by defining his niche, market, and services. If Bill were to describe his business, this is what he'd say: "I help small retailers hire and retain staff by sitting in on employment interviews, filtering resumés, and teaching small business owners the right questions to ask."

That description sounds perfectly reasonable. Bill has clearly defined his services, and that's exactly what he offers in terms of services. That and nothing more. His sole revenue source is from his direct involvement with his clients. It's never even occurred to Bill that he could be helping his clients reach their goals by offering different kinds of services.

Let's look at Sarah. She approaches it a different way. She looks at her competitors (including Bill) and says, "I help small retailers hire and retain staff by using a number of flexible service delivery methods." On the surface her description doesn't look that different from Bill's, but it is. Sarah isn't restricting herself in terms of *how* she will deliver that help (that is, her services).

For example, she notices that nobody is offering a workbook that is specifically designed to help small retailers hire better staff. She writes one and offers it both as a value-added service to go with her consulting and as a stand-alone she can offer to clients who cannot afford to hire her. By offering the book, she is also capitalizing on her knowledge of the small business market. Small retailers are really busy. She provides an alternative way to help them.

Sarah notices that competitors aren't helping small businesses sift through the hundreds of job applications they receive in response to job ads. So she creates a checklist she can offer to clients in order to walk them through the filtering process.

Realizing that many small retailers lack significant money to pay consultants, she creates an Internet-based help line on which clients from all over the world can contact her to ask hiring questions via e-mail for a small fee.

Do you see how Peggy and Bill are operating quite differently? Bill, firm in the idea he offers consulting services and only consulting services, limits his revenue and ignores alternative ways to deliver help to his clients.

Peggy, however, is open-minded. By not defining her services prematurely, and constantly looking for various ways to achieve the same goals, she's continually broadening her scope while increasing her competitive advantage. Bill is stuck.

Step-by-Step Service Definition

Here's how to determine your service offerings. Identify your special and unique skills. Investigate the market. Look at your competitors and identify areas where client needs are going unfulfilled.

Define your niche(s) and competitive advantages with statements like the following:

- Assist individuals with retirement planning
- Help people increase their fitness levels
- Assist people in undertaking home renovations
- Help government determine feasibility of engineering projects

Once you've done that, make a list of all the different ways you can help your client. These will be your potential service offerings. For example, if you are a fitness consultant, you might come up with these services:

- Offer personal training services at client's location
- Provide exercise guides in a printed brochure and over the Internet
- Develop weekly menus on an individual custom-basis
- Develop customized exercise plans for children
- Instruct aerobics classes

Do you get the idea? Your list should be much longer. Brainstorm. Write down as many services as possible. Then pick out the most likely ones in which you would have a competitive advantage, and focus on those.

Don't forget the ones you decide against. They may become more attractive in six months or a year. Finally, keep the list and continue to update it regularly.

The Least You Need to Know

- The choice of appropriate niches is an important determinant of your success as a consultant.
- Defining a niche involves considering your skills, the market, and your competitive edge.
- If you can't figure out a competitive edge, there's no reason for people to hire you instead of a competitor.
- Don't restrict your thinking about *how* you will help your clients (that is, the services you offer).

Chapter 15

Staying Legal, Solvent, and Sane

In This Chapter

- ◆ Matters of registration, licensing, and zoning
- ◆ Tips on taxes
- ◆ Advantages and disadvantages of the home office
- ◆ Your supporting cast—your lawyer, accountant, and insurance agent

Wouldn't it be great if you could concentrate all your time and energy solely on the delivery of consulting services? Like any other kind of business, a consulting business has to satisfy government regulations, including tax laws. Protection from liability and lawsuits is also important. These considerations, just like much of the paperwork consultants need to complete, are unexciting, but essential.

A discussion of zoning, business registration, insurance, and tax issues may seem boring to you but, trust me, you don't want to discover you've overlooked one of these issues after you've been sued or hit a spell of ill health.

In this chapter I'll talk about staying legal, solvent, and sane. Add "protected" to that list, as well.

Keep in mind that the purpose of this chapter is to make you aware of certain issues you need to attend to, not to give you legal advice. It's best to get advice from appropriate professionals, since laws and requirements vary, depending on country and even state or province.

Staying on the Right Side of the Law

Remember the rock 'n' roll song, "I Fought the Law and the Law Won"? You've just dated yourself, but be aware that, in business, fighting the law and winning is an uphill battle. The time and the resources involved in contesting even an inadvertent violation of regulations are costly.

Between Colleagues

Need advice on legal and business issues? The Small Business Administration is a government agency that can help if you live in the United States. Visit it at www. sba.gov. Canada has similar services. Contact your provincial or federal government and inquire about their business centers.

Consulting Confidential

Consider registering several names if you choose a sole proprietorship and if registration is not overly expensive. Here's a trick. Consider registering the domain name of your website as a company name. For example, my site is called work911.com. It makes sense to also register "The Work911 Company" as a business name. It's just a small trick to create brand awareness.

In the next three sections I'll discuss business registration, licensing and zoning, and copyrights and trademarks. The first two are issues that you'll have to deal with at the start-up process.

Business Registration

Your business needs a name, right? It should be simple. But it's not enough to have a name and use it. You must register that name with the proper authorities. There's a reason why this requirement exists, and it's to protect businesses from damage that can occur if the same name is used by different companies.

Where do you register? It depends. You are probably required to register your name with your state or province. You might need to register with the city you live in (usually as part of obtaining a business license). And in some cases there may be federal requirements. If you are not sure about where or with whom to register, check out free resources in your area. The local chamber of commerce may help, as would any other small business association. You can also contact your local government for guidance or consult a lawyer.

Before registering your business's name, you need to decide what kind of company structure you wish to own. For example, you can be a sole proprietorship, a partnership, a corporation, or even something somewhere in the middle. Different countries provide slightly different options. How do you decide? It's not a bad idea to research the alternatives by requesting relevant material from your local government.

However, it's probably a good idea to check with an accountant and/or a lawyer. The accountant will be able to explain the financial and tax implications of one company structure over another. The lawyer can explain the legal obligations involved with each of the choices, particularly for partnerships and corporations. Generally, if you want a partnership or corporation, you are going to need the involvement of a lawyer anyway.

Licensing and Zoning

You'll probably need to obtain a business license from the city you live in. Cities vary considerably in what this means and how it's done. Some cities may charge substantial fees for such a license. Some may not. Some may require you to pay special business taxes to the city. Call city hall and find out.

What about *zoning bylaws?* Such laws are enacted by cities usually to restrict the kinds of activities that can occur in any specific part of the city. For example, an area zoned as residential cannot contain business enterprises, unless an exception or variance is sought.

If you are going to have a formal office outside your home, zoning bylaws shouldn't be an issue, provided your office is part of an office complex. It is an issue if you plan on working from your residence, however. I know several consultants who were forced to relocate because they had inadvertently set up practices in areas where it was not allowed. Those individuals got "caught" because their businesses required clients to come to their homes. Neighbors noticed and complained.

If customers aren't coming to your home, your neighbors aren't going to have much to complain about, though you still may not be immune to zoning laws.

> **Working Words**
>
> **Zoning bylaws** are usually city laws that restrict (or permit) particular activities to specific parts of the city. For example, you might not be able to operate a consulting business out of your home.

Quick Word on Copyrights and Trademarks

Again, laws vary, but here's the quick scoop on copyrights and trademarks. Anything that is published or created is protected by copyright laws, meaning that the author or creator of the work gets to control its use. There's a common misconception that people can use someone else's material without permission, provided they don't charge anyone. Not true.

Any material that you use in your consulting and that you create is protected and belongs to you, provided you do not assign those rights to your client. Be very alert to contract phrases like "All material pursuant to the project belongs in whole to client." If the client wants to own material that you've created (let's say questionnaires or training material), it's reasonable for you to charge extra. Don't sign away rights in ignorance. As usual, consult a lawyer in your area if you have concerns.

What about trademarks? You can't copyright a name or a slogan, but you can trademark it. Let's say you develop an amazing new consulting technique that you call "hyperspace consulting." You want to make sure nobody else can use that name in their advertising or work, so you trademark the phrase. If you have a name or names that you feel are very valuable, talk to your lawyer.

Now you've got your name registered, your business licensed, and zoning covered. There's more, but before I get to that, let's talk about business location and the home office.

Location and the Home Office

For me, one of the appealing aspects of consulting is that, apart from the time I spend with clients at their locations, I spend the rest of my workday in my home office. There's no commuting and traffic, and I can work in a sweatshirt and jeans. Having a home office may be good for some, but it may not work for others. Let's look at the advantages and disadvantages.

Most consultants serve their clients by working onsite with the customer. Like myself, they don't need a separate location in which to meet with clients. I always meet the client at his or her place of business. Here are the advantages of having a home office when most or all of your customer contact occurs at the customer's location:

◆ Time savings. Depending on where you live, you can save substantial time and frustration by not having to travel across town to an office location.

◆ Ability to write off the cost of doing business from your home. You can claim expenses for various items, including the space used in your home or apartment (deducting part of mortgage or rent), utilities, and even some home improvements.

◆ Control over your work hours. Working from home means you can work when you want to. Your thinking and off-site work time can be at 3 P.M. or 3 A.M. Your client doesn't care.

◆ Control over your work environment. Like to work with the television on? No problem. Want to work two hours, exercise for an hour, and then get back to work? It's your schedule.

♦ Dress as you please. You can wear casual, comfortable clothes; I usually wear sweatshirt and jeans.

If you've been driving to a job every day, the preceding advantages probably sound like heaven. Don't be seduced, though. There are some significant disadvantages to working at home. Here are the chief ones:

♦ Difficulty separating work life and home life. Since you can work anytime you choose, you tend to work a lot more and lose the distinction of what is "home" time and what is "work" time.

♦ The challenge of dealing with family issues. For example, you might be "at work" in your home office, but your children may have trouble grasping the idea that you aren't "at home" for them to play with.

♦ Lack of structured environment. Some people don't respond well to the lack of structure that comes with a home office.

♦ Isolation. Working by yourself gets lonely. You see fewer people and have fewer distractions.

> **Consulting Confidential**
>
> I know of one consultant who has a separate entrance to his office, which is located in the basement of his home. Every morning he gets up, dresses in his suit, goes out the front door of his house, around to the side, and in the entrance to his office. Weird or what? There's a reason. He claims that it helps him be more disciplined and keeps his home life separate from his work life.

♦ Too much togetherness. If you have a home office and your spouse is also at home during the day, it can get a bit crowded. Some couples don't function well if they are together too much.

These disadvantages may not seem major, but pay attention to them and consider whether you think a home office is for you.

More About the Right Side of the Law—Taxes

Do we *really* have to talk about taxes? After all, we all know about them and have to pay them. Must we talk about them too?

Yes. If you are accustomed to being an employee, receiving a salary, and having taxes deducted, you need to change your perspective. The biggest shift is that you are now responsible for the proper tax remittances; and if you don't get them in on time, and don't budget properly, you could find yourself in a hole that will be difficult to dig out of.

The major problem is that your income can fluctuate wildly from year to year and month to month. You aren't likely to know in advance what your final revenue is going to be.

Let's say it's January. You've just landed a really big contract and feel like you can "live a little." Maybe go out and buy that new car you always wanted. But guess what? The rest of the year is a bust. At tax time you can't pay on time because you've already spent the money, anticipating you'd earn much more. That's going to cost you.

Between Colleagues

Depending on how often you have to pay taxes, you might want to put your tax money into something that bears interest or gives a return on the money. Maybe short-term guaranteed income certificates, or bonds, or money market funds. Just make sure it's a secure investment, and you can retrieve the money with little or no penalty.

Here's my suggestion. Open up a tax account at the bank. Every time you get paid by a client, take your anticipated tax rate (let's say it's 25 percent) and deposit that percentage of your fee in the tax account. Do it off the top (your gross fee). Once that money is in the account, pretend it doesn't exist.

Because you are putting your tax money away on the basis of your gross revenue (that's before deductions), you will be sure to have much more than you need to pay your taxes. You can leave the surplus there for next year (that's a nice feeling), or after you have paid your current taxes, you can transfer it into your "spending account."

Here are some other tips related to tax issues:

♦ Keep proper ongoing records of income and deductible expenses. Keep your records current as you go. Consider getting a simple financial management program to do this. Quicken is a good program for this purpose.

♦ Consider having an accountant or tax preparer do your taxes and advise you on tax issues. It's worth it, and if you run afoul of the government you will have some expert support. The tax preparation fee is also deductible.

♦ Be really clear about what constitutes tax-deductible expenses. Tax officials are particularly good at spotting claimed expenses that are unreasonable or unacceptable. Get a tax advisor to explain. Such advice is usually tax-deductible.

♦ Don't kill yourself over nickels and dimes. For example, I don't claim car expenses as deductions even though I use my car for business. Why? I'd have to keep a log of all expenses and track when I use the car for business and when not. For the few dollars I would save, it just isn't worth my time.

Insurance—Often Neglected

It's easy, amidst the hustle and bustle of getting a business going, to forget about an important protection—insurance. What kinds of insurance do you need, and what kinds of insurance are good to have?

Liability Insurance

Liability insurance protects you from the financial devastation that can result if a client wins a legal action against you for damages.

Is it common for consultants to be subject to such civil actions? Probably not. But the risk you bear is not in the frequency of such actions, but in the potential judgment from just one. Judgments in liability suits can be in excess of millions of dollars. If you carry liability insurance, your insurance company will handle the burden. And you'll still have a life and a business.

You may think you are relatively immune to such actions because you can't imagine how your consulting practices could ever cause harm, or perceived harm. But consider this. Do you think the fast-food company that was sued for having "too hot" coffee ever actually anticipated that this might happen? It's doubtful. You just never know what could trigger a lawsuit.

Another reason to investigate liability insurance is that some clients will require a statement of liability insurance before contracting with you.

On balance, it's probably worth having liability insurance. Get in touch with your insurance agent and inquire. If your insurance agent is not familiar with this kind of coverage (many aren't), look for a company that offers commercial insurance.

Life and Income Insurance

As an independent consultant, you can't take advantage of the various corporate insurance plans that might be offered by an employer. Yet it's still important to protect yourself against life's catastrophes, and here is where life insurance and income insurance can give you peace of mind.

Everyone is familiar with life insurance, so I won't go into any detail about it. However, most people are less familiar with income insurance, and that's what I'll focus on.

I'm sure it's occurred to you that as an independent consultant, you get paid only if you work. There's no "paid sick leave" for independent consultants. So what happens if you fall ill and can't work for six months or a year? How do you pay the bills? *Income insurance* compensates you if you are unable to work for an extended period of time.

You should know that income insurance will pay you a percentage of your typical earnings, usually calculated on your last few years of revenue. Say that in your start-up phase you earn $15,000 a year. You suffer an injury as a result of a car accident and can't work for a full year. What would income insurance pay you? Not much, since it would pay out based on some percentage of your past income.

Income insurance thus becomes more important as your income increases. That's because your lifestyle maintenance costs (housing, entertainment, loan payments) are likely to be higher if you are making a lot of money. Without income insurance to help you meet your commitments, you may be in serious trouble even if your disability period is relatively short. Be aware that the higher your income, the higher the insurance premiums.

Contact your insurance company for information. Make your decisions based on cost, present income, number of dependents, and so on.

> **Consulting Confidential**
>
> Many professional associations offer group health insurance for their members. If there is such an association for your area of specialization (or for consultants), you may want to investigate this possibility. Consider both local and national ones.

> **Consultant Crashing**
>
> Don't assume that your home insurance covers your business effects. Insurance companies usually insure business property at different rates. If you run a home-based office, make sure you tell your insurance company and get their advice.

Health Insurance

Since you are no longer a permanent employee of someone else's company, any employee-related health insurance you had previously no longer applies. I think everyone understands that health insurance is an absolute necessity these days to protect you and your family.

Insurance for Your Business Equipment

No matter what your specialization, you are going to have (a) a place where your business is located and (b) business equipment for conducting your business. The latter includes computer equipment, furniture, reference books, and the specific tools of your trade. So what happens if there is a fire or break-in? Without insurance, you are in big trouble.

If you run a home-based business, probably the one thing you need to do is disclose that information to your insurance company. You may have to pay some extra premiums to insure your business-related equipment, and the time to learn about that is before any disaster.

Contract Issues

A client is eager to hire you, and you've come to a verbal agreement on the project and the fees involved. Now what? It depends. It's possible to work from a verbal agreement (but it's not a good idea). You could draft a simple letter of agreement that outlines the project and details. Or you could use a formal contract.

Corporate clients may want you to sign a contract that they draft, which is fine provided you read it carefully and make any necessary amendments. Other clients may not have such standard documents and will want you to supply a contract that they can examine and sign.

Got one of those contracts? No, I didn't think so. If you need to work on the basis of formal contracts, you will need a standard contract (often called a boilerplate contract) that you can modify and submit to the client. While you can modify such a boilerplate document yourself, it's best that the basic contract be written by a lawyer experienced in contract law. Unless you are a lawyer, you aren't likely to include all the possible protective clauses that are necessary.

Between Colleagues

Whatever services you need from a lawyer, make sure the lawyer is experienced in the proper specializations. Don't go to Uncle Bob just because he's a lawyer and will work cheap, unless Uncle Bob has experience drawing up contracts.

Having a standard contract drawn up should not cost you a lot of money, and it's highly recommended. It can save you future grief.

Your Supporting Cast

I'll end this chapter by discussing your supporting cast. This is the group of people you need to have in place to help you with business-related functions. The cast will usually include the following:

- Lawyer
- Accountant or tax preparer
- Insurance agent
- People who provide you with technical help (for example, a website developer)

Think of them as your supporting team. The better you build and maintain relationships with your team members, the better off you will be.

How do you choose your supporting cast members and maintain a good relationship with them? The answers are the topics of the next two sections.

Putting the Team Together

Here's the golden rule in choosing any member of your supporting cast:

Choose people who either specialize in small business or have extensive experience working with small business.

For example, Jane might be a great criminal lawyer and happen to live next door to you, but is she the right person to advise you on contract law? Even if she'll do it for free? Probably not. You need someone with relevant experience who can provide you with top-notch service—just as you provide top-notch service to your clients. Don't be overly influenced by friends or relatives who dabble but aren't expert.

It's the same for insurance. Not every agent or company deals with commercial insurance, and many agents simply don't know enough about it to provide you with advice.

Here's another consideration. Try to have only one lawyer, one insurance company, and one accountant/tax preparer. The more you fragment your supporting cast, the less likely your team members will have all the necessary information (the bigger picture) to be of optimum value to you. You'll also save time.

Relationship Management

It's wise to maintain a good ongoing relationship with your supporting cast. Most of us don't do that. We might, for example, consult a lawyer for help on drawing up a contract and then not speak to him or her again for years, until we need their professional services again. There's nothing terribly wrong with that, but it tends to keep the supporting cast members out of the loop and out of touch with what you are doing.

If you stay in regular touch with your professional help, they will be more informed and current regarding your business. That can be helpful in preventing problems before they occur.

Let me give you an example. Jane is your accountant. She provides you with tax advice and prepares your tax returns. During the first two years of your business, you earn about $30,000 per year. During those two years, you meet with Jane twice, at the end of each year to get your tax returns done. But in your third year, you earn $120,000 (congratulations). If you meet with Jane at the end of that year, it's too late for Jane to help you develop tax strategies for that year. That can cost you a lot of money.

If, however, you talk to Jane on a more regular basis (even if it's on the phone), then Jane will know about your revenue increase and be able to help earlier.

I suggest that you try to build a more personal relationship with your supporting cast. The more they know about you and what is going on in your business, the more help they can be.

The Least You Need to Know

◆ Stay on the right side of the law even if it seems unlikely you'll get caught.

◆ Seek and accept advice from professionals who have experience and who specialize in the area of your concerns.

◆ Don't neglect your insurance options, and don't assume that existing insurance will be adequate for your new situation.

◆ Cultivate ongoing relationships with your supporting cast, and keep them informed regarding what you are doing.

Part 4

The Ongoing Business Challenge

If you're going to be in business, you have to sell yourself and your services to potential clients. Part 4 starts off with a chapter on how to market your services. You'll find lots of practical advice specifically aimed at the small consultant.

The Internet is definitely a boon to the savvy consultancy. There are two chapters devoted to using the web as a tool to connect with clients, not only as a way to sell your services, but as a way to market your intellectual capital, including articles, books, newsletters, and other materials of use to people seeking help.

How do you close the sale to a potential client who's considering the use of your services? That's the issue addressed in Chapter 19, "Getting the Contract." And how much do you charge for your services, and do you bill by the project or by time spent? These questions and more are addressed in Chapter 20, "Let's Talk About Money."

Finally, do you want to grow (with all the headaches that might involve), or do you just want to reach a level at which you're making a comfortable living and stay there? The answer isn't easy, but see Chapter 21, "To Grow or Not to Grow," for both sides of the issue.

Chapter 16

Being Seen—Your Marketing Options

In This Chapter

◆ The difference between selling and marketing

◆ Exposure, targeted exposure, and branding explained

◆ Personal-based, virtually free marketing options

◆ Marketing possibilities in various media

We live in a world where marketing is king. Poor-quality products can sell well when backed by a strong marketing campaign. Top-quality goods can fail miserably without an adequate marketing strategy.

In some ways consulting is no different. It does you no good to be top-notch if nobody knows about you. You must pay attention to marketing strategy if you plan on succeeding.

Most consultants aren't experts in marketing, a fact that makes the marketing challenge doubly difficult. Many of us stumble about until we find the right approach to marketing our services. It takes time to figure out what works.

In this chapter I'll cover the different ways you can market your services. That should help you develop an initial marketing strategy.

Marketing and Selling ... Aren't They the Same?

Think about a salesperson; say somebody selling cars or vacuum cleaners. What is his or her goal? Most salespeople, particularly those who haven't been trained in alternative ways of dealing with prospective clients, have a very simple and straightforward purpose. They want you, the customer, to purchase what they are selling. Once you've done that, their job is largely finished. In fact, after the sale is made, they don't want to hear from you again until you're ready to buy another car or vacuum cleaner.

In consulting the situation is very different. The salesperson's job is finished after the sale has been made, whereas the consultant's job is just beginning. This makes a huge difference in how one goes about creating business.

As a consultant you need to focus less on selling and more on marketing. What's the difference? In marketing you are less concerned with obtaining an immediate sale. You are much more concerned with long-term issues. Marketing simply has different goals than sales does.

A good marketing strategy for consulting services should achieve the following goals for you:

♦ Increase the chances that clients will call when their needs match your services, even if they don't right now

♦ Create a positive and professional image

♦ Build awareness of your services and competitive advantages

♦ Create a "need" for your services through client education

These goals have important implications for what you actually do as a consultant. The fundamental difference between selling and marketing lies with these goals. The perspective is a long-term one versus short-term. Marketing may include selling at some point, but the selling process is only a small part of any marketing approach.

> **Consulting Confidential**
>
> Is it possible to succeed when offering inferior services? Sadly, yes. An adept marketer can hit the big time by offering very little value. The trick is to create the illusion of value through marketing. It doesn't appeal to me, and I hope it doesn't appeal to you. For every low-value consultant who succeeds via marketing savvy, a hundred more such people fail trying this route.

> **Between Colleagues**
>
> While the value of your services may seem obvious to you, it may not be so clear to prospective clients. That's why it's important to keep in mind that your marketing strategy should educate clients, so they understand how your services can help them reach their goals.

Critical Marketing Principles

What do you absolutely need to know about marketing? Let's look at the three most important principles, even though marketing pros may cringe at the somewhat simplified approach here.

Exposure—The More the Merrier

First marketing principle: However you market, you want to reach as many people as possible. The more people who know about your services, the more likely your business will increase.

You want to reach potential clients directly, but you also want to reach people who may pass on your information to those potential customers.

Now, here's a little test. What if this is your primary marketing guideline? Is there something wrong with "the more the merrier"? Think about it for a moment, and see if you can determine the flaw. Then read the next principle.

Targeting—Not More People, but the Right People

Let's see if you've spotted the flaw with "the more the merrier." Since consulting services tend to have a narrow or restricted market, gaining exposure to the wrong people is a waste of resources. For example, if you offer consulting services to the medical profession, it's pointless to broaden your marketing efforts to include manufacturers. It's not that the increased exposure will harm you. It's just inefficient.

That brings me to the second marketing principle: Your marketing efforts will succeed to the extent that you have targeted exposure. *Targeted exposure* means that you get your message to those people who (a) have an interest in and a need for your services and (b) are in a position to decide to hire you or advise people who can hire you.

Branding—Long-Term Prominence

Branding means creating an awareness and a familiarity with the name of a product or company, along with positive associations related to that name. It is the third marketing principle.

Branding is best understood by looking at an example. Consider companies like Ford, Coca-Cola, and Pepsi. Seen any of their advertising campaigns lately? Have you noticed that most of their ad campaigns tell you very little about their products? They don't expect you to see one of their commercials and immediately drive to your car dealership or corner store to buy their products.

So what are they after? They are trying to associate an image with their brand name. And they want their brand to come to mind whenever you think automobile or soft drink or thirst, and they want you to have positive associations with the name.

The idea is that when you are shopping you will consider their products first, because you are familiar with the name and have positive associations with it. They aren't concerned with selling you something now; rather, they want you to buy things from them forever.

What's the connection with the marketing of consulting services? Well, think about it. Isn't brand awareness consistent with your long-term business goals? As a consultant, you aren't as concerned about selling your services as you are with creating a positive image and keeping your products and services in the minds of prospective clients—hopefully forever.

For me, this is a critical point. Many consultants, driven by the idea they must "make the sale," neglect the longer-term context. So they create Internet websites that focus on selling, rather than on brand awareness. The result is that people visit the site, see the pitch, and stay about 20 seconds. The same applies to brochures.

Let me give you an example of branding in action. I run two websites, www.work911.com and www.articles911.com. Both have rather distinctive names and were designed to create brand awareness of my company and also of the names of the sites. I want people to remember the names and associate them with good-quality information about working life. By extension, I hope they will consider me first if they have needs I can fill.

Has it been successful? Yes. There have been over a million and a half visits to the sites, providing exposure and somewhat targeted exposure. Do they generate business? You bet.

Now that you know the three essential marketing principles, let's move on to the specific marketing options at your disposal.

Personal Approaches to Marketing

We begin with you. Believe it or not, you are an important marketing tool. That's because, in the minds of your potential clients, you, the person, and your services are seen as one and the same thing. If a client likes you, then he or she is much more likely to contact you when a need falls within your area of expertise.

Cold Calling

Many salespeople, and even consultants, stress that you need to garner exposure by making as many calls to strangers as you can and talking to them about your services. That's a technique known as *cold calling*.

There are two kinds of cold calls. One is the sales call, whose sole purpose is to sell a particular service. The second is the "get to know you call." The purpose of it is for you to introduce yourself and hopefully set up a meeting with the potential client in the hopes of creating a positive relationship that will extend over time.

I don't recommend sales calls for consultants. Success rates are poor, and it will be clear to the people you call that you are out for the sale—not to mention that most people are uncomfortable making these calls.

The "get to know you call" has some potential, provided you handle it correctly. Focus on arranging a face-to-face meeting so the prospective client can get to know you and, above all, so you can get to know the client. Your approach should be 75 percent listening and asking questions, and 25 percent talking and informing clients about your services. If you do arrange the meeting, you can leave more-detailed printed material about your services and how you can help the client.

Between Colleagues

Cold calls are best used to set up an in-person meeting. Do you have to use cold calls to succeed? No. I don't make them.

Do I suggest trying to create rapport over the phone? No. The best way to handle this is to use the cold call as a door opener. Building rapport and confidence is best done in person.

Networking

No doubt you are familiar with *networking*, or developing contacts that can mature into business relationships. Keep in mind that networking for the sole purpose of making sales is going to brand you as a pain in the rear end—selfish. The secret to networking is to develop relationships, both professional and social, with those you want in your network. The contracts will come over time. Don't push it.

Providing Free Services

One of the best things you can do is offer free services to your community. Professional associations, chambers of commerce, and nonprofits often appreciate services such as no-fee speaking engagements. These are ideal for increasing exposure and targeted exposure, and for branding.

Because it may not be practical or even desirable to provide full-blown consulting services for no fee, I think the best option is the public speaking route. It costs nothing to do, develops your communication skills, and gives you an opportunity to strut your stuff.

Consistent with what I've said so far, never, ever do these services as sales presentations. If you provide something valuable, potential clients will see you and your services as valuable. And that means more business.

It's always useful to have items you can give away to potential clients. You probably already know that you can give away calendars, pens, and that kind of thing, and there's no harm in this. But where the real power lies is when you can give away something that is directly related to your consulting services and that also has value to prospective clients.

> **Consulting Confidential**
>
> What's the best thing about personal-based marketing? It's free (or almost free). You don't have to pay money to do it. All you have to do is spend the time doing it.

For example, for some time, I gave away free copies of several of my two-sided help cards that were related to some of my consulting services. Help cards are information sheets with a good deal of specialized information about a single topic. Often, when I do public speaking (free or paid), I include these useful aids as promotional items.

Television and Radio Interviews

Television and radio interviews can be very valuable in increasing exposure and branding. Radio is particularly easy to arrange, since most cities of any size have at least one radio station that focuses on talk shows.

I'd focus on radio first. It's easier to do well and easier to break in. How do you do it? If you have talk shows in your area, contact the talk show host or producer (sometimes the station manager) and explain the kinds of work you do and relate it to an issue that is of broad interest. For example, if you consult in workplace safety issues, then you might want to tie that in with workplace violence (a "hotter" topic).

> **Consultant Crashing**
>
> Never come across as selling a product during radio and television appearances. Let the host or interviewer call the shots. If he or she asks, tell. If not, don't. If you don't provide value to listeners on radio, for example, you won't be asked back.

You can contact radio staff by e-mail, fax, or phone. Again, remember you aren't intending to sell anything at all. You want the exposure and branding possibilities.

Go prepared with some basic contact information, such as your website address, e-mail address, and so on. I'd advise being somewhat careful about giving out phone numbers on talk show interviews. It depends on the topic. If it is an emotionally charged discussion area, better to have people contact you in ways other than by phone.

A quick note on television: The challenge with television is that it's a visual medium, so TV producers want pictures, and you need to look and act in ways that make you look good.

Local access shows are one way to obtain television exposure. Many cable companies have such local access shows and invite people to take on the responsibility of producing special-interest programs. I know several consultants who have done very well hosting such shows. Look into it by contacting your cable company.

Paid Advertising

By *paid advertising*, I'm talking about placing ads in print or other media. But is it a good idea to use paid advertising campaigns? Let's see.

In Print

With respect to advertising in print publications, you have several options. You can advertise in high-circulation, mass-market publications, or you can be more focused and place ads in smaller-circulation publications that may be more targeted to your particular audience.

In specialty areas where interest in services is restricted to a small sector of the population, highly targeted advertising is the way to go. It's cheaper and more cost-effective.

I can't advise you on how to create a dynamite print ad. I'll leave that to the experts. But I can help you become more aware of where you can place ads for reasonable prices.

No matter what field you specialize in, I promise you that there are several print publications whose audience is the exact market you need to reach. Association publications (such as those put out by your local chamber of commerce) and trade magazines are examples of publications that go to very narrow targets. For example, there are trade publications for farmers, banking executives, human resources professionals—almost any group you can think of.

Those types of publications are the ones that will produce results for you. How do you find them? That's a challenge, since most aren't sitting on newsstands. Here's a tip. Every year Writer's

> **Consulting Confidential**
>
> Small community newspapers tend to charge much less for ads than large newspapers and glossy magazines. If your services may be of interest to readers of local community newspapers, you may want to look at the possibility of advertising there.

Digest Books produces a directory of publications called *Writer's Market*. It's available in print and/or with a CD-ROM. Although it's a directory aimed chiefly at writers who want to freelance, in it you will find thousands of publications listed, along with some information about their target markets. Also included are contact names and addresses.

If you contact those publications that target your market and ask for information about advertising with them, they'll send you that information along with a few sample copies.

Something else you may not know. Ads don't always have to be boxes or pages in magazines. Some companies enclose their publications in plastic bags. You may be able to have your marketing material included in that package, along with the magazine.

Radio and Television

You also have the option of buying paid ads on radio and television. They can provide great exposure, but it's not terribly well-targeted. Effectiveness depends on whether your specialized services will be useful to those listening or watching. Paid radio and TV ads can also be expensive.

> ### Between Colleagues
>
> When placing radio or television ads, make sure you are sponsoring programs that attract the people you need to reach. If you are a sports therapist consultant, it makes sense to sponsor a sports-related show rather than a cooking show.

> ### Consulting Confidential
>
> The post office in your area may offer short seminars on direct mail marketing. Usually fees are low, and in some cases you can attend free of charge. If you plan on using bulk mail, it's nearly mandatory that you attend a course on how to go about doing it.

You might consider placing an ad in a cable TV channel guide. Most cable companies have channel guides and sell advertising on those at relatively reasonable rates. I can't vouch for the effectiveness of such ads, but they may be cheap enough for you to give them a try.

Direct Mail

Direct mail refers to mailing of promotional material via the post office. Most often the material includes a cover letter and a brochure of some kind, although some consultants may include a small freebie, like a branded bookmark.

I've used direct mail very successfully, and I think most consultants should look at it as a viable option. Direct mail can be a little more oriented toward sales than the other techniques I've discussed. But again, the best way to look at direct mail is as a relationship starter and a branding technique. You want to be remembered.

Conducting a direct mail campaign is not difficult, but there are a lot of bits to it. You need a good cover letter, attractive and informative brochures, and a list of people to send your material to. In addition, you should become familiar with post office procedures for bulk mail that can save you money, and printing and mailing services that can save you time. You don't really want to spend days stuffing envelopes.

Whom to Target? How to Get Names?

The first principle of direct mail is targeting. Since direct mail is charged on a per piece basis, you want every piece to go to someone who has a need for your services and is in a position to decide to hire you or advise someone else to hire you.

Where do you get names? The most efficient way is to purchase a mailing list (or mailing labels) collected specifically for direct mail. Typically, you'd find an ad agency or direct mail company that has a list targeting your market, and you'd purchase labels on a cost-per-thousand basis. That way you can do a large campaign or a smaller one. Be aware that most companies permit a single use per buy. Don't cheat. They'll catch you, since their lists contain "anticheat" addresses and names.

To find companies that sell this information, try your Yellow Pages under "direct mail" or "ad agencies."

If you are lucky enough to work with markets like educators or government officials, you may find it relatively easy to get personnel directories and use them as a basis for your direct mail campaigns. That's a bit less efficient, since you'll have to enter the names into your computer to produce labels and letters.

The least efficient way of identifying candidates for direct mail is to call companies that might be interested in your services and find out whom to contact. Clearly that will work only for small-scale mailings.

Consultant Crashing

Stuffing envelopes is a low-value activity. If you spend too much time on low-value activities, you aren't maximizing your time and resources. It is often worth hiring someone to do these kinds of things.

Saving Money and Time

You probably know you can save a significant amount on postage by sending your material via "bulk mail." *Bulk mail* is a class of mail that is cheaper to send but requires that you meet certain conditions in order to be able to take advantage of the lower rates. If you are interested in this class of mail, contact your post office. You can expect to sort and bundle your mail pieces by zip or postal code, and you may need to have special envelopes made up. There's a cost associated with the latter.

Should you stuff envelopes yourself? You have to trade off the value of your time (and the extent of your patience) in making your decision. Since I do mail campaigns that are small (usually under 300 per time), I will occasionally put the material together myself. Some people hire their children to do this work, which isn't a bad idea.

The other option is to hire an outside company to stuff envelopes and put the labels and postage (if needed) on the material. One company that does this is Mailboxes, Etc. Some of their stores will do the whole thing from folding to stuffing.

How Often? What About Follow-Up?

Here's an important question: How often do you need to contact the same prospective customers to have an effect? Well, the simple answer is as often as possible. Remember that your goal is to create brand awareness over the long term. That means sending material to the same people, perhaps several times a year. Keep your services in the minds of potential clients. Perhaps once every three months is a good choice.

> **Consulting Confidential**
>
> Consider including something that potential clients will keep. For example, producing a newsletter with some free articles relevant to your customer base is a great idea. It could be as short as four pages. If your newsletter is valuable, it will be circulated to others who may end up becoming customers.

If you have a limited budget, you may be better off making repeated contacts rather than contacting more people less often.

Finally, on the issue of direct mail, follow-up is very important. Here's the way you should do it. Do the mailing, and let people know in your cover letter that you will be calling them in a week or two after they receive your material. Then do that. It makes your call a little less "cold."

Internet Marketing

Finally we come to the newest marketing medium—the Internet. The Internet can be such a powerful marketing medium that it deserves special treatment. The next two chapters will deal with this valuable option in more detail. But here's an overview of where the Internet sits as of this writing.

We are currently in a period of economic collapse on the Internet. That, in itself, probably isn't very meaningful to you, but the causes behind it are important to understand.

> **Between Colleagues**
>
> Marketing on the Internet should not be used as a stand-alone strategy. Internet and more traditional ways of advertising should be interlinked. For example, your print material should point people to your website.

There was a period of time (ending in 2000) when companies were using up huge marketing budgets for advertising on the Internet. Fueled by an unrealistic hope that consumers would make the move to buying online, literally billions of dollars were poured into Internet companies, popularly called "dot coms." Most are gone now, primarily victims of financial foolishness that led to bankruptcy. Quite simply, investors and companies misread the Internet.

That said, there is no reason why you can't benefit from Internet marketing provided you understand that its major purpose is to provide exposure and branding over time. In the event that you also sell products that complement your services (as I do), just be aware that we are at least several years away from having product sales driven by the Internet.

Finally, our understanding of the Internet and workable economic models is much less complete than for other media. And it's a changing world. For example, what worked last year may not work next year, and vice versa.

I think it's worth the investment to develop and maintain a web presence. Just be aware that most business sites, consulting or otherwise, fail in achieving their goals.

In the next two chapters, I'll provide you with information about how to make your Internet presence a success.

The Least You Need to Know

- Focus on marketing and long-term exposure rather than short-term sales.
- Targeted exposure and branding are critical aspects of marketing your consulting services.
- The most powerful and the cheapest form of marketing is based on personal contact.
- No matter how you market, be sure to reach those with a need for your services and who are in a position to hire you.

Chapter 17

The Internet—Your Friend, Your Essential Friend

In This Chapter

- Ways the Internet can propel your consulting business
- Internet tools to extend the reach of your marketing
- Value: the basic Internet marketing principle
- Tips to help you max out the potential of the Internet

Ah, the Internet! Some people embrace and love it, and are even addicted to it. Some are neutral. Some see it as the devil incarnate and refuse to use it. Such reactions to a relatively new technology are not surprising.

Whatever your personal usage of the Internet and your reactions to it, this communication medium has become a tool that is almost essential for consultants. It is rapidly becoming the medium of choice for communicating with customers, potential and current. Used properly, it extends the marketing reach of any consultant, expanding markets from local to worldwide.

However, to receive the benefits available from use of the Internet, you need to understand two things: how the Internet functions as a business tool, and how you can use it effectively to gain those benefits.

In this chapter I'll help you understand why the Internet should be part of your overall business strategy. In the next chapter I'll talk in detail about how your Internet website can be used to boost your business.

The Critical Role of the Internet

Imagine running a business without a phone. Seems like a silly idea, right? Or consider trying to run a business without the use of mail or faxes. It doesn't make sense.

While it's possible to run a consulting business without using the Internet, it's just about as silly as running a business without a telephone or the mail or a fax machine. Maybe you can do it, but you don't want to do it.

The Internet is becoming the medium of choice for communication with clients. It's fast, relatively reliable, and close to essential. You need Internet access if only for communicating with clients via e-mail.

Consulting Confidential
The Internet is often underused or misused by consultants and small businesses. Because many consultants lack an understanding of how the Internet can and should be used, they have invested their time and money in creating an Internet presence with absolutely no return on investment. The cost of wasted resources is immense.

Beyond providing access to e-mail (which is nearly essential for consultants), the Internet has opened completely new opportunities for consultants. As a consultant, you can do things now that you were never able to do before. You can create reputations, not just in your local areas but across the world. You can market to clients no matter where they are. And you can learn from your colleagues in ways that simply were not possible before.

In the next sections I'll talk about the different ways the Internet can be used both in the running and in the marketing of a successful consulting business.

Client Communication During Projects

Consulting, more than almost any other business, requires timely communication with clients. In case you haven't noticed, communication via standard methods such as telephones has become more frustrating and less efficient. We're all familiar with the vagaries of voice mail, the difficulty in timing phone calls so we can actually talk to the people we need to talk to.

The previous methods of communication have become more difficult because the workloads and commitments of customers have increased over the last decade. Think about it. What percentage of phone calls actually connect you immediately with the person you need to speak with? I can tell you, as a consultant, that only about 20 percent of my phone calls succeed on the first try. I'd guess that clients calling me succeed on the first try only about 20 percent of the time, too.

Electronic mail helps address the problem of telephone communication. While e-mail is somewhat less immediate than the telephone, clients know they can send the e-mail and expect a response in a reasonable time, no matter where you are on the planet. You don't need to be in the office to reply to e-mail—likewise for your communication to clients. Provided your client checks e-mail once a day (or is expecting e-mail from you), you can communicate quickly and in great detail even though the client may not be in his or her office when you send the e-mail. Not only are e-mails a fairly fast communication method, but they also serve as documentation of conversations, and they are nonintrusive. E-mails can be read at the recipient's convenience.

 Consultant Crashing

Something to think about! Some people with eyesight difficulties can't easily use e-mail. Don't always insist on e-mail communication, since your client may have some reason for not wanting to use it.

E-mail is efficient. It allows you to keep correspondence electronically so you can refer to it days or months later. It allows you and your clients to deal with issues at your convenience.

Document Transfers

Consulting projects tend to generate documents. From proposals and contracts to final reports, documents need to be moved around. E-mail is quickly becoming the preferred way to do so, since it is very fast. For example, let's say you are asked to do a consulting proposal for a company across the country. They want it tomorrow for their decision-making meeting. What's the best way for you to get it there? As part of an e-mail message. No matter the time of day, all you need to do is attach the document to an e-mail message and fire it off. It's there within minutes, and all the customer has to do is print it out and use it. No fuss, no muss, no cost.

Can you live without e-mail capability? No. Not only is electronic document transfer a huge convenience, but we are fast approaching a time when proposals will be accepted only in electronic formats.

Let me give you another example. I offer custom-designed training to consulting clients. Typically I communicate and arrange sessions via e-mail whenever possible. But I find that my time savings is the greatest when I use e-mail to transfer documents. E-mail provides a huge time savings in transferring training manuals. No matter where the client is located, I can send a copy of the training material as soon as it is ready, and the client receives it almost instantly. Print it, duplicate it, and we're ready to go.

Even billing and invoicing can be done via document transfer or via e-mail. Not all the time, though. Many companies still require a paper invoice or bill sent directly to the accounts payable department, but that will change over the next few years.

Communicating with Interested Potential Clients

Of course the Internet is far more than e-mail. With it, you can communicate with potential customers who have already expressed an interest in your work and also you can explain your services to people who have yet to discover you.

Let's take on the first situation. You receive an e-mail from someone referred to you by a previous client. "How can you help me do what I need to do?" she asks. You can, of course, tell her on the phone, and no doubt that's a good start. But guess what? You have an Internet website that answers many of her questions. It contains samples of your work, your philosophy, and experience; and best of all, she can get the information on her own whenever it's convenient for her.

You might also use an autoresponder. An *autoresponder* is a program that receives an e-mail and automatically sends some preset information to that client. For example, if you send an e-mail to defuse@work911.com, you will get an immediate response telling you about my seminars on defusing hostility.

Look at the speed, convenience, and immediacy that you provide the client. When you provide information to the client faster than your competitors, you have an advantage.

Communicating with New Potential Clients

How can you explain your services to people who have never heard of you? And how can you make potential clients of them? The answer is marketing. Remember that the purpose of marketing is to create repeat business and new customers. The Internet allows you to create new clients, not only in your own region but in other geographic areas.

> **Consulting Confidential**
>
> Far too many consultants consider the Internet a sales tool and try to sell their wares like vacuum cleaners. That approach almost never works. What you need is exposure and reputation building, not hard sells. You want your customers to come to you.

I'm not talking about selling here. I'm talking about exposure and creating familiarity and comfort on the part of your potential clients.

Let me give you two examples. Joan owns her own consulting business. She discovers that she can buy e-mail addresses of people she can sell to via e-mail. Also she is aware of several public discussion groups related to her specialty. So she starts sending out mail to people on the list, and she posts sales messages to those public discussions. What happens? Complaints.

Lots of them. People receiving junk e-mail yell at her. People on the discussion list (important marketing targets) see her as not reputable.

Compare this approach with another one. Fred decides *no junk e-mail*. He participates in those same discussion groups, helping people as he can, and in fact rarely mentioning his business. He establishes, through his messages, a reputation for expertise. And guess what? People start checking out his website and contacting him about possible projects.

Another example: Compare two websites, one having 5 to 10 pages of promotional material—very glossy, very slick—and the second providing free articles, self-assessment tools, and resources, in addition to promotional material.

Which do you think will succeed? No contest. The second website provides potential customers with reasons to come back, because the website itself provides value. Think of it this way. Would you tune in to a television channel that aired only ads? I don't think so.

Between Colleagues

On the Internet, content is king. Your website, and any other contributions you make on the Internet in discussion groups or e-mails, must provide some value to people seeing it. Advertising, per se, does not provide value.

Internet Strategy in a Nutshell

In this section I'm going to talk in more detail about your Internet strategy and the Internet tools you have at your command. Here's a quick list of the tools available to you. If you don't know what one or two are, don't worry. I'll tell you in a moment.

- ◆ Website
- ◆ Professional discussion lists
- ◆ Private e-mail
- ◆ Newsgroups
- ◆ Autoresponders
- ◆ E-zine (newsletter) publishing
- ◆ Running professional lists

Your Internet strategy is like a spider web. Each part is linked to all the others, with your website smack in the middle. The goal of your Internet strategy is to make all of your Internet tools drive people to your website.

Here's what that means. Your private e-mail always contains a little tag at the end with your website address. When you post to a professional list, your post should include your

---

Consulting Confidential

Here's a believe-it-or-not. In my consulting practice, I make no cold calls to strangers. In a typical year I might send out (via regular mail) fewer than 800 promotional letters (often inviting people to visit my website). I don't advertise. I've been asked to speak at conferences and asked to write books. Almost all of my projects involve customers coming to me on the basis of my web presence. It's true.

---

website address. Get the idea? You want to drive people to your website because your use of the other tools leads them to believe they will gain something by visiting. And you want to make information about your services available so potential clients can come to you.

Of course, you aren't going to market using only the Net. You might also use direct mail, or ads, or whatever fits for you, but you will link them to your Internet-based marketing. For example, say you use a direct mail campaign (via regular mail) to introduce people to your services. The direct mail material should include a promo message for your website. If you publish an online newsletter, you might offer a free subscription. Interlink your tools and provide value to potential customers.

Now let's look at each of these Internet tools. I'll discuss websites only briefly because the next chapter is devoted entirely to this important tool.

Your Website

Your website serves as your calling card and your billboard, and demonstrates your competencies, abilities, and wisdom. As I said earlier, your website must provide value. People must find it useful and helpful.

Developing and running a website takes a bit of money (but not a lot), an investment of time, and an understanding of how to make it work. I'll cover websites in the next chapter, so hang in there.

Professional Discussion Lists

A *professional discussion list* is a forum (in which you generally participate via e-mail) that is focused on a profession or a specialized area. For example, there are discussion lists for trainers, human resources professionals, consultants, engineers, and so on.

Your long-term goal in participating is to create a positive reputation with potential customers and colleagues, and increase the reach of your marketing efforts. You do this by helping others, not by selling.

How Do Professional Lists Work?

Using professional lists is easy. Let's say you've found a list where potential clients and/or colleagues hang out. You follow the instructions for subscribing or signing up. Usually the sign-up procedure involves sending an e-mail to a specific address and then replying to the e-mail that the discussion list sends back to you.

Now you are subscribed, or a "member." The terms vary, and the sign-up procedures depend on the software on the other end. Follow the instructions and you'll be okay.

As other people send e-mails to the list, you will get a copy in your electronic mailbox, as will every other list member. If you see something you'd like to reply to (for example, to help someone out), all you have to do is use the reply function in your e-mail program and send an e-mail. Your e-mail then goes to the list and is distributed to all members.

Depending on list software, you may have other options. You may be able to read old messages from an archive. You might be able to choose to participate via a website rather than via e-mail, or choose to receive a single digest of messages once a day rather than each message individually. And of course, normally you can unsubscribe or leave the list anytime.

How Do You Make Effective Use of Professional Lists?

Above all, remember that you are putting your best foot forward when you respond to professional discussion lists. Here are some guidelines:

◆ When you join a list, hold off posting to it for a week or two to get a feel for the kinds of conversations that go on. Make sure you read any instructions about list rules. You want to fit in.

◆ Be helpful, open to learning, and avoid emotionally charged discussions.

◆ Set up your e-mail program to append a *signature line* to your contributions. The signature line should contain your name, e-mail address, website address, and perhaps one or two sentences about your website. The signature line should be no longer than four lines.

◆ Remember, you aren't there to sell. You are there for exposure. Act according to the list rules.

◆ Don't overpost. If you post too many messages, people get annoyed. Don't try too hard. Post once or twice a day max.

Working Words

A **signature line** is a short statement that your e-mail program places at the end of your e-mails. You define what's put there by setting it up in your e-mail program.

◆ It is appropriate to direct someone to your website and its resources if a specific question comes up. If your website contains resources related to the question, it's okay to let the list know.

How Do You Find Professional Lists?

How do you find such lists? Well, it's not always easy, but I've given you a few resources here that you can try. Several companies host thousands of discussion lists of all sorts. You can go to their websites and search for topics of interest. Two of the largest such companies are www.egroups.com and www.topica.com.

There are also a few discussion list directories, which you can also search. Try the following:

◆ tile.net/lists

◆ www.lsoft.com/lists/listref.html

◆ paml.net

Finally you can try using search engines like those at www.google.com and www.yahoo.com.

Try searching using the words "discussion list yourtopic" without the quotes, and changing "yourtopic" to your specialty. For example, "discussion list human resources" (again without quotes).

Working Words

Spam is unsolicited e-mail, and it is almost universally hated by e-mail users. Another term for it is junk e-mail. If you aren't sure whether the e-mail you're sending would be considered spam by the recipient, don't send it.

Private E-mail

Most people have a fair grasp of how to send and receive e-mail, so I'll just provide a few pointers. If these aren't sufficient, you might want to have a friend walk you through the process of sending and receiving mail.

◆ Make sure you respond to e-mail quickly. If you travel a good deal, it's possible to receive and respond to e-mail from wherever you are, provided you set up your e-mail program properly and have the appropriate hardware on a laptop computer.

◆ Try to keep your e-mail messages brief and to the point. People have short attention spans when reading messages on a computer screen.

◆ Be aware that e-mails can get lost. With critical e-mails, request confirmation from the person receiving it, and confirm receipt of mail sent to you.

◆ Make sure you set up your e-mail program to include your signature line.

◆ Above all, never ever send spam, or unsolicited e-mail. *Spam* is unrequested e-mail that is sent to people with whom you have no previous business relationship.

Newsgroups

I've included newsgroups here just so you are aware that they exist. Newsgroups (sometimes referred to collectively as "Usenet") have existed for a long time, and run differently from discussion lists. There are thousands of newsgroups on a number of topics, but you'll probably find that they are full of spam and silly arguments. They tend to be less regulated than professional discussion lists.

The guidelines for making use of newsgroups are pretty much the same as those for professional discussion lists. However, newsgroups are accessed differently than discussion lists. If you are interested in finding out how to do so, ask your Internet provider or get a friend to walk you through the procedure. It's not difficult.

Autoresponders

Probably the most underused Internet tool is the autoresponder, a software program that automatically sends out preset information whenever someone sends an e-mail message to the autoresponder address. Since the software runs on the computer that sends you your e-mail, it's best to contact your Internet provider to find out if they offer this service.

What are the advantages of using an autoresponder? The first advantage is that you can use an autoresponder to provide information about your services that you don't want to publish on your website. For example, most consultants don't publish fees. However, you may feel comfortable putting a price for services in an e-mail that is sent if someone asks for it.

A second, and perhaps the most powerful, advantage is that most autoresponders will let you know when someone requests your information. Normally, you'd receive an e-mail, which would include the name and e-mail address of the person requesting the information. Unlike websites, autoresponders let you know who has asked for information; you can then follow up. Autoresponders are efficient ways to get information almost instantly to potential clients.

How do you get an autoresponder? Many website providers provide this service at no extra charge as part of your e-mail program, and this is the most convenient way to use an autoresponder. Check with your web hosting company. If they don't offer it, other companies may provide the service for free or for a small fee.

Here are some tips on using autoresponders:

♦ Set up separate autoresponders for each specific topic or area in which you specialize. Thus, you will have an autoresponder for service 1, service 2, and so on. The information should be as complete as possible. Remember that the person receiving it is already interested in your company. Include any marketing material that makes sense. I also include prices.

♦ Make sure there are references to your autoresponders on your website, so people can see them. For example: "If you'd like detailed information about [topic], click here to get it instantly via e-mail."

♦ Be sure to follow up on requests for information. After all, these folks are interested enough to ask.

♦ When contacted by phone or e-mail by interested customers, offer them the option of using the autoresponder.

E-zine Newsletter Publishing

E-zines … in the old days we called them newsletters. You know, the short paper publications that contained concise articles, help, tips, and ads. Paper newsletters are still valuable, but the problem is that they do cost money to print and distribute, particularly if you want a "slick" look and feel.

The alternative? The high-tech electronic version of a newsletter known as an e-zine (or sometimes a *zine*). An *e-zine* is simply an electronic document, usually sent via e-mail to subscribers and containing many of the same things that are included in paper newsletters.

Working Words

An **e-zine** is an electronic document usually sent via e-mail to people who have subscribed voluntarily. Content includes useful information, articles, and updates but is limited only by your imagination.

What's the value of an e-zine? Publishing a regular e-zine allows you to keep yourself in the minds and hearts of prospective customers. That's because you will have regular contact with them (perhaps monthly or more often). If you write well, and include valuable material, you will look really good. The e-zine format is also great for informing people of new services or material available at your website.

The basic rule of e-zine publishing is the same as for all the Internet tools: provide value; be useful.

What about the technology needed? You can use the same technology that you use to run or participate in professional lists. Check out www.egroups.com or www.topica.com for help in setting up a newsletter distribution system, free of charge.

Other ways to send e-zines are through software you can purchase, or through other companies. However, I suggest starting with the egroups and topica sites just listed.

Producing a regular e-zine takes time, and you have to be able to write well. A poorly executed one damages your reputation. What about charging a fee for the e-zine? At the moment the answer is no. Don't do it. People aren't at the point where they're willing to pay any substantial amount for an e-zine, maybe in five years but not now. The hassles of tracking subscribers and collecting money simply aren't worth it. So think of your e-zine as a "free sample."

You need to market your e-zine, and that's often difficult. Include information on your website, including a sign-up box. Consider placing information about your e-zine in the signature line of your e-mail. Include the same information in any promotional materials you use.

> **Consulting Confidential**
>
> I publish an e-zine that includes one free article per issue and an update on new material on my website. The subscriber base is fairly small, about 5,000 people. Each time I send out an e-zine, traffic to my website triples.

Running Professional Lists

Your final tool? Running your very own professional discussion list. You already know about participating in a professional discussion list, but guess what? You can set up and run your own about whatever topics you'd like. And you can do it free of charge.

Perhaps there isn't a discussion list about one of your consulting specialties. Set one up and let people know about it. Or perhaps you'd like more flexibility and control in what you post? Set up your own list.

By running discussion lists, you can provide a valuable service for others interested in the same areas you are. I don't have to tell you that those people are your potential clients.

Is a discussion list hard to run? No. If it gets popular and you want to make sure it's an excellent forum, you will have to invest some time in it. Does running a discussion list require technological expertise? No, not usually. If you can send and receive e-mail and can use a web browser, you're in business.

How can you set up a discussion list? I'll refer you to the same two companies that I mentioned earlier, egroups (www.egroups.com) and topica (www.topica.com).

Your web host may also offer this service (mine does). There are other options that may require a bit more technical expertise.

Some tips. Again, aim for value. A discussion list that is valuable tends to grow. Perhaps most important, you need to let people know the discussion list exists, and that's a huge challenge. Again, mention it in promotional material. Make sure information about the list is available on your website, and post information about your new list on other relevant lists.

The Least You Need to Know

♦ You shouldn't rely only on e-mail, or even a website. Consider using other Internet tools.

♦ Internet tools work best when they are interlinked and when they reference each other, just as all the strands in a spider web connect to each other.

♦ Don't use the Internet as a selling tool but as a way to get exposure and build a reputation.

♦ Integrate whatever Internet tools you are using with the more usual marketing techniques (for example, regular mail, paper newsletters).

Chapter 18

Ins and Outs of a Successful Website

In This Chapter

- ◆ What your website should accomplish
- ◆ Why content is king
- ◆ How to design your website for success
- ◆ Why web hosts and domains are important

In the last chapter, I explained that your website serves as the central hub for your Internet initiatives. Since a well-designed website is so important to your marketing and communication efforts, I've provided this chapter to help you increase the chances that your website will contribute to your consulting business.

I'll begin by explaining what your website needs to accomplish in order to contribute to your overall consulting business. Then I'll talk about the characteristics of good websites, focusing on the consulting business.

After that, I'll help you with some of the nuts and bolts of setting up and maintaining a website. Although website design has a significant technical side, I'll try to keep the discussion as nontechnical as possible. While it's useful to understand the technology side of websites, it isn't absolutely necessary.

What Your Website Needs to Accomplish

Most businesses understand they should have a website but have only a superficial idea of what the website is there for. And many small businesses don't really have a good grasp of the details. To build a successful site requires that you have a clear sense of what you want to accomplish with your website. The following sections describe five goals of a good site.

> **Consulting Confidential**
>
> Most websites run by consultants are a complete waste of space. They accomplish almost nothing because they are poorly thought out, and the owners are not clear about what the website is for. There are hundreds of thousands of websites that have virtually no visitors and not much to offer the few visitors they attract.

Create a Positive Professional Image

Your website needs to enhance your image. Visitors (prospective and current clients) should come away with the impression that you are reputable, trustworthy, and professional. In that sense, a website is no different from any written material you produce. For example, you wouldn't produce a sales brochure full of spelling errors. You wouldn't include an adult-oriented ad in a print newsletter related to your consulting business. It's the same for websites.

Create a Sense That You Value the Welfare of Visitors and Clients

Do you remember the golden rule from Chapter 6, "Ethics: Doing the Right Things, Getting the Right Things Done"? Place the welfare of clients above your own. Your website is an opportunity to send this message to clients.

A website that is simply an online sales brochure is going to be perceived as an indicator that you are less interested in your clients' welfare and more interested in taking their money. A website that provides information and tools useful to visitors will be perceived much more positively.

Expose Your Services to the Largest Audience Possible

The more people who know about you and what you do, the better chance you have for increased business. One of the great things about having a website is that there is potential to reach a lot of prospective clients.

But it's not just a question of volume. Let's say you are a management or health industry consultant. Does it help you if your site is visited by children? No, of course not. You must reach decision makers, people in positions to hire you. So, while you want volume, or a high level of traffic to your site, you really need to have a specific kind of traffic.

Targeted traffic refers to visitors to your site who are in positions to benefit your business. You need the right kinds of visitors.

Working Words

Targeted traffic is traffic that comes from people who are in positions to help your business or purchase what you provide. In other words, you want traffic from decision makers or people in positions to advise decision makers.

Provide Easy and Fast Access to Information

The attention span of web surfers is notoriously short. Typically visitors will come to your site, take a quick look at the page they land on, and determine within 20 seconds whether they can find what they are looking for. If they don't see what they want, or an obvious way to get what they want, they go elsewhere. You've lost them.

So whatever information you provide must be front and center, and easy to find. Above all, visitors must be provided with what they want without hassle. And fast.

And the Bottom Line ... Business

Of course, the bottom line is that your website must bring in business. It so happens that the things I have described so far will help you bring in business, but let's not forget that business is the underlying goal of all the other issues. Your consulting website is not just a free public service. Thus, while we talk about image, speed, and provision of value to visitors, we are doing so with the assumption that accomplishing these goals creates more business.

Characteristics of Successful Consulting Websites

How do you create a website that will achieve these goals? That's a question and a half. In fact, that's a book in itself. Still, we can look at the most important characteristics of successful websites:

- ◆ Content (what's on your site)
- ◆ Design (what your site looks like)
- ◆ Search-engine friendly

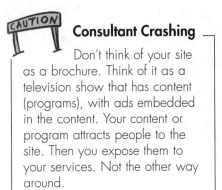

Consultant Crashing

Don't think of your site as a brochure. Think of it as a television show that has content (programs), with ads embedded in the content. Your content or program attracts people to the site. Then you expose them to your services. Not the other way around.

Content (What's on Your Site)

What's the most common mistake made by consultants with respect to their websites? Easy. It's using websites as sales brochures. Consultants who use their sites as brochures may end up with very attractive sites that have almost no visitors. Why? The site is of no value to its visitors.

So what should be on your site? The content should fall into one of two categories: free high-value content; and clear, fast-to-access, and highly visible content related to your services.

Free High-Value Content

What free high-value content can you provide? Obviously it depends on your specialization. It also depends on what will be valued and useful to the decision makers (targeted traffic) you wish to attract to your site. Let's work through an example related to my own website.

One of my targeted markets includes human resources professionals, because they are often in positions to hire me or make recommendations to hire me. My first task was to determine what kind of content they might value in a website. Information, right? Information about legal issues, downsizing, interviewing, and so on. Since I had a fair number of articles "on tap" that I had written, I put those relevant articles on my site. On the page where each articles appeared, I put information about services I provide that might be of interest to this group.

Between Colleagues

In order to provide value to visitors, you need to know your market and know the needs of the decision makers you want to attract. That's why having experience in your field is so important. When thinking about free high-value content, ask yourself, "What do my prospective clients look for and need?" Then fulfill that need.

I didn't stop there. I also knew that human resources professionals look for forms and other tools specific to the profession. So I provided access to this kind of material. Since I don't develop such things, I linked to material developed by others, in order to provide my visitors with quick access.

Getting the picture? If you are a fitness consultant, you'd want hints, tips, and articles related to physical fitness. Maybe some pictures of exercises. If you are a graphic design consultant, you might provide some free high-quality images or artwork that can be used in things like newsletters.

Fast Information About Your Services

Now let's turn to the second type of content—information about your services. You need to let people know how you can help them. Notice the phrasing. As with other forms of promotional material, you don't provide information only about your services. You slant that information to focus on how those services can benefit your prospective clients.

What kind of content fits here? Consider the following:

◆ Benefits to clients

◆ Specifics of services

◆ How to get more information

◆ Your experience and success delivering services

◆ Qualifications to deliver these services

Here's an important caution. While we talk about services, keep in mind that, as a consultant, you will provide services custom-designed to address your clients' problems. You need to explain this to visitors.

Should you post your fees on the website? The answer is no, for two reasons. First, your fees should depend on the nature of the final assignment as negotiated on a case-by-case basis. Thus, any figures you quote on a website may actually be misleading to prospective visitors. Second, at this point in the marketing process, you don't want to focus on price. You want to focus on how you can help and the value you provide.

Before I move on to website design, here's a key principle: The information about your services—the value you can provide—should be interwoven with the free high-value content on your site. Just like television programming and ads.

> **Consulting Confidential**
>
> It's amazing how many consultants provide good high-value content with absolutely no reference to their own services. I've found hundreds of excellent articles on the Internet with absolutely no links to the rest of the consultant's website and no indication of who wrote the darn things.

Website Design

It's easy to design a website. That is, if you don't care much about website success. Actually, it's easy to build an unsuccessful website, and it's not that difficult to build a serviceable website. However, it's exceedingly difficult to develop an excellent website that will build your consulting practice.

But it's worth it. You may need to enlist some expert help to get a decent website design. That's for two reasons. First, the actual design and the coding of your website require some specialized skills—skills most people don't have or don't want to learn. Second, web development is time-consuming.

Regardless of whether you decide to build the website yourself or hire someone on a consulting basis, or even a bit of both, you need to be actively involved. You can hire someone to do the coding of your site or to develop the look and appeal of your site, but you are the one responsible for the content decisions and for deciding how best to meet the needs of your website visitors. The more you know about web design, the better off you are.

There are three areas of concern in website design: the appearance of your site, the ease of navigation (moving around the site), and the degree to which your site is search-engine friendly (don't worry, I'll explain that in a moment).

Appearances Are Important

Appearances are important. If your website is cluttered, uses ugly color schemes, and is hard to read, people won't stay more than a few seconds. Here are some guidelines:

- Incorporate lots of "white space." There's a tendency to crowd as much as possible into the available space. White space (space that's not used for anything) actually makes the content on each page stand out to the viewer.

- Use shorter pages rather than longer ones. Each page should have a unique narrow focus or theme and should be compact. This helps the pages load more quickly, so the page appears faster to the visitor.

- Avoid using a lot of pictures or graphics. Use only graphics that are absolutely essential. This also speeds up page loads.

- Keep the color scheme simple. I recommend you use no more than three or four main colors. Never use black as a background.

- Use a readable font size. The size of the print on the screen should not be too small. Keep in mind that different users have different kinds of display monitors. Something that looks fine on one user's monitor may be much too small to read on another.

- Keep the variety of fonts to a minimum. There is rarely a reason to have more than two different fonts on a page. Specifically, use standard fonts like Arial, Times Roman, and Verdana. All computer systems can display these properly.

Between Colleagues

Should you design and code your website yourself? It depends. If you have the skills and programs to do so and if you enjoy the challenge and process, go for it. If not, you may want to get help.

These ideas about web design can get you started. However, there are many more design principles. You may want to read a good book on web design principles.

Navigation—How People Get Around

Navigation refers to how visitors get from one page of your website to another. Let's say your site has 20 or 30 different pages. Is it easy for a visitor to get from one to the other? Can a visitor see almost instantly what's on the other pages of your site? These questions reflect the two most important aspects of navigation design: the ease of use and the ability to see what's on the site.

Normally every page should have a navigation bar (also called a menu). The *navigation bar* is a small part of the page that shows the major sections of your website. It is usually placed at the top of each page or on the left-hand side. For example, it might contain the following links:

- ◆ About Us
- ◆ Contact Us
- ◆ How We Can Help You
- ◆ Free Resources

For a small site, your navigation bar may contain more specific links to other pages. On a large site, you'll be limited to the major categories of information on your site. That's because the navigation bar can hold only so much information. You can get around this limitation by having navigation bars or menus that expand when clicked. However, there are some drawbacks to this. For the moment, think simple.

The key things, again, are that the visitor be able to see what is available on your site and be able to access the content quickly. Therefore, your navigation bar should be prominent, use a different color than the other parts of your page, and be visible as soon as the visitor arrives. In other words, it should stand out.

Search-Engine Friendly? What the Heck Is That?

Is your website search-engine friendly? We've come to one of the most complex parts of website success. You'll see why in a moment. Think about this. Once your site is up and running, looks great and navigates well, how in heck do you let people know it's there? With millions of sites out there, people aren't likely to "stumble upon you."

Of course, you are going to promote your website in your print material and via discussion lists. But people must also be able to find you via the major search engines on the Internet.

Don't know what a *search engine* is? It's simply a website that indexes web pages. A person looking for something can go to one of these sites and type in a few words, and the search engine will return a list of sites that it thinks the visitor is looking for.

There are about 10 major search engines or directories. The main ones include Yahoo, Google, Altavista, Excite, and Open Directory Project. Some, like Yahoo, charge a fee for including your site in their systems; others include your site for free.

Now here's why search engine listings are so complex. Each one works differently and applies different rules. And these rules are changing as you read this (well almost) as search engine companies work to defeat those trying to beat the system.

Basically, you want your site to come up high on a search result list when your prospective customers type in search terms in order to try to find information you have.

Can I tell you how to do that? Yes and no. There are some basic rules that tend to be important over time and have to do with the design of your page.

Each page of your site should have a different and distinct title and file name that reflect what's on that page. The title and name should contain the words you think your visitors might use in search engines (those are called *keywords*). For example, a page on performance appraisal could have the following title "Performance Appraisal Free Help." The file name might be "performanceappraisal.html." Notice I've included the key terms "performance" and "appraisal" in both the title and the file name.

Each page of your site should include your targeted keywords within the text of the page and also in the first 200 words on your page, reading top to bottom and left to right. The keywords should appear several times in the text. The longer the page, the more times they should appear.

Each web page has what are called *meta-tags*. They include information like the title of your page and also a list of keywords to help some search engines know what your page is about. Each page should have a different title (as I said before) and keywords that apply specifically to that page. Do not use the same keywords for each page. Also note that meta-tags are becoming less important, and some search engines don't pay any attention to them.

Never try to trick search engines in order to get a higher ranking. Site owners attempt a number of methods to try to trick search engines into thinking their sites should come up more often. We needn't go into them, except to say that trying to trick the search engines is likely to result in none of your pages making it into the search engine.

In terms of search engines, you have one more option. Several companies like goto.com and findwhat.com use a system in which you pay for each click or person they send to your site. You bid on specific search terms related to your website. The higher the bid, the more likely people will visit. I'll leave you to explore this possibility by visiting these sites, but it's worth considering, since the investment can be small (but may not be).

Unfortunately this discussion is only able to scratch the surface. What I do suggest is that you read as much as possible about websites and web designs. Now let's move on to a few other web-related topics.

Some Other Website Issues

Most people contemplating the development of a website have common questions. I'll answer a few here.

Do I Need a Web Host?

First, what's a web host? The files for your site have to "live" somewhere. A *web host* is a company that provides a residence for your files and website. So, yes, you need a home for your site. However, you may already have one available. Some companies that connect people to the Internet allow their customers to build their websites on their computers. Check with the company that you use to connect to the Internet. However, keep in mind that "homes" provided by these companies may be limited in size and features.

There's another alternative. Some companies offer free website homes. In return, they usually place ads on your website. Don't use these kinds of websites for professional purposes. First, they don't do much for your professional image. In fact, if you use a free website, your visitors may see you as unprofessional. Second, you don't have complete control over your website, and the features are limited. Third, these companies are suffering financially, and there is no guarantee your website will be available if the company changes policies or goes bankrupt.

So what should you do? Pay for a reputable web hosting company. Talk to friends and colleagues to get recommendations. Don't base your decision solely on price. Let me repeat this: Don't go just by price. Lower-priced deals tend to be available from companies that provide somewhat less-reliable service. There's no point having a website if visitors can't get to it due to technical difficulties 10 percent of the time, or if the pages load too slowly. Visitors give up easily.

Consultant Crashing _____

Many neophyte web owners sign on with companies promising all kinds of things for a few dollars a month, only to discover that there's no help and no customer support, and that lots of times their sites aren't available. In fact, there's some research to suggest that web owners go through at least three Internet hosts before they find the one that works for them. Do some research, don't rely on sale hype, and pay a little more for quality.

Do I Need My Own Domain Name?

Don't know what a domain name is? It's simple. Each page or website has an address. That's the information a person types into the browser to get to a site. A *domain name* is the "house address" of your site, just like the address of your house. Your site may have different pages (like rooms), but each page is part of your domain.

There are different types of addresses. One, for example, looks like this: http://www. escape.ca/~rbacal. Escape happens to be the company that connects me to the Internet, and it hosts one of my early websites. Every person at Escape who runs a website, and has not purchased their own personal domain name, has an address that includes the www.escape.ca part.

The problem is that these kinds of names are long, and not very distinctive. The other option is to obtain your very own unique domain name. That would look like this: http://www.work911.com.

That's my newer and permanent address. It's shorter and easy to remember. There's another important reason why you must have your own domain name. Your domain name follows you around. If you have your site on Company A, and need or want to move it to Company B, people will still be able to find it under your original name. You own the name, and you decide where you want that name to point.

There are probably about a dozen other reasons to have your own domain name. It's fairly cheap, no more than $35 a year, and often less.

You need to register your name and pay for it. Companies that allow you to do this are called "registrars" or "domain registrars." Or, your web host may be able to help you with the process. Do it.

The Least You Need to Know

- Your website is much more than an electronic brochure. You need to provide reasons for people to visit it.

- It's easy to design a poor website but very difficult to design one that works well.

- Determine what your prospective consulting customers are looking for on the Internet, and do your best to provide them with free high-value information.

- At minimum it's worth paying for a good-quality web host and your own distinctive domain name.

Getting the Contract

In This Chapter

◆ What clients consider when hiring consultants

◆ Why listening is key to getting the contract

◆ How price affects contract decisions

◆ When you should respond to a request for proposal

Since consultants work on an individual contract basis, knowing how to get the contract is very important. Somehow you have to convince the client (once contact has been made) that you are the best choice for the job.

But what makes "the best choice" from the client's perspective? Of course, it varies from client to client, but we can make some generalizations about that and also about how clients decide whom to hire.

In this chapter I'll give you some insight into how clients make these decisions. I'll also talk about proposals and requests for proposals, and the concept of qualifying your customers so that you don't spend time trying to contract customers who aren't serious about hiring you.

How Clients Choose Consultants

At one point in my career, I was on the other side of the desk. My responsibilities included, on occasion, sitting in on consultant sales presentations and offering my advice on whether they should be hired. I'm going to share my experiences from that side of the desk and also draw upon information my clients have offered to explain how they hire consultants.

I'll try to translate the client's hiring process into specifics that you can use to increase your chances of being hired.

> **Between Colleagues**
>
> In order to demonstrate that you are in touch with the client's world, you need to know something about it. You may not, at least initially, know much about the company. If you are attempting to contract with a client within a context that is unfamiliar to you, ask some of your colleagues for tips and information—another reason to build a good network of colleagues.

Demonstrated Expertise and Experience

In hiring consultants, clients look for those who clearly have the expertise and experience to hit the ground running. Clients hire consultants because they don't have the time or skills to do something themselves. Remember that. If you can convince the client that you are ready and can carry out the project without increasing the client's workload, your chances of getting the contract increase.

When interacting with potential clients, focus on your relevant experience and qualifications. If you are asked about your experience with similar projects, choose one or two examples, and no more. Less is often more. By putting forth one or two examples, you make them more important. Don't overwhelm the client, and don't push your expertise farther than you need to. And don't flaunt qualifications or expertise.

Clients don't want to work with a prima donna, someone who appears to feel superior to the client. Pushing expertise too hard can be off-putting. Sure, toot your own horn but make sure there's a muffler on it.

Demonstrated Understanding of Client's Industry or Situation

One of the worst things a consultant can do is appear out of touch with the client's world and situation.

Clients want someone they don't have to train. They expect you to show your understanding of the world they live in.

Here's a somewhat trivial example, but it demonstrates what being "in touch" means. I was asked to put together a seminar for a group of social workers. Social workers tend to think in terms of clients rather than customers, and they resent the implication that the service they provide is like that in a fast-food restaurant.

As part of the meeting with the client, I made a point of saying we should entitle the seminar differently and remove the word "customer" from the title and the description. Why was this important? I demonstrated that I understood the world of social workers even before the client could bring it up. I got the contract.

The Good Listener Often Gets the Contract

While customers want to hear from you about how and why you can help them, they really want you to listen and understand them. Why is that important? Clients want you to deal with their unique situations. If you show an inability to listen and understand what they say about their situations, they will feel that you aren't able to meet their unique needs, even if the needs aren't really all that unique.

Another reason why listening is important is that a poor listener puts people off. You may be asked to present your proposal in a meeting, but if you are a poor listener and don't respond to questions in a "to the point" manner, just forget it. Listening is a vital part of making a presentation.

What does being a listener mean in practical terms? Even if you are asked to present an oral presentation about your services, try to engage those present in dialogue. Do what they ask you to do, but use questions to create that dialogue. For example, before starting a presentation, I will say, "Before I continue, I have one or two questions that would help me make this more worthwhile for you." Then I ask my questions. I integrate the respondents' answers into my presentation.

CAUTION Consultant Crashing

One consultant I know went into a proposal meeting and indicated he would use a particular survey instrument because he was familiar with it. The client didn't know much about that instrument and wanted an alternative. The consultant ended up arguing with the client, in effect not listening. The consultant had no good reason, besides his own preferences, to insist on that particular survey instrument. He didn't listen, seemed arrogant, and did not get the contract.

Remember that you have to *prove* that you are listening and paying attention. You must demonstrate understanding of what the client says to you. Refer to it. Prove you are listening.

Be very careful answering questions. A common error consultants make is assuming they understand the question when they do not. Being nervous sometimes makes it worse. Slow down and think. For example, if you aren't absolutely sure what the questioner is asking, request clarification.

Credibility and Integrity

Clients tend to choose consultants they perceive as credible, who have integrity and truly seem to have the client's welfare at heart. When pursuing a contract, you can't just announce your integrity. Trumpeting how righteous you are will likely have the opposite effect. Clients will wonder why you have to harp on it.

Establishing credibility and integrity has more to do with how you present yourself and what you say. Although slick sales pitches, an elegant appearance, and fancy brochures impress some clients, let me share with you my reaction to them. When I was in a position to do some hiring, consultants who attempted high-pressure selling immediately turned me off. Fancy clothes and fancy brochures caused me to ask the question, "If you are so good at your job, why do you need to rely on high-powered sales techniques?"

In some arenas, it may be important to have slick material and slick sales presentations. In others, not. There's no substitute for knowing your market.

Let's go back to the sales pitch. As a potential client, I looked for red flags, indications that the consultant was overselling me. As soon as I heard claims of outrageous success, or promises of results I found unrealistic, I immediately lost interest. I felt that the prospective consultant was treating me as if I were stupid, and I questioned the person's honesty.

Between Colleagues

Don't make unrealistic claims about your past successes or about benefits the client can expect. Don't try to con clients, and don't underestimate those that may appear naive.

I was particularly alert to such statements as, "We've helped our customers save $100 million over the last year." Uh-huh. That's supposed to impress me? If I could verify those numbers, it probably would. But stating something like this to a client, without any proof, is a red flag.

Gut Feeling Sense of "Fit"

Clients also want someone they feel comfortable with. It's hard to pinpoint exactly how clients decide whether the consultant qualifies in this respect, since what pleases one client may be off-putting to another.

Personally, I don't believe I can match the preferences of all clients in terms of personality and style, so I deal with this issue another way. Rather than try to make everyone comfortable with me and my style, I stay with my style. Why? Because I don't want to be too flexible about who I am. I'm honest, sometimes blunt, enthusiastic, and so on. Those characteristics tend to be helpful in gaining contracts but do occasionally put people off. That's fine.

I'd rather be genuine and present myself as I really am and let the chips fall where they may. If a client doesn't like my style and personality, I'd rather not work with that person. Dislike is a poor foundation on which to build a consulting relationship.

You can't take this attitude too far, of course. If you are arrogant, rude, and insulting, you're going to have to change those things.

Strike a balance. Don't go out of your way to please everyone at a proposal meeting, but don't ignore their comfort levels either. Show them who you are and let them decide.

Where Does Price Fit?

How much does price enter into whether or not you get the contract? It's certainly a factor, but it may be less of one than you think. I'll assume that your price structure is appropriate for your experience and expertise—not too high and not too low.

If your fees are too high compared with what the client is used to paying for similar services, that's a significant problem unless you have some qualifications that impress the customer. For example, if you have a book out on a relevant subject, that may allow you to justify a higher fee.

Oddly enough, if your price is much lower than what is typical in your market, that fact can work against you. When clients see exceedingly low prices and do not understand why, they attribute them to your inability to charge more. This worries them. If you provide a cogent reason for a low price, then it isn't as much of a problem.

In any event, clients want to feel confident they are getting good value, no matter what they are paying. If they do not believe they will get reasonable value, no matter whether you charge $1 or $1,000, you aren't going to get the contract.

Think of price in this way: In one sense, you are worth what people are willing to pay, but your job is to convey the message that you are worth whatever you charge.

> ### Consulting Confidential
>
> I tend to charge fees that are toward the high end of where I live but at the low end in larger major cities. I explain to clients in major centers that I live in an area with a very low cost of living. Rather than looking inept, I am "a good deal."

"Qualifying a Client" to Save Work

Qualifying a client refers to the process by which you determine whether you should spend time negotiating with a client or whether it's likely the client is not going to hire you anyway. Strictly speaking, qualifying won't help you get contracts, but it will prevent you from wasting time in going after contracts you aren't going to get.

I hate to tell you this but there are clients who are quite willing to string you along in negotiations, and request proposals and presentations when there's no chance you will be hired. Sometimes this is inadvertent, and sometimes it is done on purpose.

Why? Some clients (the ones you don't want to work for anyway) actually fish for free advice. They may, for example, request detailed proposals and never hire anyone, using the information contained in the proposals they've received to go ahead on their own.

Sometimes you will come across clients who seem stuck in suspended animation. Your direct contact says, "It's a cinch; we're just waiting for the head honcho to sign off." But the head honcho never does or is always "away." Or asks you to do yet another proposal presentation.

Here are some tips on this subject.

First, if you submit proposals, verbal or written, provide a decent overview, but not every specific detail. Highlight the fact that you are the best qualified to do the particular job, and don't give away everything.

Second, when negotiating, ask for and negotiate a firm timeline for a decision. Give sufficient time, but make it clear that if you do not have confirmation by that date you will withdraw. Make reasonable accommodations regarding additional requests you might receive from a client, but protect your own interests that might be affected by inordinate delays.

Third, when negotiating, try to make sure that the key decision maker is present and involved. For example, if your project needs approval of the CEO, that person should be at least marginally involved in the discussions. That's because (a) you want, and might need, CEO involvement throughout the consulting project; and (b) the involvement of the CEO is a good indication that the client is serious about hiring you. If the key decision maker is unable or unwilling to be involved, that's a warning sign.

Between Colleagues

Not only does the client interview you, but you interview the client—and make a judgment about whether you want to work with the client.

Finally, be prepared to step back from any project that's slow getting off the ground or that presents other "scents of problems." If there are delays in getting the contract, what are the chances you will get the support and resources you need to complete the project? Not good.

It's hard to back away, but, trust me, there are some clients you don't want to work for. I recall a project in which the negotiations actually continued for over a year and a half. Initially, I was asked to do a proposal, and after a significant wait I was told the client had hired someone else. About six months after that, the client called me and said the consultant they hired "didn't work out" and they now wanted me to undertake the project. That was fine, but I was alert to any signs that the client could impact the project.

Then the client asked for *another* proposal and wanted to start from scratch. After negotiating, we compromised and I sent them a short letter with just the basics. Then the client wanted something else, and then something else, and the process once again became drawn out. Finally, when the client requested a particular form of insurance document, I just backed away, told them I wasn't prepared to jump through any more hoops (I was more polite than that), and let it drop.

Who knows what would have happened if I had agreed to undertake the project. I passed on a $10,000 fee, but I have a feeling that the grief of continuing and the likely odds of failure would have made the project an ill-advised one.

The Request for Proposal Process

A *request for proposal*, or *RFP*, is a document intended to help the offering company hire the best consultant to provide services or solve an organizational problem. While RFPs are most commonly used by governments to hire consultants, other companies use this process also, particularly for large projects.

RFPs are usually sent out to consultants who are already in a database of potential vendors. Many governments, for example, will send you a standard form to complete so that you will be notified when an RFP is available for your area of expertise. Some governments will publish RFPs in publications they produce.

> **Consulting Confidential**
>
> Some consultants believe that organizations relying on requests for proposals tend to award contracts not on the basis of expertise in doing the job, but on expertise in writing proposals. There is some merit to this idea, but the truth lies in the middle. Badly written proposals guarantee you will be left in the cold. Well-written proposals don't guarantee you will get the contract.

What Does the RFP Usually Include?

An RFP typically contains information about the company making the request, usually very basic information. In addition, you'll find contact information if you require clarification.

The guts of an RFP contain two parts: details of how you must respond (deadline, format) and details about the services and/or problem the issuer is interested in. An upper fee limit or budget may also be set.

Why Do Clients Use RFPs?

To draft a response to an RFP, you need to have some sense about why your potential client is going this route. Since many RFPs come from government, let's start there.

Governments are required to have some controls over how contracts are awarded. There is an expectation that governments will choose the best person to provide the service at the lowest possible cost. The process developed to ensure fairness in awarding contracts is the RFP. This is sometimes called a tender. It's meant to be a competitive process so that decisions will be made on the content of your proposal, and not on whom you know.

Private companies who have adopted this competitive approach do so for similar reasons, to ensure that contracts will be awarded fairly and to the best applicant.

What do clients look for in the RFP? Obviously it's difficult to say, since each organization may do things a bit differently. Generally, they want to be convinced that you can do the job as it is outlined. Here are some factors they may consider:

Consultant Crashing

Be alert to signs that an RFP isn't "serious." Sadly, some organizations send out RFPs when they have no intention of hiring anybody or when they have already set up the competition so that a predetermined vendor wins. A red flag to look for? You receive the RFP so late that it's almost impossible to submit by the deadline.

- Experience and qualifications
- Realistic and practical implementation plan
- Proper staffing in place
- Anticipation of potential problems
- Cost

Some RFPs will spell out how your proposal will be evaluated, so make sure you address each and every area mentioned in the RFP. Typically before an RFP is released, the organization looking for help will create some form of point system that allocates a specific number of points to each criterion. If you don't address an important area, you can't receive the points. It's a little like missing an entire essay question on an exam.

Should You Respond to RFPs?

You'll have to decide. Let's consider both sides. If you want to work in the government sector and go after contracts of significant size, you may have no choice but to get into the proposal game. It's a huge market, one you may not want to ignore.

On the flip side, spending the time to write proposals is costly, particularly if you have to research the company and the services they might be interested in. Consider also that a detailed proposal may provide the client with a free "blueprint for success." While it would be unethical for them to use your proposal without hiring you, it does happen.

I'll share my own personal take on this process, since my primary clients are in government. I don't generally do detailed proposals or respond to RFPs. However, I make exceptions when …

♦ My area of expertise fits exactly with the expertise outlined in the proposal. In other words, I don't have to do extra research.

♦ The request for proposal gives me enough information to write a proposal that is complete. If I can't figure out what they want or how best to deliver what they want (for example, it's vague), into the trash can it goes.

♦ I estimate there is a high probability of success.

♦ The project is financially lucrative. I don't do detailed proposals for small projects.

♦ I am contacted by phone or in person by someone who will be reviewing the proposal. This tells me there is specific interest in my services, and I am more likely to respond.

Between Colleagues

When deciding whether to respond to an RFP, evaluate whether you are likely to get the contract, the time it will take to prepare the proposal, and the fit between client needs and your expertise.

I apply these criteria almost exclusively for RFPs. I will write basic one- or two-page proposals for clients who need something in writing, and with whom I've been negotiating with in person or on the phone. That's worth my time because I've "qualified" them and believe they will hire me if the basic paperwork is done.

These guidelines have proved to be fairly good ones that help me maximize my time. Perhaps they will work for you, too.

Between Colleagues

Follow up forever. Try to touch base with previous clients at least once every three months. You can make it a social telephone call or an effort to see how things are going for the client.

The Value of Referrals and References

Referrals and references play important roles in determining whether you get a contract or not. First, if someone is referred to you by a satisfied customer, you have a significant leg up over consultants who were not referred in this way.

Second, it's common for prospective clients to ask for references. They want information about how well similar projects went.

What's the most valuable thing you can do to maximize your references and referrals? Follow up. When you complete a project, keep in touch with your client. Doing so provides three advantages. First, it keeps you in the spotlight. You'll be the first to come to mind if associates of the client are looking for similar services. Second, it makes it easier to request references if you've maintained a relationship with your previous clients. Third, maintaining contact is helpful in getting additional projects from that client.

The Least You Need to Know

- ◆ Remember that even when you are asked to make a presentation, you must listen carefully to everything your client group says.
- ◆ By demonstrating an understanding of the client and his or her business and situation, you are on your way to getting hired.
- ◆ Reply to requests for proposals that seem to offer a high probability there will be a good fit. Be selective.
- ◆ Use follow-up techniques after projects are finished in order to maximize repeat business and referred business.

20

Let's Talk About Money

In This Chapter

- ◆ The different ways you can charge for your services
- ◆ Firm pricing versus flexible pricing
- ◆ Factors to consider in setting your fees
- ◆ Setting milestones for interim payments

Whether you are motivated by money or whether you consult because of the satisfactions of the job, you must pay attention to the financial side of your business.

The most common question that new consultants ask is, "What should I charge?" That's a hard question to answer, since there are no standard rates. And in fact, there is no "best" number. Nevertheless, you need to set fees and decide how to charge clients.

In this chapter you'll learn how to set fair and competitive fees and, just as important, how to collect them. I'll talk about the factors you need to consider in your fee decisions. Then it's up to you to make your own decisions.

Your Fee-Structure Options

Before I talk about how much you should charge, you need to know what your fee options are. You can charge by the hour, per project, or on a contingency basis. Let's look at each option.

Hourly Billing—Time Is Money

In the consulting world, the most common means of calculating fees is based on time used on behalf of the client. It works this way. You set an hourly rate and then record the time you spend on the project. You then bill the client for that time (called billable hours). If you are familiar with how many lawyers work, you'll recognize this as a common way of charging for legal services.

As with the other fee options, some consultants are in favor of using billable hours and others are not. Those in favor explain that they should be compensated for their time, since time is a consultant's most valuable and scarce resource. That's a reasonable justification for using a fee structure based on billable hours.

Consultant Crashing

One problem with hourly billing is that it penalizes the client if you are slow and inefficient, and penalizes you if you are fast and efficient. It also provides incentive for the consultant to work slowly.

Between Colleagues

If you decide on an hourly fee structure, you need to track the time you spend and then bill accordingly. You can do this manually, but it's best to find an accounting package that includes the capability to track billable hours.

The other position is that clients shouldn't be paying you for your time, but for the results and activities you supply to them. I think that's a justification for using a different fee structure.

I'll be honest: I don't use hourly billing. Here's why.

From an ethical standpoint, I feel that a client should know up-front what he or she will be paying for a project. Not only is that an ethical consideration, but it's a marketing consideration, since clients like to know how much they will be paying.

I don't like the idea of being penalized for being efficient, or the client being penalized for my inefficiency. It just doesn't work for me.

Finally, when you charge by the hour, you absolutely need to be sure that you and the client agree on what you will charge for. If you have to do research, will the client pay for that? Writing time? Meetings? What about driving time to and from meetings?

You also need to keep detailed logs of the time you spend on the project. The whole thing gets too complicated to suit me.

Tips for Using Billable Hours

If you decide on a billable-hours fee structure, are there things you can do to make the process work as smoothly and fairly as possible? Yes.

During the contracting stage of any project, you should discuss what you will charge for. Lay it all out for the client, so there will be less chance of dispute when the client is billed. Also, provide the client with an estimate of the number of hours you anticipate will be involved in the project. Break it down into categories, for example, meetings, report writing, and so on. Do the estimate in writing.

When you provide that estimate (which you should do in writing), consider placing an upper limit on billable hours. It need not be a firm cap and can be a flexible one. For example, you may say something like this: "Client agrees to pay $100 per hour for 100 hours. In the event that project requires more than 100 hours, client must approve additional time."

During the project, supply the client with a regular report detailing the billable hours already completed. The idea here is there should be no surprises. The more surprises for the client, the more likely you will have collection problems later on. You don't want fee disputes.

 Consultant Crashing

If you surprise a client with unexpected fees after the fact, you are more likely to have disputes about the bill. When you have fee disputes, you run the risk of late payment or refusal to pay. A simple principle for billing: Don't surprise the client.

Fee per Project: No-Surprise Billing

The most common alternative to the billable-hours fee structure is to charge per project. Charging per project involves setting a flat fee to cover the entire project regardless of the number of hours you put in.

Fee per project allows the client to know exactly what your services will cost. That's a plus, and many customers prefer the comfort of predictability.

Is it to your benefit? It depends. If you use a per-project fee structure, you need a firm idea of what the project will entail and you must be able to estimate a fee that is fair for both parties. That isn't always easy. Of course, once you set a project fee, you will also know exactly what you will be receiving upon project completion.

The biggest downside to project-based fees is when the consulting project expands beyond the initial boundaries. This can happen in two ways. First, you may discover some factors that make the project more complicated or time-consuming. For example, in the middle of a project, you realize the project will require more time than you thought initially. That leaves you with choosing to take the lesser fee or renegotiating.

The second problem occurs when you work with a client who continues to stretch the boundaries and project requirements. Let's look at a trivial example first. Your initial agreement specifies you will supply three copies of your final report to the client and present your findings to the board of directors. Toward the conclusion of the project, your client decides that 20 copies are required and asks you to present your findings not only to the board of directors but to five other groups.

If you charged by the hour, it would be easy to accommodate that, because you'd just add those hours to the bill. But on a fee-for-project basis, you're put in an awkward position. Do you refuse, since it wasn't part of the original agreement? Do you do it and take the loss? Or do you try to negotiate extra payment for these extra activities? Obviously each of these options has a downside. You're put in the position of having to trade off good customer relations for money.

Contingency-Based Fees: Getting Paid for Results

Doesn't it make sense to receive monetary benefit to the extent that your client benefits from your consulting services? Let's say you are a marketing consultant and you achieve some huge success, doubling the client's sales and revenue. If you charge billable hours, you get paid the same amount regardless of the client's increase in business. If you charge on a per-project basis, same thing.

What if you received a fee based on that increased business, let's say 15 percent of the increased revenue? This scenario, properly constructed, can bring you far more money. Of course, if you get paid only when your services pay off for the client, you may end up working for nothing.

There's a certain fairness to this arrangement. If you bring good results, you get paid commensurate with the value of your services to the client. If you don't, you get nothing.

Contingency-based fee structures are probably the least-popular among most consultants. From the consultant's view, one of the biggest problems is that the income is unpredictable, and the potential for getting paid nothing, or almost nothing, is daunting.

Contingency-based fees have some other very significant drawbacks. The first one is that it's not always easy to measure the benefits your client receives in an objective, fair, and accurate way. For example, as a training consultant how do my client and I measure the positive benefits the customer receives from my training seminars? It could be measured, but it would be difficult and challenging to negotiate measurable criteria that would work for the client.

> **Consulting Confidential**
>
> While a "pure" contingency-based fee structure may involve too many challenges and risks for you to use, it's possible to use a system whereby you get paid a base fee and then receive a bonus based on results.

A second major drawback is that the consultant is subject to factors that are not under his or her control. Let's return to the marketing example. Say that you create the best marketing plan on the planet. It is the client's responsibility to follow that plan to achieve maximum benefits. But the customer may not do so. Perhaps the company reduced its marketing budget. Or the client cut some corners, and the increased revenue is minimal. Heck, you did your job. Now you suffer as a result of factors that are beyond your control.

Between Colleagues

Criteria you use to calculate a contingency fee or bonus should be objective, measurable, and specific.

There's a third drawback here. Incorporating evaluation and measurement into a consulting project can be costly. Here's an example. Let's say you're retained to work with staff to improve customer service. You and the client agree that the success of the project will be measured using a customer survey instrument. If the ratings go up, you get paid big bucks. Consider this, though. What is the cost of measuring the improvement? In this case it could be considerable. Clients don't like that extra cost.

Finally, a fourth drawback. Contingency-based fees put the client and consultant in a somewhat adversarial situation. It is to the client's benefit to understate the benefits received, and it's to the consultant's benefit to overstate them. That's not the stuff of good, harmonious relationships.

When is a contingency fee a good idea then?

A contingency fee can work well when there are clear, easily measurable criteria for success. For example, a health consultant might charge for each pound lost. That's easy to agree upon and easy to measure.

Along with that, though, contingency fees work best when the consultant has more control over the outcomes. As you read the previous paragraph, you might have noticed the risk here. What if the client cheats and eats a dozen chocolate bars?

Also, contingency-based fees work best when the project is one in which the consultant is involved in the implementation of advice. To carry through with the weight loss example, it makes more sense to charge a contingency fee when the consultant is on the scene, cooking meals and supervising the customer to ensure that the advice is being followed. But who wants to live with the client?

Generally speaking, contingency fees carry considerable risk but have a very high upside. I don't recommend they be used on their own, but they can be part of a bonus structure. In the next section I'll talk about that and about combining fee structure methods.

Mixing and Matching

There is no reason why you can't combine these three fee structures. You could, for example, charge a basic project fee based on a set number of hours but charge on an hourly rate if that number of hours is exceeded.

Or you could use a contingency arrangement in combination with an hourly or project fee. Here's how it works.

You would charge a lower rate for a project, with the condition that if certain criteria are met (such as higher sales, increased customer satisfaction, fewer complaints), you would receive a bonus directly related to the magnitude of the improvement. The bonus is simply a reward for meeting certain agreed-upon objectives.

Thus, if the client benefits, you get paid a lot more. If the criteria aren't met, you get paid less than you would ordinarily get paid on a project basis. High upside. Limited downside.

Firm or Flexible Pricing?

Here's the situation. An organization contacts you because it's interested in using your consulting services. The project is right up your alley, but there's a problem. Your prospective client indicates they have severe budget restrictions and can pay you only about two thirds of your normal fee.

What do you do? Do you offer flexibility in pricing and accept the contract, or do you stick to a firm fee structure?

> **Consulting Confidential**
>
> A small number of consultants believe that it's okay to raise their price when a sucker comes along who seems clueless about going rates and has more money than brains. That's unethical.

Before talking about the practical issues of your decision, let's consider the ethical side. It's ethically questionable to be so flexible that some clients are paying much more than other clients for similar or identical work.

There's also a practical implication. What happens when your high-paying client discovers you delivered the same service to someone else and charged half the price? You can imagine the client being very upset, just as you would be if you and a neighbor bought identical cars and you paid $10,000 more.

The Pluses, the Minuses

Clearly, being willing to work within a client's budget is a marketing advantage. Being flexible indicates to the client that you are willing to be a partner in the process (or that you are desperate!). Quite simply, flexible pricing increases the size of your potential market. Some organizations, particularly not-for-profits or charities may have limited funding. By being flexible you broaden your potential market.

Apart from the fact that you'd be making less money than you would on a similar project, are there minuses to flexible pricing? There is the potential that clients will perceive you as desperate for the business. The way around that is to give a plausible reason why you can reduce your price for that client. On occasion, I will offer a lower price if the client is willing to carry some of the printing costs of the project. Or I indicate that my cost of living is lower than for consultants living in other areas, allowing me to offer a lower price. Once or twice, I've indicated that the lower price is a way of giving back to the community.

Apart from these significant drawbacks, I see no reason why you can't be flexible.

> **CAUTION**
>
> **Consultant Crashing**
>
> Unlike retailers, consultants don't have sales events. Doing so makes you look like you are selling a thing, and not yourself. Not a good idea.

So, What Factors Should You Consider Before Deciding?

Here are a few things to consider before lowering your price:

◆ Workload. If you are almost fully booked at a higher rate, it doesn't make sense to charge less.

◆ Public relations value. Consider whether doing something for a particular client may drive new business to your door.

◆ Size of contract. If the contract is large, it's worth being flexible, a little like a volume discount.

◆ Amount in question. If a client has a $10,000 budget for a project that normally costs $20,000, that's a huge differential. Such a big gap is different from one of only a few hundred dollars.

◆ Maybe you are desperate for the business (enough said).

> **Consulting Confidential**
>
> Should you do freebies? For example, someone wants you to speak to the chamber of commerce meeting but can't pay you. Do it if you feel it is a good marketing opportunity and as a way to contribute back to your professional community, provided it doesn't eat up too much time.

Determining Your Fees

How do you know what to charge? What do you consider when setting your fees? These are common questions with no right or wrong answer. There are at least four ways of figuring out what you should charge. Let's look at a few, remembering that setting fees isn't a scientific process.

Market Pricing

In a sense your value is what people are willing to pay for your services. Some consultants believe that you should charge whatever clients will pay, and they continue to stretch their fees to discover the "right fee."

For example, some consultants regarded as gurus in their fields will charge as much as $50,000 for a one-hour speaking engagement. Most of us normal folks realize that nobody on the planet can provide that much "value" to a client. But, people pay that. It's free market economy at its best or worst, similar to the sporting and entertainment industries.

How do consultants justify such fees? By concluding that as long as people will pay, that's what they are worth.

Most of us are never going to be able to charge huge amounts. However, if you take the position that you are worth whatever you can get people to pay, be sure to combine it with the next consideration.

Competitive Pricing

Another point of view is that you should price your services by taking into account what the competitors are charging. This is a carryover from the retail sector, where retailers are constantly examining their pricing relative to competitors'.

It makes sense to at least look at the competition. If you want to charge $500 per hour, and the going rate (what your competitors charge) is $100 an hour, where does that leave you? Either rich or broke. Let me explain. If your fees are way higher than your competition, you can make that work if you offer something spectacularly better than the competition. If you don't, your clients will go elsewhere. So if you are "special" in some way, you just might pull off the higher prices.

> **Between Colleagues**
>
> Be careful not to price your services too far below the competition. There is a belief that you get what you pay for, and you don't want to be seen as "that bargain-priced consultant."

If you believe in letting the market set your price, I suggest that you still examine where your competitors are.

Income-Needed Calculations

You can approach the fee-setting problem from another direction. How much money do you need? Once you figure out how much you need (or want to make), you can calculate an hourly rate.

Let's say you decide that you need to take home $50,000 a year gross (that's before taxes and expenses). You estimate the number of billable hours you expect, being as realistic as possible, total them up for a year, and then divide the $50,000 by the number of anticipated billable hours.

So let's say you estimate you can bill out 20 hours a week. Multiply that by 50 weeks (assuming you take some holidays). Your answer (1,000) is an estimate of your total billable hours for a year. Divide your target income by that number, and you get your hourly rate, which in this case is $50.

The calculations can be much more complicated. You can take into account tax rates, business costs, health costs, and a wide range of other things.

I've seen this method suggested for small business owners and consultants, but, frankly, I'm just not a fan. Even if I billed on the basis of hours worked, how am I supposed to know what the next year will bring? I can't, and I've been doing this for a while. Someone starting up a consulting business is going to have no idea. Any number is going to be a pure guess.

The other problem with using income-needed calculation as your only method of fee pricing is that it doesn't take into account market forces or competitors' prices. If this method is the only one you consider, you could very well be pricing yourself way too high or way too low in your particular market.

Consultant Crashing

Both income-needed and former-salary methods should never be used in isolation from market and competitive methods. If you focus only on your needs, you are likely to be completely out of step with your customers.

Former Salary Plus Benefits Calculations

A variation on the "income-needed" method is to start with the salary you used to make in your full-time job. You'd use that (or a figure above that) as your fiscal target. So let's say you made $60,000 a year. To that figure, you'd add the value of any benefits you received from your employer such as health care, pension, and so on. You'd use the same calculation method as in the previous example.

This method suffers from the same challenges as the previous one. You still have to estimate your billable hours.

The Bottom Line on Setting Fees

Any method, used on its own, is prone to problems. My recommendation is that you use a combination of methods. I think you need to consider your market and what it will bear. You need to consider what your competitors are charging for similar services, at least until you hit guru status. And I think you have to be mindful of the money you actually need. Consider all of these factors.

Other Things to Consider

I'll close this chapter by touching on some topics that don't quite fit anywhere else but are important nonetheless. I'll look at how location affects fees, and some options for structuring when you get paid.

Location, Location, Location

Believe it or not, geography plays a critical role in determining the reasonableness of your fee. For example, companies in large centers are used to paying much more for services than those in very small centers. Fees common in New York might be completely ridiculous if you applied them to clients in Madison, Wisconsin. And what you might charge in Madison might be way too low for a client in New York.

> **Consulting Confidential**
>
> When dealing with clients from different geographic areas, I often ask them what they are used to paying for similar services in their region. I use that number as one factor in quoting a fee. If it's too low, I quote my usual fee and we negotiate. If it's too high, I do the same thing.

If your practice extends beyond your geographic area (and I recommend you plan to extend your reach), you'll hit this dilemma. Your options? Use very flexible pricing, and charge more for services in more expensive markets; or price your services somewhere in the middle, and charge the same (or close to the same) fees regardless of location.

I recommend the latter. The differences in markets can be huge. Can you really live with charging your New York client three times as much as a local client? I don't think that's a good plan.

When and How to Get Paid

There are several ways to arrange payment. You can get paid in full at the conclusion of a project. You can ask for a deposit up-front and the remainder on completion. Or you can receive partial payment during the project as specific *milestones*, or preset points, are reached.

Full payment at project's end works when the project is relatively short-term and the amount of the contract is low to moderate. The reasons are simple. You need to live. You can't afford to wait six months to be paid if it's a relatively extended project. For shorter projects, let's say ones that are a week or two long, it's not a problem to wait.

Working Words

Milestones are "success points," or points in the project where significant interim goals have been met.

You can request a deposit (or partial advance payment) upon contract signing. That advance fee can include anticipated immediate expenses. When is a deposit a good idea?

Here are some situations in which a deposit (partial advance) is in order:

◆ The project requires you to put forth cash for expenses such as hotel, transportation.

◆ The project requires some "run-up" time before it begins in earnest *and* you are required to work on the project during that run-up time (for example, preparing a plan). A deposit protects you if the client backs out.

◆ You want a measure of financial commitment from the client in advance.

Finally we come to payments during the project. This fits when the project covers a long period of time, and ensures reasonable cash flow.

Normally, interim payments are tied to the achievement of specific milestones. Milestones are points in the project where significant interim goals have been met.

For example, you might contract to be paid at the following points in a long-term project:

◆ Upon completion of data gathering

◆ Upon submission and presentation of report

◆ Upon completion or implementation

Got it? Milestones are usually defined in negotiation with the client, and they need to make sense within the context of the project. They are often tied to the delivery of a particular observable service or ending point for one phase of the project.

To sum up, the payment schedule is going to depend on the nature and length of the project, and somewhat on the amount of the contract. You can mix and match these payment schedules as makes sense.

The Least You Need to Know

◆ All billing methods—hourly, project, or contingency—have different advantages and disadvantages. Make your decision based on what works best in your field, taking into account what customers are used to.

◆ Billing methods can be combined and used together.

◆ Take into account your market, your competition, and your own financial needs in determining your fees.

◆ Flexible pricing can increase the pool of potential customers, but being too flexible gives the appearance of being desperate.

Chapter 21

To Grow or Not to Grow

In This Chapter

- ◆ Why you need to consider whether to grow or not
- ◆ When you should and should not consider expansion
- ◆ How to manage the growth process
- ◆ What the alternatives are to expanding the company

If you think the business start-up process is stressful and challenging, wait until you get to the "grow or don't grow" stage.

Imagine this: In the first year, your consulting business not only pays your bills but exceeds all expectations. You're cookin', and clients are jumping onboard, clamoring for your assistance. Better yet, they come with fully stocked bank accounts and checkbooks. But there's an increasing problem. You can work only so many hours in the day. Not only do you have to meet and work with your clients, but you have all the other paperwork and responsibilities that come with running a business.

Now what? You're maxed out. Do you start turning away clients? You could try to decrease customer demand by increasing your fees. However, many consultants look to expansion as a solution to the problem.

Here's a sobering thought. Statistics indicate that small-business failures occur as a result of several factors. The most common reason is undercapitalization (not enough money to get through the start-up stage). In this case (you lucky dog), that's not your problem. Another reason small businesses collapse is failure to manage the growth of the company. You'll see why in a minute.

In this chapter I'll explain when you should consider growth. I'll also explain a few growth options and try to help you navigate around the land mines.

> ### Consulting Confidential
>
> Often the skills that bring you early success as a one-person business are not sufficient to expand your business and deal with a whole new set of tasks and challenges. At start-up, for example, audacity, creativity, and risk taking are important. If you grow your company by adding employees, all of a sudden those characteristics may hinder you. Success does bring more challenges. When you have more work than you can do, you can't ignore that. You need to deal with growth in a proactive way and think it through carefully.

The Growth Dilemma

When you reach the point where you confront the growth dilemma, here's what you'll face: You're darned if you do, and darned if you don't. Or, putting it another way, if you don't respond to customer demand, you are severely limiting your business's future. If you do expand your business, you face a whole new set of problems and challenges.

The Perils of Not Growing

Here's a common scenario: You are overworked, you can't take on more clients, you aren't seeing your family much, and you're headed for burnout. So what's the solution?

You can decide to stay exactly the same size and continue as you have, stretching yourself to the maximum. Unfortunately, the question you have to ask yourself is, "How long can I do this?" Is it realistic to live like that? Is it something you *want?* Maintaining the status quo may not be a good option.

Let's also think about your success in terms of your clients. As you hit the overworked mark, the service you provide your clients is likely to degrade. Fatigue, or just plain "rushing through," may mean you are doing a less thorough job. At best you may be hard to contact, and your response time to customer requests may become inordinately long. At worst, you may start providing poor advice and not giving enough attention to your projects.

Well, what about refusing contracts and managing the problem that way. You can do that. It's a psychologically difficult thing to do—to leave money on the table—but you can do it. In fact, if you choose not to grow, then that's one of the ways to solve the problem. It's also the ethical thing to do.

Is there a downside to this solution? Yes. If you refuse too many clients, word may get around that you aren't available. If that happens, you may see a drop in business contacts—an outcome that will affect your future business.

The Perils of Growth

So, what's the flip side? Before looking at the dangers inherent in growth, let's consider the ways you can grow. You can take in a partner, or you can hire employees to help. There are some more alternatives to growth, too, and I'll come back to them shortly.

As soon as you work with a partner or hire a single employee, you are now playing in a more complex world with more complex rules and requirements. Think about it. Here are a few of the many things you may need to address (this may vary from country to country):

- Payroll system (paying employees and having an accounting system to track salary and benefits)
- Worker's compensation arrangements
- Unemployment insurance
- Income tax remittances for employees
- Compliance with other government regulations (for example, equal opportunity, hiring, dismissal rules)
- Possible need to change business/corporate structure

In addition to this, your skills have to grow. While you may be able to manage yourself, it's a different task to manage another person: to teach, to supervise, to direct. Since lone-wolf consultants are used to being the only one in the equation, it's probable that business expansion will require the acquisition of new skills long before an employee is hired.

Expanding via partnership carries other concerns. There's basic legal paperwork, but, above all, a significant amount of time needs to be spent

Between Colleagues

Preparation involved in hiring an employee should occur way before the employee is hired. You can't afford mistakes during this growth process, since growth requires money and taking on additional responsibilities.

ensuring that the relationship between partners is strong and workable. For example, the partnership must be managed so partners share the same business goals and vision, so they can work together to achieve the same, not different, goals.

What about those details that people ignore in the partnering process? Who does what? What happens if one partner isn't pulling his or her weight? How much of the profit gets put back in the business? There are probably dozens more. These details need to be decided to make a partnership work. It takes time, and a partnership means a definite reduction of freedom.

The final peril? Money. There are two money crunch times for small businesses, two periods of danger: one at start-up and another at growth. When you hire (or take a partner), you are banking on the fact that there will be sufficient revenue to pay the employee (or split the profits with a partner). Now, if you've been making $200,000 dollars a year for the last five years and your business is stable and continuing to grow, that's a good bet. If you have had one huge year and a few lesser years, what happens if you are wrong?

> **Consulting Confidential**
>
> What about raising your fees to cut down business? Believe it or not, if you have done your job well, raising your fees probably won't reduce requests from potential customers. In many consulting areas, price is not a main determinant of being hired. You may not have less business … just more money. Of course, if you haven't done your job well, you will lose business.

Don't forget that the cost of hiring an employee goes beyond salary. It includes capital investment and other relatively long-term commitments like arranging a place for the person to work and purchasing the equipment the person needs to carry out the job. If, for example, you couple hiring an employee with also establishing a "real office," you'll have significant ongoing office expenses. What if the new arrangement doesn't work out?

The Joys of Growth

Expanding a business can be extremely gratifying, both personally and economically.

If hiring an employee means you no longer have to do what I call "low-value work" and you can focus on what you really love to do (consulting), that's a good thing. It may contribute to enhanced enjoyment, and it may free you to earn more money by using your time more effectively.

I'm not saying it *will* happen that way, only that it might happen that way. You have to factor in the time needed to hire, train, and manage; and you have to hire just the right person.

You may find that having an employee or partner increases your creativity, since you will have someone you can bounce ideas off of. This can keep you sharp.

Having someone else involved in the business may make up for any skill deficiencies you have. For example, sales and marketing may not be your thing. Having someone who enjoys it and is good can take a tremendous load off your shoulders.

Here's a question to ask yourself. Are you the kind of person who will get great satisfaction from heading a company with employees or from having a partner? Perhaps you might like the feeling of being a "player," something that comes from being bigger. Being a chief operating officer of a company of one (you) is different from being the head of a company of five or ten.

Finally, we get to money. If you manage growth properly and have the required skills, you may generate much more income than the cost incurred by having a partner or employee. After all, that's part of the point of expanding.

> **Consultant Crashing**
>
> If you hire someone, you should expect a period of learning time while the new employee finds out about the job and what you need. However, if you don't hire just the right person, you may end up with a high-maintenance employee who costs more time than he or she saves over the long haul.

> **Between Colleagues**
>
> You yourself are in the best position to decide whether to grow or not, since you know your own financial situation and your personal preferences about work. While only you can make the decision, consider talking to other consultants who have made the decision to expand.

Should You Grow? And How?

When should you give serious attention to expanding your consulting business? There is no easy answer and you'll have to make that judgment call yourself, but I can list some of the factors to consider in making your decision. In the next two sections, I'll look at when growth is worth considering and when it is a bad idea.

When Growth Is Worth Considering

Consider growth as a business strategy when you are almost sure that the addition of another person will result in increased revenue, not just staying at the same revenue level. The extra revenue should be significantly more than the cost of having an employee or partner, taking into account the following costs:

- Salary and other employment expenses
- Time spent hiring and training
- Extra costs like renting office space, furniture, and equipment, if necessary
- Maintenance costs (paperwork associated with being an employer)
- Management costs (the time you need to spend managing and guiding an employee)

Consider growth when you are financially stable and feel that the new person will be able to free you to do things that earn money directly (for example, increase your billable hours).

Expansion is also a good option when you have established a track record for revenue that is over the amount needed to carry an employee for the first year.

When Growth Is a Bad Idea

Expansion is not a good idea if you have an unstable revenue pattern. Think of it like a manufacturing company that has had up and down earnings and decides to build an additional factory to increase earnings. If it works, that's great. If it doesn't, welcome to bankruptcy. For consultants the question of expansion isn't quite so big a gamble because the capital expenditures are lower, but it's still a gamble.

If you aren't suited or skilled in managing employees, expansion may not be a good plan.

If you value the high flexibility and freedom associated with a one-person shop, consider whether you are willing to lose at least some of that. If you like consulting because of the freedom it provides you, then perhaps becoming an executive with employees isn't something you want to do.

> **Consulting Confidential**
>
> Expansion isn't the be-all and end-all. Some consultants (and I include myself) have no desire to expand and work with the additional complexities that come with expansion. Like me, you may value the independence and flexibility that come with a one-person shop. There's no shame in staying the same, provided it works for you.

Tips for the Growth Process

You've decided to go for it. Aim at the big time. So, are there things you should do to increase your chances of success?

As I said earlier, figure out the costs of having an employee, and assume that in the first year you will receive no extra revenue to cover the extra costs. This is a conservative course of action but one that protects you from getting in over your head.

Slow, steady growth is the key. Even if you have sufficient finances and business to grow quickly, use caution. Remember that the hiring process and the time immediately following a hire or partnership is going to be much more time-consuming than you might think. New employees need to learn about you and your business even if they already have most of the work skills required. The only way they can learn those things is from you. If you hire two or three people in close succession, it's going to stop you cold.

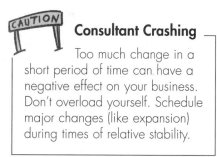

Consultant Crashing

Too much change in a short period of time can have a negative effect on your business. Don't overload yourself. Schedule major changes (like expansion) during times of relative stability.

If you grow more slowly, one employee at a time, the employee you hired first can help the second one you hire. The hiring process itself is much more complicated than you might think. For example, did you know that it is illegal to ask the age of an applicant? There are all kinds of rules involved. So before you hire, get some advice from a lawyer with labor law experience or from a human resources professional.

When hiring, take skills into account, but also consider how well you think you can get along with the person you hire. If you have one or two employees, you are going to spend a considerable amount of time interacting with them. You'd better be comfortable with them as people. The same thing applies with respect to partners. If you can't get along with a partner, you're dead.

Look to hire (or partner with) people who share your core values and principles. Assuming you are committed to a high level of customer service and ethical behavior, it's important that your employees share those values.

Hire or partner with people who have similar values but have different skills and work preferences. For example, if you are weak in the sales and marketing area, then look for someone who can supply those abilities and enjoys working in that area.

Finally, look at finding people who have the potential for increased responsibility, and give them a chance for growth. For example, you have an immediate need for someone to act as a receptionist and do some client contact work. If you hire a person who can learn and grow, you can expand the job responsibilities, further decreasing your workload while at the same time increasing that person's value to your company. In other words, consider employees as long-term investments.

Options to Growth

Fortunately, you don't have to expand your business when caught in the growth dilemma. Nor do you have to do nothing. There are several things you can do without committing yourself to hiring a full-time or even a part-time employee. Let's look at them.

Outsourcing/Contracting

The most used option is to outsource or contract with others to provide services to you. Need some marketing help? Perhaps you can hire someone to develop a marketing plan and start the marketing process; maybe a one- or two-month contract that doesn't require the person to be on the premises or make use of your business equipment will work for you. This option is more expensive in the short run but gives you more flexibility.

> **Consulting Confidential**
>
> Did you know that some companies offer short-term office rentals and receptionist services? If you have an important business meeting and want an instant office, you can rent facilities. Or if you are temporarily working away from the office a lot, you can have a receptionist who acts as if he or she works only for you but who actually works for a number of small businesses.

Sometimes subcontracting is possible. How does that work? Let's say you are a sales and marketing consultant hired by a company interested in public response to some new product lines. You can do all the work, including meeting with groups of consumers (called focus groups) to gauge their reactions. Or you can hire someone to take on the responsibility of running those groups and summarizing the data. You still are the one to interpret the data and to report to the client. In other words, you subcontract.

> **Consultant Crashing**
>
> Some consultants subcontract work on a project without telling the client who will be doing the work. That's unethical. The client should be told up-front who will be involved in the project. At minimum the client should understand that you will not be doing everything yourself.

The principle behind successful outsourcing or subcontracting is this. Subcontract the work that is low value (that is, it doesn't earn much money) in order to free yourself to carry out high-value work. You pay to get the work done, but, above all, you pay to increase the time you have to earn money. For example, you have to produce 100 training manuals for a training session you will be leading. If you did it yourself, it might take you several hours. Your time is better spent doing things only you can do, so contracting the job out to a print shop is a good choice.

Pooled Work with Others and Exchange of Services

I have two more options to discuss, and I bet you haven't considered either of them. First, you can work cooperatively with other consultants in your field and location. In other words, you cooperate to achieve a certain end in a way that is more efficient than if each of you did things independently.

Pooling work or working cooperatively is particularly effective in marketing. You may find there are four or five consultants who offer slightly different services but who offer them to essentially the same market. By working together, you can do one direct mailing to the target group, explaining the services of all the members of your cooperative. Not only can you save time in developing marketing material, but you can also save money.

Pooling or working with a temporary consulting partner is also useful if you want to take on a large project. Working with another consultant can make it more likely you will get the contract, and this arrangement saves time in both the proposal stage and the execution of the contract.

You also have the option of working out exchange of service agreements. For example, if you are a graphic designer, you may offer to design a logo and corporate image for an accountant, who, in turn, gives you advice on investments and prepares your tax returns. It's really a form of bartering.

You should know that benefits you receive through bartering of services may be taxable as earned income. Check with a tax specialist in your area.

> **Between Colleagues**
>
> Pooling resources and working cooperatively involves managing the process so all parties share the purpose of the effort and understand their roles and obligations. My experience is that this works best with people who know each other fairly well.

Better Time Management

Finally, you might want to consider improving your time management skills. If you feel you have too much work to deal with, that might be because you lack the organizational skills to work efficiently. You may benefit from reading about time management techniques or taking a course.

Obviously, if your company is on a fast-growth track, this will be only a stopgap measure. At some point even the most organized person needs to realize there are just not enough hours in the day.

The Least You Need to Know

- Expanding your business is as harrowing as starting it up. Don't underestimate the risk involved.
- Partnerships and hiring people carry hidden overhead that many business owners don't consider. The costs are not just monetary. Take into account the time that you, personally, need to spend in the hiring and training of your new employee.
- Slow and steady growth is better than rapid expansion. Minimize your risk by being patient.

◆ Before committing to expansion, consider outsourcing options, which, in the short term, may be more expensive than hiring someone but will allow you to be flexible.

◆ Consider whether being an employer or having a partner suits your personality. Would one be preferable to the other?

Part 5

The Client Relationship

You want to like your clients, and you want your clients to appreciate and value what you have to offer. Building that mutually beneficial relationship is what Part 5 covers. I start off with a chapter on how to have a realistic set of expectations about your clients and how the relationship might proceed. Regardless of the kind of services you offer, your success will be determined by your ability to work effectively with people.

What brings your clients back for more is when they actually use what you suggest and it works for them. This doesn't always happen. So Chapter 23, "Getting Your Advice Used," is about how to make sure the folks you're working for take your advice. This is followed by a chapter that explains what to do when you meet with resistance—clients who don't want to face up to the truth. And then there are what I call the clients and situations from the "dark side." You can imagine what I mean. Chapter 25, "Consulting Situations from the Dark Side," gives descriptions of such situations and how to effectively deal with them.

Finally, I conclude with Chapter 26, "Best Professional Resources on the Planet." This is a review of the books and advice I've found most useful. Along with this book, think of these resources as the consultant's consultant.

22

What to Expect from Clients and What You'll Get

In This Chapter

- ◆ Imperfect clients—get used to them
- ◆ When to say "no thank you" to a contract
- ◆ Common warning signals
- ◆ The danger of terminating during a project

One of the common errors beginning consultants make is expecting too much from clients. I think most of us start out with the idea that our clients are good, intelligent people who will work with us in good faith, know how to behave as good consulting "partners," always take our advice, and immediately see the value of what we are doing for them.

With a little thinking, you'll see that while this is sometimes the case, it is often not the case. It's not that clients are dim-witted or evil, although you may come across a few who seem to fit the first label. It's just that your clients are … well, regular people complete with strengths and weaknesses. Some of them are easy to work with, and some not so.

This attitude makes sense when you consider that consulting is primarily about people. Thus, you shouldn't be surprised when people don't act the way you expect.

Nonetheless, this attitude does indeed surprise beginning consultants. It's important to have a realistic set of expectations about your clients. Being realistic means that you will be better prepared to deal with issues that occur and you won't be shocked into inaction by totally unexpected client behavior. In this chapter I'll talk about what you can expect from your clients, the good things and the more challenging.

What You Can Hope for—The Dream Client

Are there "dream clients?" Probably. But not a lot. Should you expect to work only with dream clients? No. You should know what qualities or characteristics you hope to find in clients, but *relying* on finding them is dangerous. Very few consulting relationships are perfect, and you need to be prepared when clients don't act like you'd hoped.

So, what should you hope for?

Here's a list of dream client characteristics:

◆ Experience in working with consultants and an understanding of consultants' roles

◆ Accessible—easy to contact

◆ Willing to play an active role and not dump responsibility for success on the consultant's shoulders

◆ Committed to obtaining results rather than just the appearance of doing something

◆ In a decision-making capacity

◆ Willing and able to make decisions quickly

◆ Open-minded and willing to trust you

◆ Communicative—no hidden agendas

◆ Ethical and principled

◆ Pays on time

◆ Willingness to look at self

◆ Understands what is needed to solve own problem

Find clients who fit all of these descriptions, and you've got a project that may unfold perfectly and will probably end to everyone's satisfaction. You'll also have a client for whom you'll bend over backward to keep. However, chances are you aren't going to find this perfect client. So let's see what you are likely to get and why perfection is unlikely.

What You Will Get—The Real Client

Let's start with the very last item on our "dream client" list. It's the one that you are least likely to come across: Client "understands what is needed to solve own problem." Think about this for just a moment. Why do clients hire consultants? Usually because they have a problem they are unable to solve on their own. It doesn't make sense to expect clients to have an understanding of their own problem and its solution. If this were the case, they wouldn't need you, would they? Expect that they will be befuddled.

Sometimes clients think they know the solution and expect you to implement the solution they have already identified. That can be a huge barrier, and one I'll deal with in Chapter 25, "Consulting Situations from the Dark Side and What to Do About Them."

Can you expect clients to be able to identify the problem in any detail? No. Clients often do not have a clear idea of their problem and may not be able to explain it to you. Again, it's your job to identify the problem and then verify with the client that your diagnosis makes sense.

> ### Consulting Confidential
>
> While clients are not likely to know how to solve a problem, your job is to use what they *do* know to help them discover solutions. They have the information you need to diagnose difficulties. You have the expertise to make sense of that information.

Let's consider the other items on the list taken as a group.

Your clients are probably busy people. They are human and subject to all of the quirks and shortcomings we all have. Most of the time they mean well and want to address whatever problems they might think they have. However, it's often the case that your project is only one of a dozen things of concern to your client. Your client has a legitimate need to juggle a variety of responsibilities.

It's not uncommon for a client to hire a consultant to reduce his or her workload. It's also not uncommon for clients to be hard to contact or be less than forthcoming with information you need to have.

Be prepared for such situations and build them into your scheduling and planning. Even simple things like client communication take much longer than anticipated.

A tip: When contracting a project, see if the client will agree to prearranged meetings or phone calls held at regular intervals, and hold the client to that commitment. Consider making it part of your contract.

Client's Understanding of the Consulting Process

Things would be wonderful, indeed, if all clients understood the consulting process, their own responsibilities, and the consultant's, and embraced the consulting process in ways that would obtain the results they envisioned.

But they don't. Typically, clients lack understanding in two areas. First, they have limited experience working with outside consultants; and, second, they literally have no idea of how you work and what you need. How could they, unless they've worked with you before? That's okay. You are going to teach them.

Between Colleagues

One reason why consultants love repeat business (apart from the money) is that repeat clients have a better understanding of how the consultant works and of what is required to make a project work.

Part of your job is to educate your clients so that they understand what you need to help them and what their own responsibilities are. Don't be bashful about explaining these things to your client; begin the client education process at square one. Although you don't want to be patronizing, everyone benefits from being informed and being clear. The consulting process becomes much easier when you have the groundwork in place and all parties understand what you are going to do, what the roles are of everyone involved, and how essential it is that you be given the tools and support to do the job.

Decision-Making Hell

There are some client-side factors that consultants would like to have in place, but they are not always available. As I said earlier, you hope and expect that you will have access to decision makers so you can get the support you need. You also hope that your clients will enter into the consulting relationship with no hidden agendas. When these factors are not in place, your chances of success drop significantly.

Why are these two factors so important? As an outside consultant, you usually have limited formal power to make decisions on behalf of your client. This makes sense, since few companies are going to hand over the reins to you, even for a short time. Whether it's during the information-gathering component of a project or during the implementing of solutions, you don't decide. You advise those who decide. You can't advise if you do not have direct contact with the decision makers who do have that authority and power.

You may come across a situation in which the contact person for a particular project lacks any real decision-making power. That happens when the people who have the power delegate part of the responsibility for the project to those lower in the company pecking order.

Let me give you an example. Your initial meetings with a client occur with the CEO and one or two other people. You define the project, come to an agreement, and begin the process. However, the CEO, a very busy person, assigns a midlevel manager (let's say the human resources director) to serve as your contact. In turn, the director assigns that responsibility to a staff member.

The problem occurs when you need to have decisions made, and the only person who has the authority sits at the top of the organization. If you have direct access, that setup works well. In a delegated situation, though, you probably won't have easy and timely access. At best, everything slows down. At worst, the process comes to a shrieking halt until the decisions get made.

Clearly, this is a situation where an ounce of prevention is worth a pound of cure. Standard operating procedure dictates that you …

Between Colleagues

Always negotiate access to key decision makers. Make this a standard part of your contracting talks, explaining why it is necessary and finding out who the key decision makers are.

- ◆ identify the key decision makers.
- ◆ make clear why you need personal access to them.
- ◆ have direct access channels in place.

Attend to this from the time you start negotiating a project.

Those Darned Agendas

Here's something to think about. If your consulting project has little meaning or impact on people, you probably won't come across people who have agendas at cross-purposes to your goals. That's not always the case, but it applies generally.

However, the more far-reaching the project and the more it impacts people, the more likely you will encounter people who have motivations and agendas that are (a) hidden or hard to discern and (b) that affect your ability to achieve the consulting goals.

Hidden agendas are held by individuals who have values, motivations, or concerns (often self-serving) that cause them to oppose or derail the consulting project. For example, individual employees may be hesitant to help you gather information if they perceive that your suggestions might result in layoffs. You may come across people who, for no practical reason, want to maintain the status quo. That, too, is a hidden agenda.

Consulting Confidential

People in the middle of the company hierarchy often have a much better grasp of what goes on in their organization than those at the top. That's why it's important to involve the right people throughout the organization.

Client and other stakeholders may have other agendas they are hesitant to share—protecting their turf, empire building, and so on. As I've said many times, it's part of your job as a consultant to manage this process and ensure that hidden agendas don't end up sabotaging the project.

I'll talk more about this problem in Chapter 24, "Facing and Dealing with Resistance," but the important point here is that while you would expect (or hope) that people will act in good faith and disclose any side agendas they have, you can't count on them doing so. Consultants have to be alert to the possibility of there being events and feelings below the surface that may need to be addressed.

Now let's talk about the decisions and options available to you if you discover that the client or other players in the project are acting in ways that can damage the project. Sometimes red flags exist from the very beginning, when you are negotiating the contract. Sometimes you don't see those flags until you are in the middle of a project. You need to know your options and how to execute them.

Three Important Decisions

Once you have concluded there are things going on that may impact your ability to deliver on your project promises, you have some basic options. If problems emerge during the contracting phase and you see things that cause you concern, you can say no thank you, and cease pursuing the contract. If major concerns emerge during the project phase, you can either choose to address them or you can pull the plug. These are not easy decisions to make.

Deciding What You Can Live With

You can't decide on go/no-go issues without having a starting point. In essence, you have to decide what you can live with in terms of both the project and your business in general.

In other words, you have to identify what's important to you on both personal and business levels, identify the consequences of your go/no-go decision, and match the consequences with what's important to you.

For example, let's say you have the opportunity to sign a lucrative consulting contract with a major company. In your initial meetings, you are almost convinced that several key players have some private agendas that would not bode well for the project's success. Do you take the contract? That's for you to decide.

Here are some questions to ask yourself as you make your decision:

◆ How confident am I that I can bring these agendas to the surface and address them so they do not interfere?

- What is the "value" of this contract, in terms of money, future business, and my reputation?

- What are the consequences of not achieving the goals of the project?

- What are the rewards for taking on a tough challenge and succeeding?

- What is my personal tolerance for frustration?

- Will the project become so messy and time-consuming that I will see it as the "project from hell"?

> **Consulting Confidential**
>
> One factor I consider in terms of taking on contracts is whether I "like" the people involved. The reason I look at this is that I'm more likely to deal effectively with frustrations and challenges if I like the people involved. If I don't like them, my frustration levels grow quickly and I tend to be more mistrustful.

These questions, and similar ones you may come up with on your own, can be applied to any situation, whether prior to signing the deal or during the project. Keep in mind that you need to constantly assess the success of the project as you go.

Deciding When to Say Thanks but No Thanks

Do you know what's really painful to small consulting companies? Leaving money on the table. Actually, we all have a tendency to accept contracts when it's clear, or should be clear, that we are entering a minefield.

It's understandable. Most of us aren't rich, and money can be a much greater concern than we'd like. That said, you will come across situations in which you are better off refusing the contract. What are the conditions under which you should refuse a contract?

They can be divided into a number of categories. The first involves business concerns. There are situations in which accepting a contract is an unwise decision for purely business reasons. The prospective client may have completely unrealistic or unfair expectations about issues like fees, what you are suppose to deliver, and timing.

Here are some possible situations:

- Client has limited budget and wants to pay you much less than you believe you are worth.

- The schedule for the project is completely unreasonable. It's not possible to carry it out properly in the allotted time.

Consultant Crashing

Money corrupts, and big money corrupts in a big way. At least it can if you let it. Accepting a consulting project when you have no chance of succeeding with it (but it pays well) is not a wise or ethical choice. Let someone else get caught in that meat grinder.

◆ The amount of time you will have to put into the project impacts on other projects, and the compensation does not justify that time investment.

Do you walk away if you come across situations like these? There's no hard and fast rule. Consider the questions listed earlier. Is it possible to educate the client to be more realistic, or are the terms fixed in stone? How much do you value the total fee for the project? Balance that with the time it may take you to complete it, or the possibilities of failure.

Consider Probability of Success

The second category you have to consider is the probability of success. Probability of project success has nothing to do with money. It's completely independent. When you look at a prospective project, one of the first things you do is ask yourself, "What are the chances I can take this on and succeed so that both the client and I myself are satisfied with the outcome?"

If the answer is that you are almost certain of success, you'd probably go ahead and agree to do it, even if the situation weren't perfect. If the answer is that you're uncertain, watch out.

Generally, you want to succeed (or at least have a fair chance of succeeding) on each and every project. The reason is simple. Failures follow you around and damage your reputation. Failures don't "feel very good" either.

Let me give you a personal example. I was asked to work with a CEO on a quality improvement project and invited to meet with him and his senior executives. The CEO dominated the meeting, talking about 80 percent of the time in a way that indicated he was more concerned with impressing people than with actually improving quality. The other executives at the session either said nothing or pandered to the CEO.

What did I conclude? Having some information about this group before walking in, I found that the meeting confirmed this information. This project had no chance of success, whether I accepted it or whether the best consultant in the world carried it out. Too many hidden agendas; too much organizational illness.

What did I do? I never refused outright. As is often the case in these situations, both parties opted out. During the meeting I showed only limited enthusiasm for the process I was engaged in and laid out my perspective

Between Colleagues

When assessing your probability of success, be realistic about both the situation and your own abilities. The more expert you are at consulting, the more likely you will be to succeed; but your estimate must be based on an accurate skill assessment, needs of the situation, and your track record in similar situations.

rather bluntly, saying that "I would expect the CEO and senior executives to agree to a number of principles before I would even begin to discuss project details or draft a preliminary proposal."

What happened? They didn't hire me or offer me the contract (hurrah!). I don't think they liked me much, either. They hired someone else they could manipulate more easily. That person came in, did some limited work for them, and was actually far away when the time came to implement the quality improvement effort. What happened to the clients? Well, it was a disaster. The executives behaved badly, ended up threatening staff to try to get them onside. A number of union grievances were filed. The CEO was eventually replaced, in part because of this debacle but largely because he was poor at his job.

And what about me? I still smile when I think of how smart I was to, in effect, walk away from a project doomed from the start.

> **Consulting Confidential**
>
> There are times when you have to be blunt about what you require for successful completion of a project, even though you know the client may not be very receptive. If the client balks, fine. You've probably just saved yourself considerable grief. Courage is an important part of consulting.

Deciding to "Pull the Plug"

There's an equally, or perhaps even more difficult, decision you might be faced with. What happens when you are in the middle of a project and see it sinking (slowly or with great speed)?

How can this happen? For a number of reasons. You may have been so eager to take the contract that you overlooked potential barriers to successful completion. Your fault. On the other hand, it might have been impossible to predict challenges at the point of signing the contract. Maybe there were no hints. Or maybe the playing field changed somehow from the time you took the contract to the time you started experiencing difficulties.

What then? First, understand that pulling out of a project in the middle involves substantial difficulties, some practical, some ethical, and some legal. You should consider pulling the plug only as a last resort.

Ending the project can take place under two different situations. The first is likely to minimize the harm to you if you terminate the project. In this situation you try to negotiate an "ending" with the client, because the client also realizes that to continue is pointless or even harmful. In other words, the project is terminated by mutual agreement.

How do you broach the subject of termination so as to bring about this mutual agreement? Be honest and open, always focusing on the welfare of the client. If the client's welfare is not at stake, it's likely the client will be upset if you try to justify termination for your own reasons (for example, it's become too much work, or you now decide you aren't being paid enough). The client may not let you out of your contract.

What's the second situation? In it, the client wants to continue and you don't. That's big trouble, because you have to be concerned about legal issues connected with breach of contract. In your decision making about these situations, clarify for yourself why you want to terminate. Is it because the project is a mess and you can't fix it? Perhaps the client has become his or her own worst enemy? Or is it because you just don't want to do it anymore, or maybe the project hasn't turned out to be as lucrative as you hoped for?

> **Between Colleagues**
>
> Regardless of the reasons for project difficulties, make sure you discuss the situation with clients constructively, and stay away from figuring out who is to blame. Your goal is to solve the problem, not blame someone, if someone other than yourself is to blame.

Next, ask yourself if there is *any* way to salvage the project. Can you negotiate ways to overcome the challenges within the current contract? Keep in mind that if your reasons for wanting to terminate are not related to the client's welfare but your own, you are still bound by that initial contract and cannot terminate unilaterally.

After that, do everything you can to negotiate so that the client's needs are met and yours are not totally sacrificed. Consider termination only as a last resort. Consider unilateral termination as a means to save your life. Anything less than that and you may have to continue.

The Least You Need to Know

- What you hope you will get from clients and what you actually get are usually quite different. Be realistic.
- To prevent problems later on, negotiate access to the important decision makers at the beginning of a project.
- Knowing when not to accept a contract is important. Be alert to signals that the project may be impossible to carry out with success.
- It's always preferable to negotiate and problem-solve than to terminate a consulting relationship during a project.

Chapter 23

Getting Your Advice Used

In This Chapter

- ◆ Early warnings that signal later problems
- ◆ The importance of creating the proper "client mindset"
- ◆ Interactions as opportunities to get your advice used
- ◆ Your client—the trump card

I think most consultants want to have their advice and recommendations used and implemented. That's certainly part of a commitment to the client's welfare—a sense that the point of consulting is to help, and not just provide an income for the consultant.

Most clients (it's hard to say "all") enter into consulting relationships with the expectation that they will use the advice they receive and that using it will result in something good. It's hard to imagine a client consciously planning to ignore the advice. "Let's hire this guy, pay him a lot of money, and then ignore what he says, okay?" That's not a likely scenario.

There's many a slip between intention and action. In other words, there's no guarantee the client will follow the advice. Get used to this reality. No matter what you do, you are likely to come across clients who won't find your advice palatable or will choose not to go ahead with your solutions. If you can't accept that fact and recognize it as the client's prerogative, you are going to get very frustrated.

While it may be the client's prerogative to decide what to do with your suggestions, that does not mean you have no influence over the probability that your advice will be used. You do have influence, and it's significant. By managing your project effectively and taking on the responsibility for getting your advice adopted, you'll find your success rate improves.

That's what this chapter is about. I'll explain how to manage the consulting project so that the client is more likely to make use of your advice and to benefit from it.

The Different Ways Advice Gets "Lost"

You contract with a client. You diagnose, collect data, and do a wonderful job of drafting recommendations that you think the client will eat up. But the client doesn't. "Won't work," she says, or "It's just not the right time." Those are two common client reactions involved in the outright rejection of a consultant's recommendations. Rejection hurts and it can be messy. But at least the rejection was straightforward, and it's possible to salvage the project.

Advice isn't always lost in such a direct way, however. It can get lost in indirect ways, too; and consultants need to understand them. It's likely you'll find that these less obvious ways are far more common than the outright rejection. A consultant who ignores the possibility that his or her advice may be bent, stapled, or mutilated is liable to experience a lot of projects that look good but turn out badly.

There are two situations where advice appears to be accepted but doesn't result in successful implementation. In the first one, you get "partial implementation and acceptance." In the second, you get "agreement then a screw-up" in implementation. Both share a common characteristic: The client appears to accept the advice, moves forward in applying it, but ends up not getting what he or she wanted. That's not surprising if the client misapplies or partially applies your advice. The bottom line is that while your advice may be "used," it isn't used properly. This is a serious situation.

Wanted! Client's Desired State of Mind

For clients to accept advice and use it as intended, the client must have a certain state of mind. It's your job to help create that state of mind so the client will accept and use your advice. To do so, you need to understand what you are trying to create. That's what I'll talk about next.

Let's list some of the elements that need to be in place by the end of the project. The earlier these are in place, the more smoothly the entire project will go.

Your client needs to …

Consultant Crashing

The poor consultant limits his or her thinking to the nuts and bolts of problem solving and ignores the people side. Failure to create the right client mindset means that, no matter how good the advice, it's likely to be wasted.

- ◆ Have some sense of urgency regarding the remedying of the problems that the project is to solve.
- ◆ Have an understanding of your recommendations—a deep understanding, not just a superficial understanding.
- ◆ Trust you and your ability and lend credence to your expertise.
- ◆ Understand the consequences of doing nothing.
- ◆ Understand that partial or incorrect use of the advice is likely to make things worse.
- ◆ Understand how using your advice will benefit him or her directly—the "what's in it for me" factor.
- ◆ Have a sense of ownership of the project and understand his or her role in its success.

Let's not leave out other people who can influence the implementation of your advice. Stakeholders and employees have considerable power (sometimes formal, sometimes informal) related to what happens after you deliver your advice. By and large, not only should you create the proper state of mind in your direct client, but you should also do so with stakeholders and other players.

Warning Signs That Trouble Lies Ahead

To ensure that your advice will be used, and used properly, your standard operating procedures should include creating the "right state of mind" in your client. Your effort to do this should begin at the first contact with the client and extend past the point where you have presented your findings.

Between Colleagues

To determine the level of commitment and sense of urgency associated with your project, don't rely solely on what the client says, but on what the client does to back up his or her words.

Still, even with this effort on your part, you need to know the warning signs that might indicate potential problems in getting your advice adopted.

Some of these signs occur early, even in the contracting stage; others appear during the project, and perhaps the most serious occur when you present your advice. In the next three sections, I'll look at the warning signs in each stage and explain what you can do about them.

Red Flags Early in the Process

Are there any early red flags or signals in the consulting process that might indicate the client will end up as a "nonimplementer"? There are.

During the initial contact and contracting phases, be alert to clients who seem to lack an urgent desire to address the issues they say they want addressed. How do you know? You can't reach inside the client's head or read the client's mind, but there are observable signals that may give you pause.

For example, if the process of coming to an agreement is slow, or you believe that the client is procrastinating, these are early signs of trouble. While it may be true that your client is very busy, it's also probably true that your client isn't placing enough importance on solving the problems that your consulting project is designed to address. People find the time to solve really important problems.

Suppose your client is difficult to contact. Phone calls are not returned promptly and meetings are delayed. Those are other signals.

Here's a third: Your client indicates the project is "high priority" but delegates responsibility for it so far down in the organization that you are dealing with someone with no authority and little status. In one consulting project I was involved in, the client (an executive) was quite adamant about the importance of the project but delegated the responsibility for the project to the least-capable person available. The logic in handing off the project to this person was, "He didn't have much else to do."

Here's a different early warning sign. Your client delays project approval in order to consult with a number of other people in the organization—ostensibly to achieve some consensus on whether they should hire you. There's a variation on this theme: the dreaded committee. It's not uncommon for clients to form committees to search for a consultant, and arrange the final contract. This is actually a form of delegation, and the idea behind it is sound, at least on the surface—involve stakeholders in the decision-making process.

In practice, delegating to a committee may indicate your client will not be giving you the support you need later on. What you want from your client is the ability and willingness to make decisions, and you want a personally involved client. Some clients are so caught up with the notion of building consensus that they become paralyzed.

Committees, by the way, can be major barriers to having your advice used. Why? It's simple. The more people involved in deciding to use your advice, the more likely your advice will be tabled.

So, Now What?

What do you do if your "distance early warning system" identifies any of these red flags? First, let's explore your options, keeping in mind that we are talking about signals that pop up before you actually sign the contract.

You have the option of ignoring the warning signs and forging ahead. You also can refuse the project. Or you can discuss these issues with your client. Since you don't know for sure whether there will indeed be problems, the obvious choice is to meet with the client to clarify issues and to create a client mindset that will increase the likelihood your advice will get used.

How do you do that?

Arrange a face-to-face meeting with your client. I think that's better than a phone discussion, but if all you can get is a phone call, go with that. If the client delays, explain that it is important to meet now to avoid problems in the future.

At that meeting, your task is to create the necessary client mindset so that the project succeeds, assuming that it's offered to you and you accept. That means helping the client understand the consequences of doing nothing, and clarifying the client's priorities. Associated with this is coming up with an action plan to make sure you have access and to ensure that the project will not be delayed further.

On the surface, the best way is to tell the client what to do—in other words, you lay down the law. That's not a good strategy for two reasons. First, you don't have the contract yet. If you lean on the client at this point, you probably won't get the contract. Second, telling or ordering people to do things is just about the worst way to create a mindset.

Your strategy is to lead the client to the "right" conclusions and the right action. Your tools include questioning, listening, and a little explaining. Perhaps the best way to understand this strategy is to look at an example.

Jackie has been trying to sew up a contract to supply consulting services to the XYZ Company. Her client, Mary, has struck a committee to make the final decision about the contract, and it's been two months—no decisions and no apparent

Between Colleagues

Leaning on the client (applying pressure) can be a way of not getting hired if you have concerns about the project and only want to do it provided the proper conditions exist.

progress. Jackie knows that even if she gets the contract, chances are her recommendations are going to die on the committee table. So she arranges a meeting with Mary.

Jackie says: "Mary, I think the committee can be a valuable resource during this consulting project. Still, I think we need to clarify how you want to be involved in the project and how we should proceed at this point. First, I need to know whether you feel this is a must-do project or a nice-to-have. Is this something you feel must get done?"

Mary (the client) responds: "If, for some reason, we don't get this project going, what do you see as the consequences?"

Mary might ask a number of follow-up questions with the aim of helping the client clarify the importance of the project. Now it's time to move to identifying some solutions.

Jackie says: "Mary, we obviously agree on how important this is and that it can't be delayed much longer. It's just too costly to wait. What we need to do is figure out how we can speed up the approval process. How can we do that?"

If Mary refuses to address these issues, then it's time to lay the cards on the table. This is how Jackie might do it.

Jackie states: "Okay, I think that if we delay any further, the chances of success diminish. So, if we don't come to an agreement by September 17, I'm going to have to withdraw from consideration. It's up to you and the committee how to proceed."

Between Colleagues

When negotiating a project, get the client to commit to the idea there is one *final* decision maker at his or her end. Committees are less problematic if one person has the final decision. Ideally, the buck stops with the direct client.

Do you see the pattern here? You want to ask the right questions so you get the right answers. If you don't get the right answers, then you need to provide some limits and indicate the consequences if things don't change. That may involve drawing a line or setting a final date after which point you are no longer interested.

You aren't going through this exercise to provoke anyone. Nor are you doing it to display your "power" (you don't have any anyway). You do it because you know that unless you get certain issues fixed now, there's little chance the project will progress well, and less chance your advice will be taken seriously and used effectively.

Red Flags During the Project

When you see warning flags during the negotiation of a consulting agreement, it's not a pleasant situation. But it is far more workable than if these warning indicators emerge during the project. Once in the middle of a project, you have no "stick" (refusal to continue) to wield. Sure, you could walk away from the project, but that's not a practical solution. Besides, warning signals, unless they seriously impede the course of the consulting intervention, are not sufficient in themselves to terminate an agreement.

In short, your remedies are limited to the use of your interpersonal skills and abilities to persuade your client and the stakeholders to back the project and follow through.

Since your concern right now is to make sure your advice doesn't go unheeded, let's focus on dealing with those warning signals. In addition to the ones listed earlier, be alert to any kinds of resistance coming from stakeholders or anyone else connected to, or affected by, the project, particularly if you aren't going to be around for the implementation phase. You'll be amazed at how people in the organization will lobby against implementing your advice, after the fact. Thus, your goal is to bring any and all key players onboard and keep them there. This is largely a public relations effort that involves creating a sense of ownership of the project amongst key players and looking for signs of skepticism and discussing things with the "skeptics."

Here are some suggestions:

◆ Bringing people onside is important throughout the project. Use each interaction to bring people onside.

◆ Keep people focused on how things will be better if the problem you were hired to address is fixed.

◆ Use the same communication process to address warning signals as the one that was outlined earlier. Approach lead people to assess their own feelings about the project, and use "telling" in limited ways (and only after softer methods haven't worked).

◆ Deal with outright resistance immediately. If you can't counter that resistance before you tender your advice, chances are your advice won't be implemented.

Between Colleagues

Every single interaction with any of the client's personnel must be seen as an opportunity to enlist their support so that your seeds of advice will fall on fertile ground.

Red Flags at the Reporting Stage

I can't overstate the importance of the oral presentation of your findings and advice. In the ideal world, you'd want everyone excited to hear your advice and looking forward to implementing your ideas. That could happen, and it's more likely to happen if you've laid the groundwork earlier in the project. But often it won't be the case. Even if most people are onside, one or two people may not be.

Presenting your report is one of the last chances you have to create a final commitment to your recommendations. This is particularly true if your involvement is to end when you have reported your findings.

Let's go over the critical aspects of the presentation. You must give enough information that your client and any other attendees understand the problems you identified, the data you used to draw your conclusions, and the options and solutions you are suggesting.

Not only must they understand the options, but they must buy into them. They will be more likely to buy in if they understand the logic behind the options. So lay out the reasoning, and focus on the importance of the options. Map out the consequences of not doing anything, of delay and procrastination, and state clearly how those things will affect the attendees individually.

Consultant Crashing

The inferior consultant sees his or her job as providing facts during the presentation of results. The superior consultant understands the critical issue is getting the key players to support the findings.

This last bit is important. It's one thing to map out consequences to an organization. However, it's another to point out consequences to individuals, because then the consequences seem much more immediate, personal, and real.

Be persuasive but not overbearing. Invite comments and deal with them nondefensively.

How Do You Know There's Trouble?

You're at a meeting and you're presenting your results. What signs do you look for that might indicate your advice is less likely to be used? The following actions on the part of your audience could indicate trouble:

 ♦ Looks and actions that indicate indifference or uninterest

 ♦ A focus on minor details rather than on the important ideas you have presented

 ♦ A lack of questions and comments

 ♦ The withholding of feedback on the ideas

Now what? You may still have a trump card you can play. If you see these signs amongst the stakeholders, arrange a private meeting with your direct client.

Explain your concerns in the process of debriefing (or discussing) the presentation meeting. Now invoke the involvement of your client. Here's one way to do it.

"Mike, there were some signs I saw at the meeting that suggest there's going to be a struggle to get these recommendations implemented so they can succeed. I'd like to hear your perceptions about how the meeting went, and how you and I can work together to finish this off so you get the maximum benefits."

Then you devise an action plan that specifies what actions the client must take to make sure the project actually generates benefits and doesn't become a waste of time and effort. By the end of that meeting, the client should have a plan outlining what he or she needs to do. The plan might include inspirational leadership, constant reminders to staff, or even a heavier hand.

> **Consulting Confidential**
>
> Provided your direct client supports your recommendations (and you should know that before presenting your findings publicly), the project need not be derailed at this late date as long as your client takes an active role in getting your recommendations implemented. It's your job to define that role with the client.

Implementation Screw-ups

If there is significant resistance by key players, and it hasn't been turned around by the time the advice is implemented, the chances of a successful implementation drop considerably. At this stage, you may not have sufficient influence to turn the situation around, particularly if you have no implementation involvement.

If you are involved in implementation, remember that your job is not just to oversee the nuts and bolts of any changes introduced, but to build and maintain momentum for the changes. It's the interpersonal things—the people parts—that are still important. Yes, you want that computer system installed in the "right way." But the key to that is making sure everyone involved understands what the right way is, and supports it.

So, if you can, keep your finger on the pulse. Keep on top of the implementation. Be an active presence and hopefully a trusted one. Above all, ensure that all the key players understand why doing things a certain way is important in terms of their benefits. Then surface any resistance, and allay concerns as they occur.

You can't guarantee success. You can only lay the groundwork for successful implementation. In the event that your recommendations are not used or are implemented poorly, identify the things you could have done differently; then next time, do things differently.

Don't go nuts about these things. Remember that while you are responsible for bringing the project off, there are some situations in which no one could possibly succeed. Don't blame yourself or the client. Simply learn from failures.

> **Consultant Crashing**
>
> We all experience failures or partial failures. Good consultants learn from them and don't repeat them. Poor ones blame others and end up repeating the same mistakes.

The Least You Need to Know

◆ Put credence in what people do, rather than in what people say.

◆ Better to lay the groundwork for getting advice accepted early than to wait until the advice is tendered.

◆ You can provide the best advice in the world, but if you don't create a proper "client mindset," it may be for naught.

◆ If the presentation of your results surfaces warning flags, talk to your direct client privately and as soon as possible to draft a plan to counteract any resistance.

Chapter 24

Facing and Dealing with Resistance

In This Chapter

- ◆ An inevitable challenge—resistance
- ◆ Active, visible resistance versus hidden resistance
- ◆ Strategies for reducing and preventing resistance
- ◆ Tactics for turning resistance into something constructive

No matter what your consulting specialization, you will face resistance. It comes in many shapes and forms, and can occur at various times in the consulting process. You must be prepared for it.

Before talking about why people resist, let's clarify what resistance means in terms of consulting. *Resistance* is a normal part of the consulting process and is characterized by an unwillingness to give credibility to the project, a desire to avoid involvement, or a hesitation to implement advice.

Resistance can occur as part of your relationship with your direct client, or it can rear its head in other members of the organization who need to be involved to make the project succeed.

In this chapter I'll help you prepare to deal with resistance. I'll talk about how to recognize resistance, why it occurs, and how to deal with it productively.

What Resistance Looks Like

Resistance takes two forms. The first, and most obvious, is active resistance. The second, and perhaps more important form, is passive resistance. Let's see what both of them look like so you can recognize them and deal with them.

Active and Visible Resistance—You Can't Miss It

Active resistance is out in the open. Generally, it's hard to miss. The best way to explain active resistance is to look at an example.

Let's say you are presenting your conclusions to a group of senior executives. Several of the people at the meeting are fairly clear about their opposition to your suggestions. Erika interrupts and challenges you, trying to overpower you. Jake is just plain negative, saying things like, "It's just not going to work" and "That's all fine and dandy for other people, but it's not going to work in my department."

Consultant Crashing

Don't be lulled into a false sense of security if you are not seeing active resistance. The resistance most likely to harm you is beneath the surface, because if you aren't able to see it, you won't be able to deal with it.

This is active resistance. Jake and Erika are actively working at cross-purposes with you. You know it, and they aren't hiding it. The fact that you can see it is both a good thing and a bad thing. It's a good thing because you know where you stand and can address the resistance. It's a bad thing because the only thing that stands between you and consulting oblivion (at least on this project) is your ability to handle the active resistance.

But what about the others in the group? Does silence mean they are with you? Let's look at passive and less-visible resistance.

Passive, Less-Visible Resistance—Invisible Termites

Passive, less-visible resistance is resistance that is there but isn't obvious. People may be uncomfortable with what you are doing or saying, but they will say absolutely nothing in front of you. Let's return to our example. Mary sits quietly during your meeting, saying very little. Nothing in her behavior indicates whether or not she's with you. Things change, though, as soon as you leave. Not 10 seconds after you leave the room, she starts lobbying to prevent your suggestions from being implemented. She begins the process during the meeting itself (as soon as you've left) but also approaches the other executives in private to bring them onside—her side.

There's one more resisting person in the group (my, this is a true consulting horror story). Edgar says nothing in front of you, and he says nothing to his colleagues during the meeting. But Edgar is politically savvy. Recognizing that the CEO supports your recommendations, he knows he's better off saying nothing. His attitude is: "Fine, if this consultant and the CEO think they are going to get anything from my department, they have another thing coming." He's prepared to work behind the scenes to sabotage the project.

These are examples of passive resistance. It's like having termites in your house and not knowing it until your house falls down around your ears. You have to be aware that an infestation is possible, even likely. You need to look for it. Once you find it, you may be able to devise strategies to deal with resistance in a productive way.

> **Between Colleagues**
>
> Although dealing with resistance is frustrating, it's part of the job. Do your best to maintain lines of communication with the significant players so they will be more comfortable expressing their concerns.

Why Do People Resist?

People resist change for a number of reasons, and that's really what I'm talking about here—resistance to change. Although it's not possible to cover all the reasons why people resist change, I'll discuss the major ones.

Mistrust of Your Direct Client

Let's say the CEO of a major company hires you to address some issues about recently lowered productivity. You analyze the problem and come up with some great ideas to improve productivity, none of them noxious or difficult for employees to accept. But they don't accept them. When it's time to get employees onboard, there is a lot of both passive and active resistance. How could this be?

If your direct client (in this case the CEO) is seen as untrustworthy by employees, and you come up with suggestions that are associated with the mistrusted CEO, those suggestions are going to be treated with suspicion, even if they are excellent. Being linked to a mistrusted person can cause major problems.

> **Consulting Confidential**
>
> The less you know about your client and the client organization, the more likely you will face strong resistance. If you know ahead of time that a CEO is not well thought of, you can structure the process so it's less likely to produce resistance. If you don't know, you get blindsided.

Mistrust of Outsiders, or "Not Invented Here"

Some organizations develop a culture or mentality that regards anything coming in from outside as suspicious or not relevant. Sometimes it works the other way, and to the consultant's advantage. That is, the fact that a consultant from outside makes recommendations can be a factor in getting the changes made.

Symptoms associated with this source of resistance include comments like, "Well, that would never work here" or "This consultant doesn't understand us at all."

There's also the possibility that people involved in your project may have a mistrust of consultants in general. Don't dismiss this possibility. People who have had bad experiences with consultants because of incompetence or arrogance on the consultant's part will be far more resistant to consultants and their advice in the future.

Inertia, or the "It's Fine Now" Mentality

In physics there's a principle that states: A body in motion tends to stay in motion, and a body at rest tends to stay at rest. The same applies to organizations and individuals.

People tend to want to continue what they are doing, most often because it's familiar. It's surprising to think that people would prefer to do things that are clearly not working when they have the option of changing things. But it happens all the time.

Symptoms of this source of resistance include comments like, "Gee, there's nothing wrong with the old way" and "Why are things always changing around here?" and "This new way is just too hard."

> **CAUTION**
>
> ### Consultant Crashing
>
> Never assume that you have the track record, qualifications, or brilliance to have your ideas accepted without some resistance. I don't know of any consultant on the planet with enough status to avoid resistance entirely.

> **Consulting Confidential**
>
> When faced with a raft of internal political barriers, it's tempting for consultants to throw up their hands and blame any failures on the client. Remember that one reason you are hired is your ability to work within that environment and make it more effective. It is part of your job.

Internal Politics, or the Hidden Agenda

Sad to say but many consulting projects hit the rocks due to a lack of understanding and to the effects of internal politics. People in organizations are human. Some are ambitious, some selfish, and some exceedingly political. Their hidden agendas can affect whether they are receptive to participating in a project or implementing your suggestions. For example, a vice president hoping to be promoted to CEO might resist changes that make the existing CEO look good.

As another example, your advice might mean diminished power for, let's say, midlevel managers. Some will have no problem with that, particularly if they aren't political game players. Others, however, may see these changes as threatening. That's a hidden agenda.

Like situations in which your client is not seen as trustworthy, situations with hidden agendas can be addressed *if* you know they exist. The problem is you may not look for a hidden agenda. Be alert to internal politics that may interfere with your project. Anticipate. For example, in drafting a set of recommendations, ask yourself who is most likely to feel threatened.

What You Want to Do Is Dumb

I know a number of consultants who don't consider the possibility that the advice they give is just plain off the mark. No matter how good you are, or think you are, there will be times when your ideas don't fit. They really won't work, and people will resist in a rational way.

Or, your ideas may not be dumb, but they may have serious implications for some people. You'd expect that people who might lose their jobs would be resistant, even if the chances of an actual job loss were slim.

So remember that it's possible you will come up with solutions that won't work. Solutions you develop may be good for some and really bad for others.

Above all, when faced with resistance, your starting point is to take a critical look at yourself, what you've done, and your suggestions. Consider the perspectives of the various parties. Of course, you should be doing this throughout the life of the project, way before you tender final recommendations.

Why Do People Resist in Passive or Sabotaging Ways?

I think most consultants acknowledge that while people may disagree with their suggestions, well-meaning people can work together to ensure a good outcome. As a consultant, you need to be able to deal effectively with active resistance. What's much harder is to deal with the more passive forms of resistance, because the tactics used appear sneaky and underhanded. Passive or behind-the-scenes resistance feels like sabotage. Why do people do it? Why don't they just come out and say what's on their minds?

In most cases passive or behind-the-scenes resistance is not intended to damage you personally (although it can have that outcome). People who engage in this are probably not evil, but they react to stressful situations in unconstructive ways, often because they don't know how to deal with the situation more constructively.

Some cultures, for example, have very strong pressures to ensure that open conflict doesn't happen. Even in North American culture, where we seem to relish conflict in our entertainment media, the truth is that a good proportion of people do not handle open conflict well. Even though they may find it interesting to watch on television, they can't handle it in their personal or work lives.

Passive resistance, then, often reflects an individual's discomfort and lack of skills related to open conflict and disagreement. Therefore, they work the backroom to express their disagreements.

Between Colleagues

You don't want to be naive about potential attempts to sabotage projects. Realize that people may do this kind of thing because they don't know any other way to act. Realize also that some people are just nasty.

If you understand this, you are likely to be more tolerant and less angry when backroom tactics are used in relation to your project. Above all, it's important that you do not react angrily unless there is a constructive outcome to expressing your anger.

That said, some people are "game players" (as opposed to "team players") who have learned that passive resistance works for them. These are the people you have to watch for and sometimes approach bluntly.

Resistance Anticipation and Prevention

Dealing with resistance has two parts. One has to do with how you deal with resistance as it occurs; for example, how you react if someone is argumentative at a project meeting.

The other part has to do with anticipating and preventing resistance in the first place. Thankfully, there are a number of things consultants can do to reduce resistance throughout the project. That's what I'll talk about here.

Stakeholder Involvement from Square One

Stakeholders are people whom you must have onboard in order for the project to succeed. In some cases, this might include senior executives; in others, union personnel. Stakeholders can include regular employees if their cooperation is needed for the project to succeed.

Working Words

A **stakeholder** is a person who is needed for your project to succeed and/or a person who will be affected by the consulting project.

To identify the stakeholders for a specific project, ask yourself (and perhaps your client) this simple question: "Who is in a position to kill this project stone dead?"

The supplementary questions are, "Who is going to be affected by this project, and what is their ability to prevent the project from achieving a successful outcome?"

Once you've identified stakeholders (and it should be one of the very first things you do), you have to get their involvement early on. Let me give you an example. I was once involved in a consulting project at the behest of a CEO. I was retained in an advisory (generally powerless) position. Once the working committee completed its work and compiled recommendations, one of the members was asked to present them to senior executives (essentially vice presidents). It was a disaster. Almost all of the executives resisted the recommendations. Why? Because they had not been sufficiently involved in the project from the start. They didn't see it as "theirs."

Ultimately, this resistance occurred as a result of a number of mistakes on the part of people in power positions on the project, including the CEO, but also other project participants. Because of the resistance, the project failed.

What should have happened? Once the CEO defined the project, at least generally, the next step should have been individual meetings (in person) with each senior stakeholder. They should have been shown the respect they deserved by virtue of their positions. Since these stakeholders were essential to project success, they should have been accorded the importance that comes with that power. Interestingly enough, other stakeholders at lower levels in the organization were included early on, and those people were supportive and anxious to see changes made.

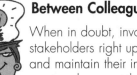

Between Colleagues

When in doubt, involve stakeholders right up-front, and maintain their involvement and support throughout the project by using face-to-face communication.

Asking the Right Questions

When negotiating a project, the questions you ask can help you get an overall perspective of the situation and anticipate any future resistance. Here are some good questions to ask your client (and perhaps others involved in the project):

- ◆ Has anything gone on in the organization that might cause difficulties for what we are doing? For example, things like downsizing or mergers?
- ◆ Are there any specific people whom you feel are going to be uncomfortable with what we are planning to do?
- ◆ Is anything coming up in the organization that I need to know about?
- ◆ What would staff say if I asked for their opinions of you (where "you" is the client hiring you)?
- ◆ Are there people who might see this project as threatening or who might lose something as a result of the project?

Ongoing Stakeholder Communication

Major stakeholders need to be cultivated throughout the project. One common error is to assume that because stakeholders have been involved at the beginning, and their ideas solicited, they will continue to be supportive. Not true.

The goal here is to make this project "their" project. It shouldn't be your project or even the CEO's or client's project. It must belong to all the players.

To ensure that the goal is reached, you need to communicate in an ongoing way with these stakeholders. The most effective way to do that is through direct contact. Face-to-face meetings are best, telephones next best. Other methods like memos and e-mail are not recommended. That's because you need to gauge where the stakeholders are at, and you can do that best in person.

Consultant Crashing

Want to fail? Contact stakeholders at the beginning of the process and then forget about them. Don't ask their opinions, and don't let them know what's going on until it's time to report.

What should this communication with stakeholders include? There are a number of things. You need to explain the purpose of the project and how it will make their lives better—it's good to remind people of this throughout. Give updates on where things stand, what's been done, and what's next. But above all, you need to ask questions of the stakeholders, and check out things as you go. Ask for their opinions and advice, and whenever possible include them in your consulting process.

Clarity Up-Front

Resistance prevention involves doing your best to ensure that everyone is clear about the project and knows who is doing what. Each person must know his or her own role and responsibilities. It's easy to assume that stakeholders will be able to read your mind and know where they fit into the whole thing. Don't make that assumption. During the contracting phase, and also when you are involving stakeholders, make sure you map out their roles and your own roles, too. This process involves you explaining, but it also works very well if you ask stakeholders how they feel they can be involved.

Between Colleagues

Here's a simple preventive step. Ask people how they think they could best contribute to addressing the issues that you were contracted to deal with. Listen.

Nonexpert Mode

Finally, let's talk about the image you project. You certainly don't want to project an image of incompetence or stupidity. Neither do you want to come across as a cocky, arrogant expert. Presenting an image like that is equivalent to painting a giant bulls eye on your back. People will resist and sabotage just to take you down a peg.

Remember, you aren't an expert until you demonstrate that you are, and you will never be as expert about a company or situation as the people who work and live in that context every day. Finally, remember that your job isn't usually to order people about, to give speeches from the mount, or pass on tablets of stone. Your job is to consult—to work with people to make something good happen.

What to Do When Resistance Happens

Prevention is great, but it's unrealistic to expect that you can totally eliminate resistance through prevention. You will face both active and passive resistance, so let's talk about tactics you can use to turn resistance into constructive outcomes. I'll explain first how to deal with active resistance and then with passive resistance.

Countering Active Resistance

You're at a meeting involving some stakeholders in your consulting project. It's early in the project, and one person, Sam, drops the boom on you. In a two-minute tirade, he lets everyone know he thinks the whole project is a waste of time. Just for effect, he drops the term "B.S." into the tirade. What do you do?

First, realize that how you handle this moment will determine whether the project fails or succeeds. Not just because Sam is being difficult, but because all the other stakeholders are watching you. Blow this one, and you lose all of them.

Here's what you don't do:

- ◆ Argue
- ◆ Try to persuade Sam of the merits of the project (yet)
- ◆ Go head-to-head with him
- ◆ Get upset, because as a professional consultant you are being paid to deal with just these situations

Here's what you should do:

- ◆ Acknowledge
- ◆ Inquire and ask for clarification
- ◆ Throw the ball back in Sam's court

Here's a response: "Sam, it's clear to me that you have serious concerns about the project, and I need to understand those" (acknowledgement). Then you ask Sam some specific questions about his concerns. Don't ask general ones, because you'll just get general answers.

Next, move to eliciting specific suggestions from Sam. You are trying to shift Sam from bashing the project to making constructive suggestions. Here's how you might put it.

"Sam, I'm sure it would help all of us here if you could offer some suggestions that you feel would be better ways to go about this. None of us wants to go in the wrong direction or waste resources, and things are flexible enough that we can change things."

If Sam stays negative, you stick with the preceding approach. Invite him to offer constructive alternatives and refuse to engage in argument.

Something else you should do, regardless of how the meeting ends, is arrange to speak to Sam in private. Use the same techniques. Acknowledge his concerns. Indicate that his opinions are important. Ask for suggestions. It's not complicated to do this, but it takes self-control and some sophisticated communication skills.

What about more private situations? What if Sam is sweet in public, but in private (with you) he is negative, nasty, and unpleasant? Same tactics. Acknowledge, and ask for input. There is one twist though. Sometimes people will take shots at you in private because they feel protected. If this happens, indicate to Sam that you feel his concerns should be heard by the rest of the stakeholders, to see if others agree with him. Then see what happens. That might stop the negative behavior and in-your-face resistance. If not, then the issue should be considered in a more public forum with the other stakeholders.

Here are some general guidelines for countering active resistance. You can apply these no matter what the situation:

Consulting Confidential

Some issues are best worked out privately, and some in groups. Dealing with objections can be done privately or publicly, but doing so privately is a good first step. With people who are nasty and unpleasant in private, it's best to deal with their concerns when others are present.

- Never argue. Limit your participation in debate.

- Don't act defensively. If your ideas are attacked, move off the attack by putting the onus on the other person to come up with better ideas.

- In group settings, keep in mind that groups will defend a person whom they see as the target of an unfair attack. Let the group support you. Invite them to express their opinions.

- Never lose your temper. In some very rare situations, expressions of passion can work, but not usually.

Dealing with Passive Resistance

The way you deal with passive resistance depends on a lot of factors, so it's hard to give a recipe for each scenario. However, here's a general pattern.

First, discover it. Second, surface it and bring it into the open. Third, deal with it as you would any active resistance once you've brought it into the open.

Generally, if you are on the ball, you will see hints that some nonconstructive things are going on in the background. You may be treated coldly by someone. Someone else may be "too busy to meet with you." Or you may just get a feeling that something is not quite right.

How do you surface resistance, when you don't know where things stand? By finding out where things stand. Approach the person, and ask if something about the project is bothering him or her. Phrase it in a helping way and not an accusatory way.

Once you've brought the resistance out in the open, ask the person if there are any specific things that would put his or her mind at rest, or would make the person more comfortable with what's being done.

This works if the number of passively resisting people is relatively small. If the number is large, then that's an indication something is seriously wrong or that you just aren't going to get people onside.

> **CAUTION**
>
> **Consultant Crashing**
>
> Do not ignore resistance if it is coming from a number of people. Don't treat it as insignificant. Reassess and diagnose the source of that resistance.

This latter situation *can* happen. You're hired to decide how to downsize a company to maximize its profits. People either know that or suspect that. In such a case, you are likely to encounter resistance no matter what you do or how you behave. Yes, you can minimize it by being compassionate, understanding, and supportive, but you aren't going to eliminate the resistance.

If you have a lot of passive resistance from multiple people, and there isn't an obvious explanation for it, look to your consulting process. Perhaps you've messed up somewhere, and the process you've chosen needs to be changed. Maybe you need more active involvement from stakeholders, or perhaps something you don't know about is operating. At this point, you go back to your client to discuss possible causes.

I'll end this chapter with a tactic I haven't mentioned before. If your client has sufficient power and positive regard within the organization, it may be necessary to further involve him or her. This involvement may be gentle: The client can lend credibility to the project by speaking to groups or individuals. Or the client's involvement may be … well, less gentle. Some projects can succeed only if the client (senior executive) lays down the law. That's not a preferred solution and is likely to drive resistance underground. It should be used as a last resort, and you should advise your client along those lines.

The Least You Need to Know

◆ Resistance is a common occurrence and is normal.

◆ A significant part of your job as a consultant is to prevent and deal effectively with resistance.

◆ Fighting resistance head-on (for example, arguing, persuading) doesn't work. Use the resistance to increase communication.

◆ Here's the resistance fighting pattern: (1) surface, (2) acknowledge, (3) send the ball to the other person's court, and (4) follow up and stay on top of things.

Consulting Situations from the Dark Side and What to Do About Them

In This Chapter

- ◆ What to do when your client is the problem
- ◆ How to deal with preconceived solutions
- ◆ When to halt project expansion
- ◆ How to discourage window-shoppers and brain-pickers

By now, you understand that consulting is not a simple process. Nor is it an easy one. Projects can go awry for a number of reasons—some connected to you and your abilities, and some connected to your client and the client's situation.

Since your job is to anticipate and deal with client-related difficulties, you should be aware of the most common difficulties that occur in the consulting process. More important, you need to understand how to handle them once you've identified them. In this chapter, I'll look at these common problems—consulting situations from the dark side—and explain how to handle them.

When Your Client Is the Problem

After reading the previous chapters in this book, you now understand that your clients aren't perfect, right? Bottom line: If your clients were perfect, they wouldn't need you. If your clients always made good decisions and understood their own problems, they wouldn't need you. Keep those thoughts in mind. Dealing with difficult consulting situations is part of your job.

Between Colleagues

Clients tend to see themselves in an overly positive light and can be blind to their own contributions to their difficulties. Part of your job is to help them define their own nonconstructive contributions.

Since you will come across situations in which your client (or people associated with the project) create barriers to project success, you should have a general strategy for dealing with these situations. I'll distinguish between two different contexts, since each needs to be handled somewhat differently. First, what if your direct client is the problem? Second, what if the problem lies with other people in the organization and not specifically with your direct client?

The Client from the Dark Side

You've been working on a project and, truth to tell, it doesn't feel right. In fact, the information you get is that the consulting project is being negatively affected by the actions of the person who hired you, or by the perceptions people have of that person. What might that situation look like?

Perhaps your direct client is a poor leader or manager. Maybe the person is too authoritarian, isn't a good decision maker, or has poor people skills—there's a wide range of behaviors your direct client could engage in to interfere with the project. Or the client may be totally blind to the causes connected to the reason why you were hired in the first place. What do you do?

Consulting Confidential

A common problem occurs when a client hires you to solve a problem in the organization. After collecting data and hearing from other people in the organization (and observing the client directly), you are sure the problem is actually caused by the person who hired you. This happens more often than you'd think. Always be prepared.

Here's the strategy:

- Surface the newly identified cause.
- Present data and impressions.
- Clarify with client.
- Explain consequences.
- Pursue agreement on new course of action.

Let's walk through these steps with the help of the following scenario. Here's the situation. Mary is the CEO of a company and has hired you to address what she perceives as poor morale and work teams that aren't working together very well. When you begin talking to people in the organization, patterns emerge. You learn that many of the employees in the organization have negative perceptions of the CEO. They see Mary as unable to delegate responsibility and too involved in the everyday decisions that should be made by the work teams. You realize that no matter what you do with the employees (for example, team building), unless Mary does things differently, nothing will change.

The Steps Explained

Begin by broaching this subject with your client. In other words, *surface the issue.* There's no way around this. You *must* involve your client in solving this problem, and it has to be done promptly. How do you do it? Here's an example.

Working Words

Surfacing the issue means that you take a problem or issue that lurks below the surface and you shine a light on it so people can discuss it and deal with it in the open.

In a private meeting (only you and Mary present), you say: "Mary, I've spent the last week talking to people in your organization, and I think that you do indeed have some team issues that we need to look at. I think they can be addressed, but I'm going to need your help. Can I run through some of the things I've found out, and where I think we need to go?"

After you get consent, continue: "As we talked about when you hired me, I think there are some barriers to effective team functioning. Some have to do with the way the teams are structured, some have to do with a lack of team skills, and some have to do with your involvement in the team process. I can help you with the first two, but you and I need to work together to solve the third one."

Notice that you are broaching the subject in a nonthreatening and nonblaming way. This is the approach you must use throughout the process.

Next you *present your data* more specifically, with a brief interpretation of that data. It might sound like this: "Mary, a number of team leaders have mentioned that they feel they would have better team functioning if you gave them more decision-making authority and stood back a bit more from the everyday decision-making process. I think that's something worth pursuing before we plan on doing any other team-related intervention."

If you have more-specific data, this is where you use it, keeping in mind that you should never identify the specific sources of the data.

Consultant Crashing

When talking with the client, you must protect the confidentiality or sources of your information. If you say something like, "Tom said you're a lousy manager," you've broken an implicit or explicit "contract" with the people you have to work with.

Now you *clarify*. The clarification process shifts the conversation away from you and your findings, and onto the perceptions of the client. It could sound like this: "Mary, is it possible that there is something to this? Are there areas where you feel you could change the way you do things to help support the teams?"

At this point, one of two things will happen. Mary may say yes, and then the conversation turns to the establishment of a new course of action agreement. You may be able to skip the next step, explanation of consequences, although it's still good to walk the client through them.

The second result may be that Mary is resistant to the notion that she needs to change what she does. Then it's time to *describe the consequences* of doing nothing in that area.

You could do so like this: "Mary, I know you anticipated doing some team-building sessions to improve productivity here, and that's still a good idea. But even if we do that, and employees learn new skills, I don't believe you are going to get what you want. In fact, if we do that, and everything else stays the same, things may get worse. At best you'd be wasting your money on those activities. On the other hand, if you're willing to make a few small changes in how you deal with the teams, I think you will get what you are looking for. So that you have some idea of what I'm recommending, I'll just go through two or three things you can do that might be helpful, okay?"

Notice you're telling Mary that it's not to her benefit to maintain the status quo. You're also doing this in a nonblaming way, and hopefully in a nonthreatening way.

Mary will either buy in or continue to resist. If she continues to resist, then you continue to try to explain consequences and deal with the resistance by trying to surface her feelings and objections about making changes.

Between Colleagues

When giving recommendations that involve changes in your direct client's behavior, limit your suggestions to two or three things. Don't overwhelm the client, since that's guaranteed to create anger and defensiveness.

Whether Mary buys in to this or not, the final step involves *creating agreement* on a new course of action. If she's "with you," then the discussion continues, and you provide a few recommendations about what Mary can do and a course of action to implement those recommendations. If she's not "with you," you have decisions to make. Do you continue with the original plan? Do you alter it somewhat? Can you live with the consequences of not dealing with the major barrier to better team functioning? Can Mary?

That's the basic process. If you handle it well, you have a pretty good chance of getting the client onboard.

What If the Barriers Lie with Other Stakeholders?

You may encounter a situation in which the barriers lie not with the direct client, but with people who work for the direct client, or other stakeholders. For example, midmanagers may balk at the consulting process, treating it with suspicion and resisting throughout the whole process. Or, employees may not be forthcoming with information or involvement.

You have two options for handling people who are being uncooperative. The first is to use the strategy just described. It works equally well with direct clients and stakeholders. Your second option is to work with your direct client to devise a strategy that will encourage other stakeholders to participate more enthusiastically.

That strategy may involve invoking the power and authority of the client. It may involve more active support and persuasion on the part of your client. At its extreme the direct client may exert significant pressure on other stakeholders, although that should be left as a last resort.

> **Consultant Crashing**
>
> Clients with power are sometimes too quick to use it in consulting situations. It's your job to rein in this power. Ordering or coercing people to cooperate only drives resistance underground, where you can't deal with it. That's often what happens if the approach is too heavy-handed.

Dealing with the Client with Preconceived Solutions

From the consultant's point of view, the best situation occurs when the client has an open mind and has not overconstrained the range of solutions, or even how the problem is defined. That's not always the case. Clients may not contact you until they've already identified the problem and its causes and decided on a solution.

That wouldn't be a bad thing, except that in many cases the client's preconceived notions are wrong. If you go along with the subtle or not so subtle pressure to implement a specific solution, you can end up in charge of a consulting project that will not benefit anyone.

There are two main points of intervention when working with such clients. One involves identifying the situation during the contracting phase and dealing with it before the project begins. The second involves working with the client during the project to help "open the client's mind."

Let's look at each of these interventions.

Dealing with Preconceptions from Square One

You need to assume that most clients are going to have some preconceptions about the causes of their concerns and will have some possible solutions as well. Where clients vary is in their willingness to entertain the possibility that their preconceptions are inaccurate or not complete. It's your job to encourage open-mindedness from the beginning of a project. If you set this up properly, the client will be more receptive to your interpretations throughout the life of the project.

You may recall that in Chapter 7, "Beginning the Consulting Intervention," I discussed the difference between the presenting problem and the root problem. Let's review. The *presenting problem* is the problem or issue that is put on the table by your client. The *root problem* is the actual problem that must be addressed for success. They are not always the same thing.

At the beginning of the project, your task is to use your skills to encourage the client to be open to the root problem. The best way to explain how this works is to look at an example.

It's your first meeting with Jack, your prospective client. His company, at least according to Jack, has high overhead and lower productivity than he would like. He's looking for a consultant to come in and recommend where staff can be cut. That's the presenting problem. As a seasoned consultant, you know there are a lot of factors that may contribute to low productivity, and that cutting staff may not be the solution. At this point you don't know what's needed. However, your goal is to ensure that your solutions will be given credence even if they differ from Jack's preconceptions. How do you lay this groundwork?

Now is the place to use your questioning skills. By using questions, you gather information, of course, but you also broach the subject of alternative interpretations. Here are some questions you can use:

> **Consulting Confidential**
>
> Clients always have preconceived ideas about the nature of their problems and possible solutions. If clients are open-minded, those preconceptions need not be problematic. It's the close-minded clients, the ones who already "know the score," who are the challenges. It's often these people who contribute actively to their own problems.

> **Between Colleagues**
>
> Treat client preconceptions as hypotheses that must be tested. Don't accept them blindly. Neither should you throw them out until you have determined they are not accurate.

- How sure are you that your productivity is lower than it should be?

- What evidence do you have that you might have too many employees?

- How committed are you to reducing your staff?

- If we find there are other ways to solve the productivity issue, would that be something you could live with? (You might provide examples.)

Do you see what you are doing here? You are trying to create some doubt in the mind of the client about his preconceived way of looking at the problem.

You're also determining whether you should go ahead with the project. It may be that you judge the preconceptions to be so strong that this project would not be worth undertaking, because it's going to fail.

Dealing with Preconceptions During a Project

If you lay the groundwork for open-mindedness from the beginning, you are much less likely to have to deal with preconceptions during a project, at least from your direct client. If preconceptions do occur, you would use the techniques discussed in Chapter 24, "Facing and Dealing with Resistance."

You are most likely to hit preconception barriers during (a) preliminary reports and communication and (b) at the point where you present your final recommendations but before the implementation phase.

Now you have to rely on your persuasive skills and your ability to explain how you've arrived at your conclusions. Your client thinks the solution is to do "x," and you've concluded that another course of action is indicated. Explain your conclusions. Present data. And most important, run through the consequences of doing "x" versus following the course of action you've outlined.

It may be that your client refuses to accept your conclusions. That's part of the consulting game. If that's the case, you have the choice of continuing along the path the client wants or ending your involvement.

The Creeping, Growing, Changing Project

Clients have a habit of adding new pieces to projects. One thing about consulting projects, they don't seem to grow smaller over time; they get bigger. This isn't too much of a problem if you charge an hourly rate, but if you charge a total project fee, you can end up doing more and more for the same fee. Here's a quick example from the information technology field.

You're a computer consultant and your client retains you to design a database system. Seems simple and straightforward. You work with the client to define the needs of the system and the content of the database. After you've started developing the system, the client phones you and wants three more fields of information added. Several days later, the client wants something else added. And on and on. You end up having to do a lot of reworking.

What's the solution to this problem? Use a drop-dead date. What's that? A *drop-dead date* is the final date that changes can be introduced into a project. So with the consent of the client, you set a date after which no additions or changes can be incorporated. The idea here is to encourage the client to think through everything beforehand, so you don't have to rework everything.

This works well for projects in which the solution is fairly clear up-front. To make a drop-dead date work, you should also use the *sign-off* process, in which all parties agree to the final details or plan.

Between Colleagues

If you use a drop-dead date, always have a sign-off meeting just prior to the drop-dead date. It's also good to have a sign-off document that specifies the details of the finalized project.

Here's how it works. As the drop-dead date approaches, you sit down with your client and define the final specifications of the solution. In our database example, it might mean defining the data fields, the reports needed, and so on. To proceed, your client (and any significant stakeholders) must sign off, or agree, to these final specifications.

From that point the project is pretty much etched in stone.

The Flawed Implementation Situation

We all like to have our ideas implemented and implemented in ways that work for the client. If there's one thing that drives consultants nuts, it's situations in which the recommendations are used but the way in which they are applied almost guarantees failure.

There are two kinds of flawed implementation situations, each somewhat different. One applies if you have been retained not only to offer recommendations, but also to be involved in implementing them. The second applies if your role in the project officially ends at the point you tender your suggestions.

Between Colleagues

The key to implementation success is for you to be involved in it, either informally, through follow-ups, or more formally, as part of the contract. You should follow up anyway, even if it's not part of your formal responsibilities.

When You Haven't Been Contracted to Implement

Chapter 10, "The End Game—Recommending, Reporting, Implementing," discussed consultants who make recommendations, and consultants who both recommend and implement. Obviously it's easier to ensure that the implementation process is done correctly if you are contracted to do so. What if you aren't? Are there things you can do to increase the probability the client will do it "right"?

Yes, and again the watchword is prevention.

First, your final report (or recommendation) should be detailed enough that it provides enough information to the client to implement. Consider including a detailed action plan and specifying critical points and possible pitfalls that are likely to occur in the implementation process. The more general your recommendations, the more likely the implementation is going to get messed up.

Doing such detailed reports may require more work on your part. It's worth the investment. What you are doing is increasing your value to the client. You are also more likely to enhance your consulting reputation if clients find they can implement your suggestions *and* receive the results they hoped for. It's a small but valuable use of your time.

> **Consulting Confidential**
>
> Some consultants actually window-shop or pick the brains of their colleagues. This is a bad thing. The most common tactic is for a consultant to pretend to be a potential client in order to determine what to charge for his or her own services. It's tacky.

Second, even if you aren't officially involved in the implementation in an ongoing way, you can contribute to it. Here are two possibilities. As part of your initial contract, indicate you will be available on a limited basis as an implementation troubleshooter. Factor that into your fee structure. The idea here is that if the client encounters glitches, you are available to guide him or her through.

The second possibility is simply to follow up on an informal basis. This is highly recommended. Let's say you submit a final report containing a number of suggestions, and your official involvement ended at that point. There's nothing stopping you from contacting the client to find out (a) how the implementation is going and (b) whether you can provide additional help, on either a paid or unpaid basis.

There are huge benefits to following up like this. It shows you are concerned with your client's welfare. It's a good way of creating repeat business with that client. And, of course, you keep a hand in increasing the success of the implementation.

The one caution is to make sure you don't get roped into doing too much free work.

An Assortment of Difficult Situations

Of course, there are a number of other situations you may encounter. In the previous chapters I've discussed many of them, but let's review.

The Delayed Approval Client

You've met with the client. She indicates they "probably" will hire you. "I'll call you by the fifth," she says. No call by the fifth. You follow up. No decision has been made. This occurs several times. What do you do?

First, consider how much you need the business? If you really need it, you can hang in there. What you must consider, though, is whether the client's current behavior is going to continue once you have the contract. So the bottom-line question is, "Do I want to work with a client who moves so slowly?"

> **CAUTION**
>
> **Consultant Crashing**
>
> Consultants who allow themselves to be "kept waiting" for approval are likely to end up also "waiting" during critical parts of their consulting projects. Assume that slow-to-approve clients are also going to be slow-to-do-everything clients.

Here's one option. Clarify where the delays lie. That won't speed up the process of approval, but it gives you additional information you may need during the project. The reasons for the delay are critical. Maybe the CEO is in Pango Pango. Or maybe there is internal disagreement about hiring you. If it's the former, it doesn't mean much. If it's the latter, you need to know.

Finally, give a drop-dead date. Indicate to your client that if you do not have a firm go-ahead by the specified date, you will assume the answer is no and you will allocate your time elsewhere.

Window-Shoppers and Brain-Pickers

Believe it or not, some clients are window-shoppers or, worse, brain-pickers. The window-shopper is just testing the waters and isn't serious about hiring a consultant. The brain-picker is worse. He or she pretends to be interested in hiring you but does so to get free advice. Again, there's no intention to pay you for your expertise.

The problem is that you cannot definitively distinguish who is a serious prospective client and who is window-shopping or brain-picking. The nature of consulting is that you are occasionally going to put in time trying to get contracts from people who will never hire you.

If you absolutely refuse to give details of how you would handle a consulting project, you are going to lose legitimate prospects. The best you can do is limit your wasted time, since you can't eliminate these kind of people. Here are a few tips.

When asked to prepare a written proposal, indicate that any proposal is tentative and that the details have to be worked out once the contract is signed. This is a legitimate condition, since you determine the details only after data gathering. You might map out how you would work to define the problem, but at the proposal stage you haven't done that work yet. Hence, you can't provide detailed solutions.

Limit the time you will spend on initial contracting meetings. For example, indicate to prospective clients that you will be glad to spend an hour (or whatever seems reasonable) to discuss their needs. If they decide to go further, then you must have an agreement in place.

Again, use drop-dead dates. Have an initial meeting. At the end of that meeting, make sure you and the client agree on a date at which the project becomes dead. If the client wants more involvement after that date, consider carefully whether it's worth your time.

Between Colleagues

When placing a limit on contracting meetings, consider the size of the potential contract. The larger the contract, the more time you should spend.

The Least You Need to Know

- When the client is the problem, use this strategy: Surface, present data, clarify, explain consequences, and renew agreement.
- Client preconceptions are best dealt with during the contracting phase.
- Follow-up is important to ensure your recommendations are implemented successfully.
- Limit your lost time with window-shoppers and brain-pickers, but recognize you can't totally eliminate them.

Chapter 26

Best Professional Development Resources on the Planet

In This Chapter

◆ Find out which books are "must-reads" for consultants.

◆ Develop your specialized skills.

◆ Learn more about the business side.

◆ Sharpen your consulting process skills.

One of the central themes of this book is that the consultant's stock-in-trade is made up of the skills, knowledge, and wisdom related to the consulting process and the consultant's specialization.

I've focused on what you need to know to begin a consulting practice, but it's understood that consulting success is based on a commitment to expand your abilities and stay up-to-date in your field. Professional development isn't a nicety, but a necessity.

This chapter is dedicated to identifying both specific and general resources you can use to develop your abilities. Some resources are specific. For

Between Colleagues

Here's a quick tip: Each month read at least one book that helps you develop your business skills or your consulting skills. Do this forever.

example, I suggest some "must-read" books. Other resources are more general. You may have to do some searching to find these resources in your local area. Some of the suggestions are free or low-cost. Others can be more costly.

Remember one thing: The more you learn, the more you have to offer your clients. And that means more business and a more successful consulting practice.

Absolutely Must-Reads for All Consultants

I can't overstate the importance of professional and personal development. Focus on building your skills related to the consulting process and the business side of consulting.

There are hundreds of books about these topics. Are there writers who stand head-and-shoulders above the rest? Yes. Peter Block and Herman Holtz are almost mandatory.

The Work of Peter Block

If there is a single person regarded as the "professor" of consulting, it must be Peter Block. A consultant since 1966, one of his specialties is providing seminars for consultants, but he's also written several books on the consulting profession.

Unlike some "gurus" who tend to deliver less than their hype would suggest, Peter Block is the real deal, and his reputation is rightly deserved.

Many people consider Block's book *Flawless Consulting—A Guide to Getting Your Expertise Used* as the consultant's bible. Its focus isn't so much on the business end of the consulting business but on the process of building successful relationships with clients. Even though this book emphasizes business and management consulting, make no mistake about it: It applies to any consulting relationship, simple or complex, regardless of context.

Between Colleagues

Some books are worth buying; some can be borrowed just as well from the library. If you buy only two books on the consulting process (besides this one), it's worth buying the books by Peter Block described here.

If you've never read it, get it. It's published by Jossey-Bass. Most bookstores should be able to order it for you, or you can order online via amazon.com: www. amazon.com/exec/obidos/ASIN/0787948039/ bacalassoci.

You might also consider another book by Peter Block, *The Flawless Consulting Fieldbook and Companion*, also published by Jossey-Bass. It's a "field book" with lots of examples, including dialogues between consultant and client.

The Work of Herman Holtz

If Peter Block is the "don't miss" expert on consulting process and skill, Herman Holtz may be the most prolific writer on the subject of the business of consulting. It's hard to count the number of books he has published on the subject, but it's probably in excess of 100.

Since there are so many, it's difficult to recommend any specific one beyond *How to Succeed as an Independent Consultant*, published by John Wiley & Sons. While it does not neglect the process of consulting, its strength is that it covers so many of the business aspects involved in the consulting business. Whether you want to enhance your understanding of proposals and proposal writing, marketing, fees, presentation, or dozens of other topics, this book is highly recommended.

Since he has published so many books, your local bookstore is unlikely to carry more than a very few. I'd recommend researching his books on the Internet from amazon.com. Unfortunately, Mr. Holtz passed away in 2000, so there will be no more new books by him.

Between Colleagues

Don't forget about your public library system. Of course it's an invaluable resource for books, but it is also great for finding professional associations and other more obscure items. Don't be shy about approaching your reference librarian for help.

Developing in Your Specialization

I've said it before. Consulting skills + expertise in your specialization = consulting success. So how do you develop, expand, and update your knowledge in your own specialization? Let's look at some resources.

The Articles Indexing Directory Project

For those of you involved in business consulting of any sort, one of the best online resources is the Articles Indexing Directory Project. It contains articles on over 60 work-related topics (for example, human resources, quality improvement, training, workplace violence). There's also material on business practices, ethics, and the consulting process.

This site happens to be one of my own sites, developed initially to help me research various

Consultant Crashing

Don't feel you have to follow any specific path for professional development. There are so many ways to learn. You should identify the ways you prefer to learn (alone, in groups, by reading, online) and pursue those first. That way, professional development activities are more enjoyable.

business topics. When I found that it took me too long to find relevant articles on the Internet, I started keeping the best ones in a directory. As my directory evolved, I decided to make it available to the public at no charge.

The directory contains articles reviewed for quality and relevance on a wide range of work-related topics. New articles are added regularly. At the time of this writing, there are over 1,200 articles listed. The only problem is that you can spend days on the site! Access it with any website browser by going to www.articles911.com.

Internet Search Engines

The Internet can be a great resource for developing your specialty-related skills. Regardless of the areas you practice in, you are bound to find information about what's going on in your field and find other people with whom you can share expertise.

As I've already mentioned, it's also an ideal way to research books you might want to buy. It's always available, and you don't have to trek to the local library.

The problem is that there is *so* much information available about almost everything, it's hard to find what you want. The solution is to learn how to use Internet search engines efficiently. Search engines provide the ability to search the Internet for information based on specific search terms. For example, let's say you want information about consulting seminars offered by Peter Block. You'd go to a search site, enter the words "Peter Block consulting seminar," and you'd get a list of sites with information on that topic.

> **Consulting Confidential**
>
> If you don't have access to the Internet, you should probably arrange it. However, there are other alternatives. Most public libraries and "Internet cafes" offer Internet access for a nominal fee, or even for free.

Search engines aren't equal. Some are excellent. Some are terrible. The good ones tend to index more of the Net than the terrible ones and are better at giving you what you want, and only what you want. That said, finding things on the Internet always takes longer than you'd expect.

My recommendation for the preferred search engine? Google.com appears to have one of the largest and most up-to-date indexes. Probably not as good are the search engines Yahoo.com and overture.com (formerly goto.com). They have decent content, but websites now pay to be included. That sometimes causes the search results to be less useful.

Consider using search engines to find …

- ◆ Professional associations relevant to your specialty and close to your location.
- ◆ Books related to your specialty.
- ◆ Others in your field with whom you might interact.

◆ Special-interest discussion lists on topics important to your professional development.

Professional Associations/Conferences

Consider getting involved in professional associations. These are usually not-for-profit organizations that bring together people from specific professions. For example, there are associations or societies for engineers, doctors, trainers, human resources professionals—almost any group you can think of.

There are several kinds of associations. If you are interested in staying in touch with people in your specialization, regardless of whether or not they are consultants, look for an association specifically targeted to your specialty. If you are interested in learning from people in your specialty who are also consultants, that's a narrower field. It's easier to find the former than the latter, but you'd be surprised how many associations cater specifically to consultants. Here are some examples:

Between Colleagues

Not only should you consider joining an association, but consider contributing to it in some way. This kind of volunteer work puts you in touch with more people and is a great networking opportunity.

◆ National Bureau of Professional Management Consultants

◆ Professional and Technical Consultants Association

◆ National Association of Legal Search Consultants

◆ National Association of Computer Consultants

◆ Association of Bridal Consultants

◆ American Association of Healthcare Consultants

One caution about associations: Some are legitimate and recognized not-for-profit associations; however, some are run by individuals to turn a profit and may be disguised as non-profit. Look for the first. Shy away from the second. Look for associations that have regular elections to choose their executive officers. That's a distinguishing feature of legitimate associations.

National associations often have local chapters that hold regular meetings and publish regular newsletters. Both can keep you up-to-date in your field. Some associations, particularly large ones, hold major yearly conferences. While attending can be expensive, conferences are really the best way to find out what's going on in your field. Best of all, they tend to be exceedingly energizing and refreshing.

Some companies put on conferences on a "for profit" basis. Some of these conferences can be excellent. Some are not useful due to the level of commercialism. It's always good to ask around and get the opinions of others who might have attended in the past.

Between Colleagues

Conferences can be expensive to attend and often require travel. Try to attend a minimum of one large conference once every two years—more if possible. Put aside the money. Before choosing a conference, ask around about quality.

Finding associations and conferences can be challenging. Probably the best way is to ask others in your field. Failing that, Internet search engines can be helpful. For example, let's say you are interested in human resources associations. You could search using the following words: "human resources association." To find something in your area, you might add your province or state to the search words. Substitute "conference" for "association" if you are looking for conferences.

Teaching as a Way of Learning

Here's something many people don't think of as a professional development activity. Consider teaching courses at your local college or adult education institution. How can this help you develop your content knowledge?

Teaching forces you to stay current and learn your topics well enough to teach them to others. You'll also find that teaching provides an opportunity to learn from the participants in your classes. Since many of the participants will be from your target market, they will help you keep current about potential clients' concerns and issues.

One side benefit is that you develop new contacts in your community, and that can help in business development.

Developing Your Business Skills

If you work in a very specialized field, keeping up can be difficult, since there may not be that many resources for professional development in your specialty. Not so for business skills. Whether you need to learn how to write a proposal, prepare a loan application, market more effectively, or design your own brochures, it's likely you'll find resources in your local area. The best part is these resources may not be costly at all.

Free or Almost-Free Expert Help

If you are new to the business side of things, you may not know that governments sponsor organizations that can help you with the intricacies of both starting and running small businesses. They exist to help develop the small business sector, which is a major component of the economy.

In the United States, there is an organization called the Small Business Administration (SBA for short). The best way to learn about its services is to visit its website (www.sbaonline.sba.gov) or contact your local SBA office. Here's a brief rundown of what it offers.

The SBA offers extensive services for start-up businesses, including information about local laws, developing business plans, and much more. Also available is personal and private counseling help related to your business issues.

The SBA's "Small Business Classroom" offers online courses in a number of areas, including business planning, e-commerce, and self-assessment. Its Internet site includes over 3,000 links to other useful and often-free resources.

There's so much available from the SBA that I can't even scratch the surface, but this is a "do not miss" resource.

If you are in Canada, a similar service is run jointly by the provincial and federal governments. The various offices are referred to as "Canada Business Service Centres" (note the Canadian spelling of "centre"). They offer services and information in French and English and have online help. You can visit their provincial offices or access their information by phone or fax.

They offer a small business toolbox, explanations of relevant government programs, and various information guides. For more information about the Canada Business Service Centres, go online to www.cbsc.org. Regional offices also have good business-related libraries. One particularly nice feature is that there are toll-free lines to each of the provincial offices.

> **Consulting Confidential**
>
> Prior to the Internet, you'd have to actually live in a country to take advantage of the services its government supplies to small business. Nowadays, with so much online, you can use at least some of a government's resources via the Internet. If you live in another country, don't hesitate to visit these sites in addition to finding out what your own government supplies.

Education and Training Possibilities

Unless you live in a remote location, chances are you have access to education and training opportunities. Many of these are available fairly cheaply.

Opportunities range from entering a formal degree program at a university, enrolling in a college certificate program, or taking courses offered by extension or adult education institutions, including your local school boards. The first two require longer-term

Between Colleagues

Local, short courses offered by school boards or some adult education schools tend to be practical but sometimes lack depth. University courses tend to be a little less practical but provide more depth. Choose according to your needs.

commitments and fit best if you want to acquire formal or academic qualifications. They can be expensive. The third requires only that you be available for the hours the course is offered. Some may require a commitment of a few weeks, once a week; some more. Costs are generally low, and teachers are usually drawn from the community and have a lot of practical knowledge and experience.

Where to start? Every university, college, and most school boards offer adult education courses. Contact these organizations and ask about their adult education courses.

If you happen to live in a very isolated or rural area that lacks resources close by, don't despair. Over the last 10 years or so, more and more organizations have set up distance learning programs, where you can learn, and even obtain degrees, without having to attend "live." Using various methods, including the Internet, videos, projects, and so on, these can be useful. Contact universities or colleges in your state or province to inquire. If they don't have anything suitable, you can look farther afield, since distance really isn't an issue.

Get Mentored, Get Networked

What's a mentor? A *mentor* is someone with experience, knowledge, and wisdom who agrees to take you under his or her wing, to help you develop. Generally it's someone you already know, like, and respect. While some people actually look for a mentor as if they were looking for a job, and see it as some sort of formal arrangement, I don't think it works that way. You can be "mentored" by a number of people, and you need not call it mentoring. Personally, I call it "having lunch" or "getting together for a drink" or "picking someone's brain."

Consulting Confidential

Most people (even consultants) are willing to share their expertise with newer members of the profession. After all, it's flattering. When you have the opportunity to share your expertise, do so. Give back to the community.

Regardless of how you set this up, the point is to learn from that person. For example, let's say you attend a chamber of commerce get-together and meet a few people with business know-how. You can approach them to ask if they'd mind if you call them once in a while to pick their brains. Over time, these relationships may become full-fledged mentoring relationships.

I've spoken about the importance of networking as a business strategy and as a method of marketing yourself. I believe the most significant advantage to building a network is to learn. Make the effort to build relationships with a range of people with different abilities and skills, and you will have readily available help and opportunities to learn.

Developing Your Consulting Skills

Developing and improving your consulting skills is very similar to developing your business acumen, except it's a bit more difficult to find resources.

Let's summarize your options. Most of the options in the following list are ones that I've already mentioned. However, the last three are new ones, and I'll focus on them in the next sections.

You can build your consulting skills in the following ways:

◆ Reading

◆ Joining a consultant's association or group, local or national

◆ Developing relationships with potential mentors

◆ Drawing on a network of more-experienced consultants

◆ Attending conferences for consultants

◆ Attending training seminars for consultants

◆ Attending training seminars not designed specifically for consultants but that address skills often used by consultants

◆ Accessing professional Internet-based discussion groups

The last three deserve a bit more discussion.

Attending Training Seminars for Consultants

You can learn a lot about the consulting process and develop your skills by attending seminars designed to teach you about the consulting process. Or, you may learn very little. Since fees for these kinds of courses can be quite high, let me give you a few tips about how to decide what to attend, or even *if* you should attend.

Between Colleagues

So many consulting skills are common to other professions. Consider taking more-generic courses in things like negotiation, public speaking, and group dynamics, even if they aren't designed specifically for consultants.

I'm not a fan of a lot of training for consultants. There's good stuff out there, but keep in mind that anybody can offer such a course just by announcing they are doing so. In looking at options, here's a list of things I'd suggest:

◆ Try to contact the seminar leaders and talk to them before registering. Ask them about content and process.

◆ Consider paying more and going to a seminar offered by a leading authority. Going to a seminar put on by Peter Block's company, although it may cost more and require travel, could be worth much more than a local, lower-cost seminar.

◆ Before registering, talk to peers about their experience with the program in question. Ask the offering company for references.

◆ Make sure the seminar leader has experience and a track record in areas similar to your practice area.

◆ Look for a money-back guarantee.

Training Courses to Learn Often-Needed Skills

While I think it's worthwhile to attend a seminar designed specifically for consultants, it may be more practical and beneficial to build skills you use as a consultant but are not specific to the consulting process. These seminars are more likely to be available locally, since they are not quite so specialized. What kinds of skills and seminars do I recommend?

Here's a list of skill areas relevant to the consulting process. In fact, I consider them essential to the consulting process. You should be able to find seminars on these topics in your area:

◆ Listening

◆ Facilitation and group skills

◆ Negotiation

◆ Conflict management

◆ Public speaking and other communication skills

◆ Mediation skills

Professional Internet Discussion Lists

While the Internet is useful for finding information, one of its greatest strengths is its ability to allow you to get in touch with other consultants and pick their brains. I think it's worthwhile to seek out and join discussion lists where people of like mind and interest hang out and share information or help each other with professional issues. The discussions on these lists are public, so you can get help and tips from a number of people, many of them with significant expertise in the consulting arena.

Just to give you an idea of what's available, let me tell you what's around in my areas of practice. I am involved in discussion lists on training, human resources, performance management, conflict, and workplace communication, to name a few. On those lists are practitioners, employees, and other consultants interested in the same subjects. I can learn not only by participating, but also by simply reading the messages that come through. At the very least, they help me keep a finger on the pulse and keep current. I find the most benefit from discussions dealing with some of the thorny issues most consultants face.

How do you find professional discussion lists on the Internet? Try visiting www.egroups.com and www.topica.com, since they are the most common hosts for these kinds of lists. Those sites can explain how to participate, and you can search these sites to find lists of interest. Once you find a list of interest, you can probably ask list members about other resources. That's the easiest way.

Consultant Crashing

Don't be a discussion list "taker." If you help others, people will be willing to help you. If you participate only when you need something, people will be less helpful.

The Least You Need to Know

♦ An effective consultant is someone who keeps learning and makes professional development an ongoing commitment.

♦ Highly recommended are books by Peter Block and Herman Holtz.

♦ Read at least one book a month to expand your skills in your specialization or to develop your consulting skills.

♦ Professional associations, mentoring, and making use of your professional network are all an important part of continuous professional development.

Appendix A

Glossary

autoresponder A program that automatically responds to a received e-mail by sending material you have previously specified.

billable time The time for which you will be directly compensated, the financial bedrock of your practice.

bonus A reward for achieving specific objectives as negotiated and specified in the original contract.

branding Creating an awareness and familiarity with the name of the product or company, along with positive associations.

competitive edge Something you have to offer or some characteristics of your services and company that competitors do not have or cannot deliver.

consulting A process that involves a disinterested or neutral party in the provision of advice, problem solving, and services, and the application of a number of tools specific to the consulting role.

discussion list *See* professional discussion list.

drop-dead date The final date that the client can introduce changes to the project.

executive summary A short, concise description of the project, its purpose, and your recommendations, usually at the beginning of your report.

e-zine An electronic document usually sent via e-mail to people who have subscribed voluntarily, with content including useful information, articles, and updates, limited only by your imagination.

implicit contract *See* psychological or implicit contract.

income insurance Insurance that compensates you if you are unable to work for an extended period of time, usually as a result of health problems.

infrastructure development Acquiring the equipment you need to succeed.

iterative process A process that repeats. The answers may be different each time, but the process itself is the same.

liability insurance Insurance that protects you against claims and legal actions related to any harm, real or alleged, that might occur as a result of your consulting business.

milestones "Success points" or points in the project where significant interim goals have been met.

multiple income streams Different ways and sources of making money.

navigation bar (or menu) A small portion of your web page that shows and links to the major sections on your site.

niche A relatively narrow area of practice or corner of the consulting world, one where you have considerable expertise and where you have a significant competitive advantage over your competitors.

noncompete clause A contractual agreement that you will not practice in the same area of specialization for some particular period of time after you have left the company.

overhead time The time you spend that is not directly compensated for by the client; it includes marketing, client meetings, and paperwork (like making sure your taxes are in order).

presenting problem The surface-level issue or problem presented to you by the client.

probing Using follow-up questions that are based on what the respondent has told you, for the purpose of refining the person's answer.

process skills The tools every consultant needs and uses to ensure that his or her advice and recommendations are as informed as possible; process skills include interpersonal communication, group facilitation, data gathering, and diagnostic skills.

professional discussion list A forum (usually conducted via e-mail) that is focused on a particular profession, interest, or process.

professionalism The image you project through competence, actions, and words that makes you a trusted and reputable practitioner in the eyes of your clients and colleagues.

psychological or implicit contract Includes the formal arrangements you make with a client *plus* a set of assumptions about the project that may or may not be shared by consultant and client.

qualifying a client   Determining whether your potential client is likely to hire you or not.

request for proposal (RFP)   A formal document sent to potential consultants that outlines the specifics of a consulting project and requests proposals to address the consulting need.

resistance   A normal part of the consulting process, characterized by an unwillingness to give credibility to the project, a desire to avoid involvement, or hesitation to implement advice.

signature line   A short statement your e-mail program places at the end of your e-mails, which you set up in your e-mail program.

skills cascading   Using your existing skills to provide opportunities for you to learn new things that will be of value.

spam   Unsolicited and almost universally hated e-mail; also known as junk e-mail.

specialty-related skills and knowledge   The basic and advanced knowledge and skills required to work in your chosen field and needed in order for you to provide expert advice to clients *and* be seen as credible by prospective clients.

stakeholder   A person whose involvement is necessary for your project to succeed and/or a person who will be affected by the consulting project.

surfacing the issue   Taking a problem or issue that lurks below the surface and shining a light on it so people can discuss it and deal with it in the open.

targeted exposure   Getting your message to those who need your services and are in hiring positions.

targeted traffic   Website traffic that comes from people who are in positions to help your business or purchase what you provide—in other words, decision makers or people in positions to advise decision makers.

unintended outcome   A by-product or side effect of a course of action, generally not anticipated, but sometimes foreseeable.

zoning bylaws   Usually city laws that restrict (or permit) particular activities to specific parts of the city.

Resources

If this book has served to get you more interested in consulting than ever, there are lots of places you can go for additional information and help.

Further Reading

In Chapter 26, "Best Professional Development Resources on the Planet," I gave you some books I consider to be among the most useful to consultants. I include a few more here.

Ashford, Martin. *Con Tricks: The Shadowy World of Management Consultancy and How to Make It Work for You.* New York: Simon & Schuster, 2000.

Biech, Elaine. *The Business of Consulting: The Basics and Beyond.* San Francisco: Pfeiffer & Co., 1998.

———. *The Consultant's Quick Start Guide: An Action Plan for Your First Year in Business.* New York: John Wiley & Sons, 2001.

Biech, Elaine, and Linda Byars Swindling, Esq. *The Consultant's Legal Guide.* San Francisco: Jossey-Bass, 2000.

Cohen, William. *How to Make It Big as a Consultant.* 3rd ed. New York: AMACOM, 2001.

Cope, Mick. *The Seven Cs of Consulting: Your Complete Blueprint for Any Consultancy Assignment.* Upper Saddle River, NJ: Financial Times Prentice Hall, 2000.

Greenbaum, Thomas L. *The Consultant's Manual: A Complete Guide to Building a Successful Consulting Practice.* New York: John Wiley & Sons, 1990.

Holtz, Herman. *The Complete Guide to Consulting Contracts.* Chicago: Dearborn Trade, 1997.

———. *The Consultant's Guide to Proposal Writing: How to Satisfy Your Clients and Double Your Income.* 3rd ed. New York: John Wiley & Sons, 1998.

Kishel, Gregory, and Patricia Kishel. *How to Start and Run a Successful Consulting Business.* New York: John Wiley & Sons, 1996.

Maister, David. *True Professionalism: The Courage to Care About Your People, Your Clients, and Your Career.* New York: Touchstone Books, 2000.

Maister, David, Charles H. Green, and Robert M. Galford. *The Trusted Advisor.* New York: Touchstone Books, 2001.

Phillips, Jack. *The Consultant's Scorecard: Tracking Results and Bottom-Line Impact of Consulting Projects.* New York: McGraw-Hill, 2000.

Raisel, Ethan. *The McKinsey Way.* New York: McGraw-Hill, 1999.

Shenson, Howard L. *The Contract and Fee-Setting Guide for Consultants and Professionals.* New York: John Wiley & Sons, 1990.

Sheth, Jagdish, and Andrew Sobel. *Clients for Life: How Great Professionals Develop Breakthrough Relationships.* New York: Simon & Schuster, 2000.

Silberman, Melvin. *The Consultant's Toolkit: High-Impact Questionnaires, Activities, and How-to Guides for Diagnosing and Solving Client Problems.* New York: McGraw-Hill, 2000.

Weiss, Alan. *Getting Started in Consulting.* New York: John Wiley & Sons, 2000.

———. *Million Dollar Consulting: The Professional's Guide to Growing a Practice.* New York: McGraw-Hill, 1997.

———. *The Ultimate Consultant: Powerful Techniques for the Successful Practitioner.* San Francisco: Jossey-Bass, 2001.

Since consultants are often engaged in training and in the recommendation of resources to their clients, I would like to call your attention to a series of basic management books that I have found useful. It is the "Briefcase Books" series. These books average about 200 pages each and deal with many different topics. It is a series for which I have written one of the books and for which I have a high regard. Here's a list of currently available titles:

◆ *Communicating Effectively*

◆ *Conflict Resolution*

◆ *Customer Relationship Management*

◆ *Effective Coaching*

◆ *Empowering Employees*

◆ *Hiring Great People*

◆ *Leadership Skills for Managers*

◆ *The Manager's Guide to Business Writing*

◆ *Managing Teams*

◆ *Motivating Employees*

◆ *Performance Management* (I wrote this title)

◆ *Presentation Skills for Managers*

◆ *Project Management*

◆ *Recognizing and Rewarding Employees*

◆ *Skills for New Managers*

There is a website devoted to the series that includes information about each title and has training discussion guides that you can download for use with the books. Go to www.briefcasebooks.com for more information.

Associations

There are several associations for consultants. Here are some of the main ones:

Association of Management Consulting Firms
521 Fifth Avenue, 35th Floor
New York, NY 10175
Phone: 212-697-9693
Fax: 212-949-6571
Website: www.amcf.org

Known as the premier professional association for management consulting firms.

Institute of Management Consultants
521 Fifth Avenue, 35th Floor
New York, NY 10175-3598
Phone: 212-697-8262
Fax: 212-949-6571
E-mail: office@imcusa.org
Website: www.imcusa.org

American Consultants League
30466 Prince William Street
Princess Anne, MD 21853
Phone: 410-651-4869
Fax: 410-651-4885
Training professionals in the business of consulting.

International Council of Management Consulting Institutes
858 Longview Road, Suite 200
Burlingame, CA 94010-6974
Phone: 1-800-568-5668
Fax: 650-344-5005
E-mail: icmci@icmci.org
Website: icmci.org/icmci
The international association of national institutes that certifies individual management
consultants with the designation CMC.

National Bureau of Certified Consultants (NBCC)
2728 Fifth Avenue
San Diego, CA 92103
Phone: 619-297-2207
Fax: 619-296-3580
E-mail: nationalbureau@worldnet.att.net
Website: expert-market.com/nbpmc

National Speakers Association
1500 South Priest Drive
Tempe, AZ 85281
Phone: 602-968-2552
E-mail: nsamain@aol.com
Website: www.nsaspeaker.org
NSA is an international association of more than 3,700 members dedicated to advancing
the art and value of experts who speak professionally.

Websites

- American Society for Training and Development (ASTD)—www.astd.org   One of the best sites for information on every type of management topic. If you are involved in any type of training, you should know about this site.

- Briefcase Books—www.briefcasebooks.com   Features titles from the Briefcase Books series, books on basic management topics that are ideal for use with clients.

- Complete Idiot's Guides—www.idiotsguides.com   Provides information on other books in the *Complete Idiot's Guide* series that you can use with clients. Includes a wide variety of management titles.

- Consulting Base—www.consultingbase.com/docs/sidenav/sitemap.shtml   A very good site with lots of resources and links.

- Consulting Central—www.consultingcentral.com   A very good site for consulting information. Lots of resources and links here.

- Consultant Resource Center—www.consultant-center.com   Provides articles and gives other resources available to consultants.

- Ducks-in-a-Row—www.ducks-in-a-row.com   Developed by a consulting company that offers services to get organized. A good example of a simple but effective site; it offers a great service.

- Findarticles.com—www.findarticles.com   A very valuable site if you're looking for articles on specific topics that might have appeared in many different magazines.

- HR-Guide.com—www.hr-guide.com   Tons of links on every type of issue dealing with human resources. Could be very useful to a consultant dealing with any kind of HR topic.

- The Institute of Management and Administration—www.ioma.com   A great site for articles on many different management topics that are available online from IOMA's many different e-zines. A good resource.

- International Guild of Professional Consultants—www.igpc.org   Includes resources to help consultants improve their professional abilities.

- National Consultant Referrals, Inc.—http://204.52.210.18/newreq.htm   A referral service for companies looking for consultants.

- ProSavvy—www.prosavvy.com   A site for consultants and for companies looking for consultants. Lots of good resources here.

- Quintessential Careers—www.quintcareers.com/consultant_jobs.html   Lots of links to opportunities for consultants and freelancers.

- Resources for Consulting from the-shelf.com—www.the-shelf.com/consult.html   A variety of resources here, most for sale from the United Kingdom. Some may be useful.

- Search4Consultant—www.search4consultant.com Just what it says, a site that allows you to search for consultants by state and category. A good place for a consultant to be listed.
- Society for Human Resource Management—www.shrm.org Includes lots of resources dealing with HR management and management in general.
- Society of Professional Consultants—www.spconsultants.org Lots of useful resources for consultants, including articles, e-zine links, a speaker's bureau, and more.

There are many more sites available. Do a search on google.com or other search engines using queries such as "consultant resources," "how to consult," or some other specific entry with quotes around it. If you enter just the word "consulting," you will get thousands of hits that won't be very useful to you.

E-mail Discussion Groups

Consulting (for consultants in all areas, focusing on the consulting process)—To subscribe, send an e-mail with this message: subscribe consulting.

Address: majordomo@quality.org

HC-CON (consultants in health care fields)—To subscribe, send an e-mail with this message: subscribe hc-con.

Address: majordomo@quality.org

Learning-Org (forum on learning organization concepts and shared experiences)—To subscribe, send an e-mail with this message: subscribe learning-org.

Address: majordomo@world.std.com

TRDEV (training and development)—To subscribe, send blank e-mail message. This discussion group is especially recommended. Very active and a good way to network with colleagues and maybe potential clients.

Website: groups.yahoo.com/group/trdev

Address: trdev-subscribe@yahoogroups.com

Magazines and Journals

Besides the journals in your specialty, you will also find many magazines dealing with business subjects that you might be interested in. Here are a variety of magazines that are worth exploring.

◆ *Across the Board*—www.conference-board.org   Published 10 times a year, this is a general business magazine with lots of articles of use to consultants.

◆ *Business Horizons*—www.kelley.indiana.edu/Horizons   This is the business magazine published by the Kelley School of Management at Indiana University. A notch below the *Harvard Business Review*, but a good journal to keep up with. Available in most libraries.

◆ *Consulting Magazine*—www.consultingcentral.com/magazine/maginfo.html   This is a great magazine for consultants, available by subscription and online.

◆ *Harvard Business Review*—www.hbsp.harvard.edu/hbr/index.html   Probably the premier management journal for those seeking to keep up with management trends and techniques. Well worth subscribing to.

◆ *Industry Week*—www.industryweek.com   Its mission is to cover, analyze, and present the best management practices to executives in the manufacturing sector and its supporting service industries. Lots of stuff of interest to consultants. Available free if you qualify. Many articles also available online.

◆ *Journal for Quality and Participation*—www.aqp.org/pages/jqp   Published bimonthly by the Association for Quality and Participation. This journal often includes articles of interest to consultants and accepts articles from consultants.

◆ *Performance Improvement Journal*—www.ispi.com   Published by the International Society for Performance Improvement, it often includes articles of use to consultants in a variety of fields.

◆ *Quality Progress*—www.asq.org/pub/qualityprogress   Published monthly by the American Society for Quality, this is the foremost magazine dealing with quality management topics, including HR, training, and teamwork. Often includes articles of interest to management consultants.

◆ *Sloan Management Review*—mitsloan.mit.edu/smr/index.html   Published quarterly, this is like the *Harvard Business Review* except the articles tend to be based on research and are longer than in *HBR*. Often includes useful material for consultants.

◆ *Strategy+business*—www.strategy-business.com   Published by Booz-Allen & Hamilton, this magazine features articles and book reviews by prominent researchers, executives, and Booz-Allen consultants.

◆ *Strategy & Leadership*—www.mcb.co.uk/sl.htm   This magazine, formerly published by Strategic Leadership Forum, offers thoughtfully written articles by prominent consultants, professors, and executives. Regularly includes articles of use to consultants and accepts articles from consultants for publication.

◆ *Training*—www.trainingmag.com   One of the premier magazines for the training profession and more. Always includes articles and tools of use to consultants in many fields.

◆ *Training & Development*—www.astd.org/virtualcommunity/td_magazine   The ASTD's monthly magazine, it also includes lots of articles and tools consultants will find valuable.

◆ *Workforce*—www.workforceonline.com   Formerly *Personnel Journal*, this magazine regularly includes articles of interest to consultants, especially in HR issues. Many of its articles are available online.

Index

S